W9-BCU-189

Assessment in Higher Education

Issues of Access, Quality, Student Development, and Public Policy

A Festschrift in Honor of
Warren W. Willingham

Assessment in Higher Education

Issues of Access, Quality, Student Development, and Public Policy

A Festschrift in Honor of
Warren W. Willingham

Edited by
Samuel J. Messick
Educational Testing Service

LAWRENCE ERLBAUM ASSOCIATES, PUBLISHERS
1999   Mahwah, New Jersey   London

Copyright © 1999 by Lawrence Erlbaum Associates, Inc.
All rights reserved. No part of this book may be reproduced in any form, by photostat, microfilm, retrieval system, or any other means, without prior written permission of the publisher.

Lawrence Erlbaum Associates, Inc., Publishers
10 Industrial Avenue
Mahwah, NJ 07430

Cover design by Kathryn Houghtaling Lacey

Library of Congress Cataloging-in-Publication Data

Assessment in higher education : issues of access, quality, student development, and public policy / edited by Samuel J. Messick.
p. cm.
"This volume commemorates the career contributions to research on higher education of Warren W. Willingham. It contains the proceedings of a conference held in his honor at Educational Testing Service in March, 1995"—Pref.
"Bibliography of Warren W. Willingham": p.
Includes bibliographical references and indexes.
ISBN 0–8058–2107-4 (alk. paper)
1. Universities and colleges—United States—Examinations—Congresses. 2. College students—Rating of—United States—Congresses. 3. Universities and colleges—United States—Entrance examinations—Congresses. 4. Willingham, Warren W.—Congresses. I. Messick, Samuel.
LB2366.2.A874   1998
378.1'664—dc21   98-25282
                                                                          CIP

Books published by Lawrence Erlbaum Associates are printed on acid-free paper, and their bindings are chosen for strength and durability.

The final camera copy for this work was prepared by the author, and therefore the publisher takes no responsibility for consistency or correctness of typographical style.

Printed in the United States of America
10 9 8 7 6 5 4 3 2 1

CONTENTS

List of Contributors   xi

Preface   xiii

Bibliography   xv
Warren W. Willingham

PART I
PRELUDE   1

Chapter One   3
The Changing Face of Higher Education
    Assessment
Samuel Messick

PART II
ENHANCING STUDENT ACCESS AND SUCCESS
IN HIGHER EDUCATION   9

Chapter Two   13
Personal Qualities and Human Development in
    Higher Education: Assessment in the Service
    of Educational Goals
Arthur W. Chickering

Chapter Three   35
Assessment to Improve College Instruction
K. Patricia Cross

Chapter Four   47
Assessing and Credentialing Learning
    from Prior Experience
Morris Keeton

Chapter Five   57
Commentary
Feedback and Reflection in
    Facilitating Further Learning
Wilbert J. McKeachie

Chapter Six   63
Commentary
Characteristics of Assessment in Support
    of Student Access and Success
Sister Joel Read

PART III
EXPANDING ADMISSIONS TESTING   69

Chapter Seven   73
Implications of Standards-Based
    Reform for Admissions Testing
Robert L. Linn

Chapter Eight   91
From 2 to 3 Rs -- The Expanding Use of
    Writing in Admissions
Hunter M. Breland

Chapter Nine   113
A Theory-Based Framework for Future College
    Admissions Tests
Howard T. Everson

Chapter Ten   133
Commentary
Expanding the Breadth and Depth
    of Admissions Testing
Richard E. Snow

Chapter Eleven   141
Commentary
Interpreting Scores in Context to Identify
    Student Potential
Fred A. Hargadon

PART IV
POLITICS AND PUBLIC POLICY
OF HIGHER EDUCATION ASSESSMENT   145

Chapter Twelve   147
Assessment of Higher Education Quality:
  Promise and Politics
Peter T. Ewell

Chapter Thirteen   157
Assessment, Student Development, and Public Policy
Alexander W. Astin

PART V
ISSUES OF EQUITY AND FAIRNESS IN
HIGHER EDUCATION ASSESSMENT   177

Chapter Fourteen   181
Computer-Based Testing for Examinees with Disabilities:
  On the Road to Generalized Accommodation
Randy Elliot Bennett

Chapter Fifteen   193
Directions in the Assessment of Linguistic Minorities
Richard P. Durán

Chapter Sixteen   203
Human Diversity and Equitable Assessment
Edmund W. Gordon

Chapter Seventeen   213
A Systemic View of Test Fairness
Warren W. Willingham

PART VI
PROSPECTS   243

Chapter Eighteen   245
Technology and the Future of Higher
    Education Assessment
Samuel Messick

Author Index   255

Subject Index   259

CONTRIBUTORS

Alexander W. Astin
University of California,
  Los Angeles

Randy Elliot Bennett
Educational Testing Service

Hunter Breland
Educational Testing Service

Arthur W. Chickering
George Mason University

K. Patricia Cross
University of California,
  Berkeley

Richard Durán
University of California,
  Santa Barbara

Howard Everson
The College Board

Peter Ewell
National Center for Higher
  Education Management

Fred A. Hargadon
Princeton University

Edmund Gordon
Yale University and the College
  Board

Morris Keeton
Institute for Research on Adults
  in Higher Education

Robert L. Linn
University of Colorado

Wilbert J. McKeachie
University of Michigan

Samuel Messick
Educational Testing Service

Sister Joel Read
Alverno College

Richard E. Snow
Stanford University

Warren W. Willingham
Educational Testing Service

PREFACE

This volume commemorates the career contributions to research on higher education of Warren W. Willingham. It contains the proceedings of a conference held in his honor at Educational Testing Service in March, 1995, along with introductory and concluding chapters and interstitial commentary by the editor.

As indicated by perusal of Willingham's bibliography, which directly follows this Preface, his work addresses most of the major issues that animated higher education over the past half-century. Accordingly, both the conference and this volume were organized around some of these salient issues having increasing currency for the 1990s. These include enhancing student access, development, and success in higher education; transforming admissions testing to meet expanding educational needs; resolving the politics of accountability by assessing quality outcomes of higher education; accommodating human diversity with equity and fairness; and, capitalizing on computer and audiovisual technology to prepare students for a technology-dominated future.

Neither the conference nor this volume could have occurred without the help of many people. Special thanks go to Nancy Cole, Henry Braun, and Ernest Anastasio for their support of the enterprise. Acknowledgments are also gratefully extended to the following individuals who served as chairpersons or discussants at the conference:

> Ernest Anastasio, Executive Vice President, ETS
> Joan Baratz-Snowden, Deputy Director, Education Issues,
>   American Federation of Teachers
> Henry Braun, Vice President, ETS
> Paula Brownlee, President, Association of American
>   Colleges and Universities
> Nancy Cole, President, ETS
> Frederick Dietrich, Vice President, The College Board
> Eleanor Horne, Corporate Secretary, ETS
> Donald Steward, President, The College Board

Thanks are also due to Kathleen Howell for her assistance in making travel and conference arrangements and for transcribing conference presentations.

Finally, special recognition goes to Ann Jungeblut, the sine qua non of the entire effort, who supervised all aspects of the conference arrangements and was responsible for transforming unedited chapters into camera-ready copy in the production of the book. She reviewed the entire manuscript more than once, reworking many passages in the process, and her numerous suggestions, often gentle but sometimes insistent, were especially helpful in improving the content and style of the sections I wrote.

Samuel Messick

BIBLIOGRAPHY

Warren W. Willingham

Books and Monographs

1997 [with Cole, N. S.] *Gender and Fair Assessment.* Hillsdale, NJ: Lawrence Erlbaum Associates.

1993 [with Johnson, L.]. *Program Research Review.* Princeton, NJ: Educational Testing Service.

1990 [with Lewis, C., Morgan, R., & Ramist, L.]. *Predicting college grades: An analysis of institutional trends over two decades.* Princeton, NJ: Educational Testing Service.

1988 [with Ragosta, M., Bennett, R. E., Braun, H., Rock, D. A., & Powers, D. E.]. *Testing handicapped people.* Boston: Allyn and Bacon.

1985 *Success in college: The role of personal qualities and academic ability.* New York: College Entrance Examination Board.

1982 [with Breland, H. M.] *Personal qualities and college admissions.* New York: College Entrance Examination Board.

1977 *Principles of good practice in assessing experiential learning.* Princeton, NJ: Council for the Advancement of Experiential Learning.
[with Manning, W., & Breland, H.] *Selective admissions in higher education: A report of the Carnegie Council on policy studies in higher education.* San Francisco: Jossey-Bass.
[with Valley, J., & Keeton, M.] *Assessing experiential learning--A summary report on the CAEL project.* Princeton, NJ: Council for the Advancement of Experiential Learning.

1976 [with Associates.] *The CAEL validation report.* Princeton, NJ: Coop-
      erative Assessment of Experiential Learning.
      Validity and the Graduate Record Examination Program. Princeton, NJ:
      Educational Testing Service.

1974 *College placement and exemption.* New York: College Entrance Exami-
      nation Board.

1973 [with Associates.] *The source book for higher education.* New York:
      College Entrance Examination Board.

1972 [with Ferrin, R. I., & Begle, E. P.] *Career guidance in secondary educa-
      tion.* New York: College Entrance Examination Board.
      The no. 2 access problem: Transfer to the upper division. Washington,
      DC: American Association for Higher Education.

1970 *Free-access higher education.* New York: College Entrance Examina-
      tion Board.

1969 *Patterns of admission for transfer students.* New York: College Entrance
      Examination Board.

1965 *A report to the trustees of the College Entrance Examination Board: Re-
      search and development.* New York: College Entrance Examination
      Board.

Articles and Chapters

1990 [with Lewis, C.] Institutional differences in prediction trends. In W. W.
      Willingham, C. Lewis, R. Morgan, & L. Ramist, *Predicting college
      grades: An analysis of institutional trends over two decades* (pp. 141-
      158). Princeton, NJ: Educational Testing Service.
      [with Rock, D. A., & Pollack, J.] Predictability of college grades: Three
      tests and three national samples. In W. W. Willingham, C. Lewis, R.
      Morgan, & L. Ramist, *Predicting college grades: An analysis of insti-
      tutional trends over two decades* (pp. 239-251). Princeton, NJ: Edu-
      cational Testing Service.

1989 Research and assessment: Tools for change. In C. H. Pazandak (Ed.),
      *Improving Undergraduate Education in Large Universities. New Di-
      rections for Higher Education, No. 66* (pp. 27-40). San Francisco:
      Jossey-Bass.

Standard testing conditions and standard score meaning for handicapped examinees. *Applied Measurement in Education, 2,* 97-103.

1988 Admissions decisions. In W. W. Willingham, M. Ragosta, R. E. Bennett, H. I. Braun, D. A. Rock, & D. E. Powers, *Testing Handicapped People* (pp. 133-141). Boston, MA: Allyn and Bacon, Inc.
[with Powers, D. E.] The feasibility of rescaling. In W. W. Willingham, M. Ragosta, R. E. Bennett, H. Braun, D. A. Rock, & D. E. Powers, *Testing Handicapped People* (pp. 133-141). Boston, MA: Allyn and Bacon, Inc.
Standard testing conditions and standard score meaning for handicapped examinees. *The Score.* Circle Pines, MN: Newsletter of Division 5 of the American Psychological Association.
Testing handicapped people--The validity issue. In H. Wainer & H. I. Braun (Eds.), *Test validity* (pp. 89-103). Hillsdale, NJ: Lawrence Erlbaum.

1983 Measuring personal qualities in admissions: The context and the purpose. In R. B. Ekstrom (Ed.), *Measurement, technology and individuality in education: New directions for testing and measurement, No. 17* (pp. 45-54). San Francisco: Jossey-Bass.

1982 [with Ramist, L.] The SAT debate: Do Trusheim and Crouse add useful information. *Phi Delta Kappan, 64,* 207-208.

1980 The case of personal qualities. *College Board Review, No. 116,* A1-A8.
[with Hartnett, R. T.] The criterion problem: What measure of success in graduate education? *Applied Psychological Measurement, 4,* 281-291.
New methods and directions in achievement measurement. *New Directions for Testing and Measurement, 5,* 73-80.

1978 *Some educational and social implications of University of California v. Bakke.* (A series of working papers on implications of the Supreme Court's decision in the Bakke case.) New York: The College Board.

1976 Critical issues and basic requirements for assessment. In M. T. Keeton and Associates, *Experiential learning: Rationale, characteristics, and assessment* (pp. 224-244). San Francisco: Jossey-Bass, Inc.

1974 Predicting success in graduate education. *Science, 183,* 273-278.
Transfer standards and the public interest. In *College transfer: Working paper and recommendations from the Airlie House Conference, December, 1973* (pp. 26-49).

Working toward a new agenda in graduate admissions. *Proceedings of the Fourteenth Annual Meeting of the Council of Graduate Schools,* Phoenix, AR (pp. 8-20).

1973   Access to higher education--an overview. In W. W. Willingham & Associates, *The Source Book for Higher Education: A critical guide to literature and information on access to higher education* (pp. 1-11). New York: College Entrance Examination Board.

1971   Educational opportunity and the organization of higher education.   In *Barriers to Higher Education* (pp. 1-20).   New York: College Entrance Examination Board.

1970   Free-access college: Where they are and whom they serve.   *College Board Review, 76,* 6-14.   New York: College Entrance Examination Board.
       The importance of relevance in expanding post-secondary education.   In *Trends in post-secondary education* (pp. 69-84)   Washington: Government Printing Office.

1969   Transfer students: Who's moving from where to where and what determines who's admitted?   *College Board Review, 74,* 4-12.

1968   [with Pasanella, A. K.]   Testing the educational and psychological development of young adults--ages 18-25.   *Review of Educational Research, 38*(1), 42-48.

1967   [with Ed.]   Invasion of privacy in research and testing.   Special supplement to *Journal of Educational Measurement.*

1966   Sociological research at the College Entrance Examination Board.   *Sociology of Education, 39*(4), 391-396.

1965   The application blank as a predictive instrument.   *College and University,* 271-281.
       The effect of grading variations upon the accuracy of predicting freshman grades.   *College and University, 40,* 159-164.
       Graduate record examinations aptitude test (Review).   In O. K. Buros, Ed., *The Sixth Mental Measurement Yearbook* (pp. 461-463).   Highland Park, NJ: Gryphon Press.
       Miller analogies test (Review).   In O. K. Buros, Ed., *The Sixth Mental Measurement Yearbook,* (pp. 472-473).   Highland Park, NJ: Gryphon Press.

1964 An empirical evaluation of three types of college grade scales. *Journal of Educational Measurement, 1,* 69-72.

Estimating the number of different selection decisions resulting from the use of alternate predictor composites. *Journal of Applied Psychology, 48*(5), 302-304.

On the evaluation of academic progress. *Journal of Educational Research, 57,* 371-373.

Freshman grades and educational decisions. *Journal of Engineering Education, 54*(10), 329-332.

The interpretation of relative achievement. *American Educational Research Journal, 1*(2), 101-112.

Validity of several methods of expressing high school achievement level. *College and University, 40,* 49-54.

1963 Adjusting college predictions on the basis of academic origin. *Yearbook National Council on Measurement in Education, 20,*1-6.

Erroneous assumptions in predicting college grades. *Journal of Counseling Psychology, 10,* 389-394.

Evaluating the academic potential of transfer students. *College and University, 38,* 260-265.

[with Ambler, R. K.] The relation of the Gordon personal inventory to several external criteria. *Journal of Consulting Psychology, 27*(5), 460.

1962 College performance of fraternity members and independent students. *Personnel and Guidance Journal, 41,* 29-31.

[with Strickland, J. A.] Conversion tables for Otis Gamma and Scholastic Aptitude Test. *Personnel and Guidance Journal, 41,* 356-358.

Evaluating previous academic performance. *Proceedings of a Conference on Institutional Research on College Students.* Atlanta: Southern Regional Education Board.

Some remarks on disseminating test scores. *The Newsletter.* Regents of the University System of Georgia, No. 7.

1961 *Essentials of psychological testing* (2nd ed.). (Review). *Educational and Psychological Measurement, 21,* 505-506.

Review of elementary statistical methods, by Helen Walker & J. Lev. *Educational and Psychological Measurement, 21,* 510-511.

1959 On deriving standard scores for peer nominations with subgroups of unequal size. *Psychological Report, 5,* 397-403.

Estimating the internal consistency of mutual peer nominations. *Psychological Reports, 5,* 163-167.

Non-medical correlates of medical complaints. *Journal of Aviation Medicine, 30,* 29-34.

Note on the computation of $\Phi/(\Phi)_{max}$. *Psychological Reports, 5,* 606.

1958 Confidence and correctness in comparative judgment. *Perceptual and Motor Skills, 8,* 227-230.

[with Jones, M. B.] On the identification of halo through analysis of variance. *Educational and Psychological Measurement, 18,* 403-407.

Interdependence of successive absolute judgments. *Journal of Applied Psychology, 42,* 416-418.

[with Nelson, P., & O'Connor, W.] A note on the behavioral validity of the Gordon personal profile. *Journal of Consulting Psychology, 22,* 378.

Performance decrement following failure. *Perceptual and Motor Skills, 8,* 199-202.

The relation of age to success in flight training. *The Journal of Aviation Medicine, 29,* 136-138.

1956 [with Furchtgott, E.] The effect of sleep-deprivation upon the thresholds of taste. *The American Journal of Psychology, 69,* 111-112.

The organization of emotional behavior in mice. *The Journal of Comparative and Physiological Psychology, 49,* 345-348.

Technical Reports

1987 *Handicapped applicants to college: An analysis of admissions decisions.* (CB Report No. 87-1; ETS RR 87-1). New York: College Entrance Examination Board.

1986 [with Morris, M.] *Four years later: A longitudinal study of Advanced Placement students in college.* (CB Report No. 86-2; ETS RR 85-46). New York: College Entrance Examination Board.

1976 [with Nesbitt, H. S. Eds.] *Implementing a program for assessing experiential learning.* Princeton, NJ: CAEL.

1974 [with Burns, R., & Donlon, T.] *CAEL working paper no. 1: Current practices in the assessment of experiential learning.* Princeton, NJ: Educational Testing Service.

1971 [with Ferrin, R.]. Practices of southern institutions in recognizing col-
      lege-level achievement. *Higher Education Surveys Report No. 3.* Palo
      Alto, CA: College Board Examination Board.
      Professional development of financial aid officers. *Higher Education
      Surveys Report No. 2.* Palo Alto, CA: College Board Examination
      Board.

1970 Admission of minority students to midwestern colleges. *Higher Educa-
      tion Surveys Report No. 1.* Palo Alto, CA: College Board Examination
      Board.
      Higher education surveys: Description of the model. Palo Alto, CA:
      College Board Examination Board.

1963 *Academic characteristics of women students at Georgia Tech* (Research
      Memorandum 63-6). Atlanta, GA: Office of Evaluation Studies,
      Georgia Institute of Technology.
      The application blank as a predictive instrument (Research Memorandum
      63-10). Atlanta, GA: Office of Evaluation Studies, Georgia Institute
      of Technology.
      A comparison of the entering classes of 1957 through 1962 (Research
      Memorandum 63-2). Altanta, GA: Office of Evaluation Studies,
      Georgia Institute of Technology.
      *The effect of grading variations on the efficiency of predicting freshman
      grades* (Research Memorandum 63-1)   Atlanta, GA: Office of
      Evaluation Studies, Georgia Institute of Technology.
      An empirical evaluation of three grade scales (Research Memorandum
      63-11). Atlanta, GA: Office of Evaluation Studies, Georgia Institute
      of Technology.
      *Evaluation of an artificial language test as an indicator of success in
      freshman language courses* (Research Memorandum 63-4). Atlanta,
      GA: Office of Evaluation Studies, Georgia Institute of Technology.
      Intramural migration and selective retention of students (Research
      Memorandum 63-9). Atlanta, GA: Office of Evaluation Studies,
      Georgia Institute of Technology.
      Three dimensional visualization and success in architecture (Research
      Memorandum 63-5). Atlanta, GA: Office of Evaluation Studies,
      Georgia Institute of Technology.
      Variation among the grade scales of different high schools (Research
      Memorandum 63-3). Atlanta, GA: Office of Evaluation Studies,
      Georgia Institute of Technology.

1962 *The analysis of grading variations* (Research Memorandum 62-9). At-
      lanta, GA: Office of Evaluation Studies, Georgia Institute of Technol-
      ogy.

A comparison of the entering classes of 1957 through 1961 (Research Memorandum 62-2). Atlanta, GA: Office of Evaluation Studies, Georgia Institute of Technology.

[with Ambler, R.]. *Comparison of methods for deriving peer nomination scores.* Pensacola, FL: U. S. Naval School of Aviation Medicine.

Longitudinal analysis of academic performance (Research Memorandum 62-8). Atlanta, GA: Office of Evaluation Studies, Georgia Institute of Technology.

Possible biases in Scholastic Aptitude Test scores (Research Memorandum 62-8). Atlanta, GA: Office of Evaluation Studies, Georgia Institute of Technology.

A reanalysis of the College Board achievement tests as predictors of freshman grades (Research Memorandum 62-7). Atlanta, GA: Office of Evaluation Studies, Georgia Institute of Technology.

Scatterplots showing the relationship between ability measures and freshman grades (Research Memorandum 62-3). Atlanta, GA: Office of Evaluation Studies, Georgia Institute of Technology.

Selecting students for an honors program in elementary German (Research Memorandum 62-4). Atlanta, GA: Office of Evaluation Studies, Georgia Institute of Technology.

1961   *Aptitude and performance of freshman who voluntarily withdraw* (Research Memorandum 61-2). Atlanta, GA: Office of Evaluation Studies, Georgia Institute of Technology.

An evaluation of a study hall program for intercollegiate athletes (Research Memorandum 61-8). Atlanta, GA: Office of Evaluation Studies, Georgia Institute of Technology.

A comparison of the entering classes of 1957 through 1960 (Research Memorandum 61-3). Atlanta, GA: Office of Evaluation Studies, Georgia Institute of Technology.

Contribution of the College Board achievement tests to prediction of freshman grades (Research Memorandum 61-7). Atlanta, GA: Office of Evaluation Studies, Georgia Institute of Technology.

Evaluation of the College Board achievement tests (Research Memorandum 61-10). Atlanta, GA: Office of Evaluation Studies, Georgia Institute of Technology.

Interrelations among performance measures, I: Chemical Engineering (Research Memorandum 61-13). Atlanta, GA: Office of Evaluation Studies, Georgia Institute of Technology.

Interrelations among performance measures, II: Mechanical Engineering (Research Memorandum 61-14). Atlanta, GA: Office of Evaluation Studies, Georgia Institute of Technology.

Norms for second year students (Research Memorandum 61-1). Atlanta, GA: Office of Evaluation Studies, Georgia Institute of Technology.

On the evaluation of academic progress (Research Memorandum 61-12). Atlanta, GA: Office of Evaluation Studies, Georgia Institute of Technology.

Progressive decline in freshman grades of preparatory school graduates (Research Memorandum 61-5). Atlanta, GA: Office of Evaluation Studies, Georgia Institute of Technology.

Reanalysis of freshman grade prediction (Research Memorandum 61-4). Atlanta, GA: Office of Evaluation Studies, Georgia Institute of Technology.

The relation of spatial aptitude to performance at Georgia Tech (Research Memorandum 61-1). Atlanta, GA: Office of Evaluation Studies, Georgia Institute of Technology.

Some attitudes expressed by transfer students from junior colleges (Research Memorandum 61-11). Atlanta, GA: Office of Evaluation Studies, Georgia Institute of Technology.

1960 *On the interpretation and use of standardized test scores* (Research Memorandum 60-1). Atlanta, GA: Office of Evaluation Studies, Georgia Institute of Technology.

1959 *Methods for deriving standard scores for peer nominations with subgroups of unequal size* (MR005, 13-5001, 1, 27). Pensacola, FL: U. S. Naval School of Aviation Medicine.

1958 *The comparative validity of two rating forms* (MR--5, 13-5001, 1, 18). Pensacola, FL: U. S. Naval School of Aviation Medicine.

Biographical information and time to complete training (Special Report No. 58-10). Pensacola, FL: U. S. Naval School of Aviation Medicine.

Confidence and correctness in comparative judgment (Research Project NM 14 02 11 Subtask 12). Pensacola, FL: U. S. Naval School of Aviation Medicine.

The effect of training experience on student attitudes about naval career (Special Report No. 58-17). Pensacola, FL: U. S. Naval School of Aviation Medicine.

The identification of future failures among marginal disciplinary cases (Special Report 58-30). Pensacola, FL: U. S. Naval School of Aviation Medicine.

A note on peer nominations as a predictor of success in naval flight training (Project No. 16 01 11 Subtask 1, Report No. 14). Pensacola, FL: U. S. Naval School of Aviation Medicine.

The sentence--completion test as measure of morale (Project NM 16 01 11 Subtask 4, Report No. 4). Pensacola, FL: U. S. Naval School of Aviation Medicine.

1957   *External factors related to DOR attrition: Month attrited and character-istics of pre-flight class* (Special Report No. 57-6). Pensacola, FL: U. S. Naval School of Aviation Medicine.

Interdependence of successive judgments. I Comparative judgement. II Affective judgment. III Absolute judgment (Project NM 14 02 11 Sub-task 12, Report No. 2). Pensacola, FL: U. S. Naval School of Aviation Medicine.

A study of morale of pre-flight and primary flight training (Special Report No. 57-17). Pensacola, FL: U. S. Naval School of Aviation Medicine.

[with Bair, J., & Seale, L.]. *Extension of duty for first tour reserve naval aviators* (Special Report No. 56-26). Pensacola, FL: U. S. Naval School of Aviation Medicine.

PART I

PRELUDE

Higher education has been moving from an era dominated by selection of high levels of talent, with a consequent emphasis on admissions testing, to an era concerned with broadening the range of talent, with a consequent emphasis not just on selection but also on assessment for student growth and development. This change has brought with it a heightened attention to the diversity of the student population as a means of expanding the base of talent. At the same time, the burgeoning of computer and audiovisual technology is facilitating the development of alternative self-directed modes of learning and problem solving as well as of alternative modes of assessment. Hence population diversity compounds with a potentially explosive diversity in learning and assessment to highlight the issues of equity and fairness in education and testing.

In Chapter 1, Samuel Messick introduces these themes and emphasizes the intersection of equity and fairness with issues of access, quality, diversity, and accountability in higher education. As introduction to the volume, Messick briefly outlines how the remaining five parts address these issues in the contexts, respectively, of student development, of admissions testing, of the politics of accountability, of fair assessment responsive to human diversity, and of the technological future of higher education.

1

THE CHANGING FACE OF HIGHER EDUCATION ASSESSMENT

Samuel Messick
Educational Testing Service

For most of this century, the face of higher education assessment has displayed a singular countenance. Admissions testing was its salient feature because student selection was the primary function that assessment served. However, as we enter the 21st century, the face of higher education assessment is progressively changing. The lines of character associated with validity and equity will be deepened, but many of the age spots and wrinkles will be rejuvenated by technology. The intent of this change is not merely cosmetic but, rather, regenerative.

We are not simply contemplating a technological face-lift to better serve the old function of selection but, instead, the reconstruction of a genuinely new face to serve new and expanded functions and purposes. For years the main function of assessment in the academy was selection to maximize the level of talent as an outcome of higher education. Then around mid-century there began a growing concern for selection to broaden the range of talent, which brought with it a concomitant concern for cultural and group diversity. Now the twin goals of high levels and broad ranges of talent are coming to be addressed more and more not only through selection but also through student growth and development, which greatly expands the role of assessment in higher education. Admissions testing becomes less salient as more emphasis is placed on assessment for instructional guidance and placement, for career guidance and decision making, for the improvement of instruction and student performance, for the certification of learning and competence, and for the evaluation of program quality.

The expanded purposes of higher education assessment constitute the main topics of this volume, but they are addressed not just in functional terms but also in terms of a number of cross-cutting issues that entail competing social values

3

and consequent tensions and tradeoffs. These include the issues of access, quality, diversity, and accountability, all of which feed into higher-order concerns about public policy with respect to higher education goals and outcomes. An integrating thread that weaves through all of these issues is the concept of equity, especially as it bears on social justice in education and on fairness in assessment.

From the perspective of equity, the main issue with respect to access is the ethical defensibility of any limits, especially the need to isolate ideologically based barriers from the practical constraints of distributing scarce resources. With respect to the quality of higher education, a central concern is the ethical basis of the criteria of excellence, in particular whether excellence constitutes the achievement of institutional and faculty repute or of student growth and development. With respect to diversity, an important issue is the balancing of concern for group parity with individual as well as institutional and societal benefits. With respect to social justice in education, which for many is the ultimate basis for accountability, the equity issues are often phrased in terms of equal access and treatment as well as equal opportunity to learn. However, as will be seen throughout this volume, the diverse value bases for social justice are more complex than this (see also, Deutsch, 1975; Messick, 1989; Nozick, 1974; Okun, 1075; Rawls, 1971). The plain fact is that not all inequalities are inequities (e.g., see Heller, Holtzman, & Messick, 1982). In education, for example, equitable treatment may not be equal treatment but, rather, treatment sufficient to the need.

This complexity stems from a pluralism of social values that creates tensions and the need for tradeoffs both in pursuing educational goals and in establishing the fairness of assessments that support those pursuits. In effect if not in original intent, this volume attempts to clarify the nature of this complexity, especially as it bears on the fairness, validity, and usefulness of higher education assessment.

Another integrative thread is the role of computer and audiovisual technology not only in improving the efficiency and power of all the functions of higher education assessment, but also in revolutionizing the delivery of higher education itself. Indeed, technology and equity are joined, not in battle but as warp and woof of the social fabric of higher education. The two are difficult to disentangle without severely damaging that fabric. Technology has enormous potential to improve equity in education and assessment if its availability becomes widespread, but also to exacerbate inequity if its effective availability is uneven.

Hence the application of technology in education is itself an equity issue, but it is not a new equity issue. In essence, it is another instance of a long-standing and profound social problem, namely, equity in the availability and distribution of effective educational resources, which is at the heart of the problem of inequitable opportunities to learn. One of the thrusts of this volume is that technology is only superficially part of the *problem* of equity in education and assessment. Rather, it is a basic and perhaps inevitable part of the *solution*.

In summary, Part I of this volume has outlined the topical content to be addressed, namely, assessment for admissions, placement, guidance, student development, instructional improvement, the certification of learning and competence, and the evaluation of institutional excellence. These assessment topics are treated not just in the functional terms of their contributions to higher education, but also in terms of the cross-cutting policy issues that they perennially evoke. These are primarily issues of access, diversity, quality, and accountability. A more fundamental policy concern permeates all of these issues, namely, a concern for equity and fairness. Finally, computer and audiovisual technology is viewed as a promissory means of improving equity by, among many other things, enhancing network access to a variety of self-directed learning resources in ways that circumvent many institutional, social, and financial barriers.

Part II focuses on assessment for student development, for the improvement of instruction, and for credentialling experiential learning that occurs outside the academy. Emphasis is placed on the development not only of the knowledge, skills, and personal qualities constituting the aims of liberal education, but also of those required for career success and for mature adult functioning. This section also introduces a theme to be reprised in several later sections. This recurrent theme is that developed competence should be revealed in performance and not just knowledge, thereby sounding an incipient call not only for performance assessment but for performance-based pedagogy in higher education.

Part III argues that admissions testing in higher education needs to be revamped. In part, this is a recognition of the fact that as the purposes of assessment in higher education are expanded, some of them, especially those bearing on placement and guidance, might be well-served by enhanced testing in the admissions process. The press to transform admissions testing also stems from the need to keep pace with the standards-based reform movement in elementary and secondary education, with its reliance on performance assessment as the primary instrument for changing teaching practices and modes of student learning. If student learning of complex skills becomes performance-based (as well as often being computer-based), then admissions testing also needs to become performance-based so that students can demonstrate their competence in the same form in which it was learned. This raises questions of the relevance of the assessment mode to the learning mode and of fairness in affording students a congenial means of expressing their competence. Other factors facilitating the reconstruction of admissions testing are recent advances in computer technology, psychometric modeling, and cognitive psychology. These advances should lead to the assessment of a broader array of constructs validly interpretable in terms of cognitive processes relative to standards and not just performance levels relative to norms.

Part IV addresses issues of public policy that arise when the assessment of higher education quality becomes enmeshed in the politics of accountability. A key issue is what the criteria of excellence ought to be. Should the criteria reflect high quality faculty and students or institutional reputation or successful student development? The current political consensus appears to call for a new accountability in terms of return on investment to society as a whole, which translates in part to a demand for value-added outcomes of higher education in the form of student growth in knowledge, skills, and character over and above what students entered college with. It also translates in part to a demand for societal input into what the outcomes of higher education ought to be. However, it turns out that the substance of desired outcomes politically relevant to the new accountability differs little from traditional goals of liberal education, except for a heightened emphasis on affective and motivational as well as cognitive aspects of competence. And once again, there is an insistence that developed competence be demonstrable in performance and action, not just in knowledge and theory.

Part V examines the social values of equity and fairness as they bear on the validity and usefulness of higher education assessment. Equity issues are addressed in terms of the appropriateness and effectiveness of educational practices for serving the needs of disabled, linguistic minority, and culturally diverse students. Fairness issues are addressed in terms of the comparability of score meaning and action implications in assessing the knowledge, skills, and other competencies of individuals from diverse educational, linguistic, and cultural backgrounds. The issues of both equity and fairness are framed in the context of human diversity broadly conceived, which goes far beyond a concern for accommodating group differences to a concern for appropriately assessing individual differences. Because the range of within-group individual differences consistently dwarfs any between-group differences, it is felt that the problems of equity and fairness will not be ultimately resolved without understanding and accommodating the major sources of individual differences in learning and performance. Until that happy time, however, Part V concludes with practical recommendations for increasing test fairness as comparable validity across all stages of the assessment process as applied to diverse individuals, groups, and contexts.

Part VI focusses on the technological future of higher education assessment as well as of higher education itself. The advent of computer and audiovisual technology introduces the prospect of alternative self-directed modes of learning that will lead to a widening and deepening of individual differences in learning and thinking styles. Technology also instigates both a rapidly changing environment requiring enhanced flexibility in learning and problem solving as well as the development of new information-processing skills for capitalizing on the new media. These and other consequences of technology will need to be addressed by higher education and its supporting assessment system as the academy attempts to prepare students for a technology-dominated society. Part VI concludes by broaching the possibility that as the academy confronts these new educational needs, its whole mode of operation may itself be technologically transformed by the advent of the virtual university.

Thus the face of higher education assessment is changing because the needs of higher education are changing. These needs are changing because technology is dramatically transforming not only modes of assessment but also modes of learning and problem solving. The overarching concerns for equity in education and fairness in assessment become paramount in this era of societal flux, especially as they intersect with issues of access, quality, diversity, and accountability in higher education. These are the themes of the present volume, as they are also major themes in the work of Warren Willingham, whose career contributions to research on higher education this volume celebrates.

REFERENCES

Deutsch, M. (1975). Equity, equality and need: What determines which value will be used as the basis of distributive justice? *Journal of Social Issues*, *31*(3), 137-149.

Heller, K. A., Holtzman, W. H., & Messick, S. (Eds.). (1982). *Placing children in special education: A strategy for equity*. Washington, DC: National Academy Press.

Messick, S. (1989). Validity. In R. L. Linn (Ed.), *Educational measurement* (3rd ed., pp. 13-103). New York: Macmillan.

Nozick, R. (1974). *Anarchy, state, and utopia*. New York: Basic Books.

Okun, A. (1975). *Equality and efficiency: The big tradeoff*. Washington, DC: The Brookings Institute.

Rawls, J. A. (1971). *A theory of justice*. Cambridge, MA: Harvard University Press.

PART II

ENHANCING STUDENT ACCESS AND SUCCESS IN HIGHER EDUCATION

For generations academicians have debated the goals of higher education and the nature of good teaching as well as how to take into account and capitalize upon experiential learning outside the academy. These debates have become sharper over the years because of increased diversity of the student population and increased productivity demands on postsecondary institutions, as well as some expanding aspirations as to what higher education should contribute to society in an increasingly competitive global economy. In anticipating the revolutionary role that multimedia and computer technology might play in higher education, Holtzman (1976) saw the challenge as fundamentally substantive and pedagogical, with technology offering a promissory means to expand educational ends:

> There is a call for education that is less routinized and more personalized, for education that not only imparts adopted knowledge but implants adaptive thinking, for education that does not just master belatedly the solutions of the past but that solves creatively the problems of the present and foresees realistically the issues of the future. (p. 24)

Daunting as this call may sound, there is little hope of heeding it without systematic information and feedback about student goals, student characteristics and experiences, and student development as well as about teaching practices and educational contexts. The collection of such systematic information and its effective use in feedback to students, teachers, administrators, and policy makers is at its core a problem of assessment, not technology. However, as will be seen, technology is critical not only to the development of efficient and convenient assessment and feedback systems, but also to the radical enrichment of the kinds of problem-solving skills and thinking processes that can be validly assessed. But before capitalizing on technology, we first need assessments that address the pedagogical needs—that aim to foster student development, to improve teaching practices, and to recognize and capitalize upon learning that occurs not just in formal educational settings but also in a wide variety of nonformal learning contexts such as the home and the workplace. These are precisely the issues that Part II of this volume attempts to address.

In Chapter 2, Arthur Chickering focusses on the primary and most fundamental issue in all measurement, namely, what qualities or constructs should be assessed for what purposes. He begins by articulating personal qualities that higher education should foster in student development. These qualities are derived not just from the goals and values espoused in formal institutional rhetoric, but also from the latent values that really drive institutional practices. Under the best of circumstances, for an "institution of integrity," the espoused values and institutional practices should, of course, be aligned.

Chickering then makes the case that there is a strong congruence between these personal qualities typifying the aims of liberal education and the cognitive and interpersonal competencies as well as motivational characteristics required for successful careers. Furthermore, he points out that these qualities and competencies are also closely aligned with major dimensions and stages of human development. This permits him to outline how different orientations toward knowledge and different motives for learning, as well as different teaching practices, can either reinforce particular developmental stages or else facilitate stage progression. Thus, assessment of the identified personal qualities and competencies, with feedback for self-directed learning and improved teaching, is in the service of meeting the aims of liberal education, of fulfilling requirements for career success, and of developing mature adult functioning.

In Chapter 3, K. Patricia Cross analyzes the essential features of assessments aimed at improving teaching practices. As did Chickering, she begins by identifying the important qualities or constructs that should be assessed for these purposes, namely, the salient behavioral characteristics of good college teachers. Most of these characteristics have been incorporated into student rating scales for evaluating teaching, and feedback from such evaluation has proven effective in changing teacher behavior, especially of poor teachers. However, the end-of-course timing of these evaluations does not provide immediate feedback, nor is the educational context of particular lessons or class experiences taken into account.

As a remedy for these shortcomings, Cross champions a number of Classroom Assessment Techniques, whereby both teacher and students together appraise student learning with immediate feedback that is highly context-specific. Many of these techniques, such as the Minute Paper and the Punctuated Lecture, are not simply assessment devices but also pedagogical strategies for involving students in monitoring and reflecting on their own learning. Hence, a key feature of assessment to improve college instruction is that the assessment should not only be informative to teachers but also instructive to students.

In Chapter 4, Morris Keeton traces the checkered history of attempts to assess and credential learning from students' experiences in nonformal learning contexts such as the workplace. Essential to this assessment of learning that occurs experientially prior to or outside of college—assessment that is basically judgmental in nature—is the recognition that reliability and validity can be attained through careful training of judges to apply clear performance standards. Much of this assessment is portfolio-assisted, to use Keeton's term, in the sense that multiple forms of a student's prior experiences are compiled, from which inferences about the level and amount of relevant experiential learning are evaluated.

Such attempts to infuse higher education with sound assessment of experiential learning are important for at least two reasons. One is that recognition of experiential learning opens access and facilitates progress of an increasingly diverse student clientele. The other reason is that the availability of sound procedures for assessing experiential learning should increase the likelihood that hands-on practice of desired skills will become a more integral part of formal instructional experiences, thereby making higher education more performance-based as well as theory-based.

In Chapters 5 and 6, Wilbert McKeachie and Sister Joel Read, respectively, offer commentary elaborating points stimulated by the three previous chapters. McKeachie emphasizes that feedback often leads to improvements in teaching and learning but is no panacea. Indeed, he outlines conditions needed for feedback to be effective. Prominent among these are feedback that stimulates student involvement and reflectiveness and that is generalizable and fosters development of transferable skills to advance further learning. Sister Joel Read focusses on six characteristics of assessment aimed at supporting student access and success, prime among which are validity and reliability but also other features bearing on issues of comparability, fairness, and value. She emphasizes that to facilitate student access and success across the curriculum, the assessments should be diagnostic and provide feedback not only about current status but also about directions for improvement.

REFERENCES

Holtzman, W. H. (1976). Education for creative problem solving. In S. Messick & Associates (Eds.), *Individuality in learning* (p. 23-33). San Francisco: Jossey-Bass.

2

PERSONAL QUALITIES AND HUMAN DEVELOPMENT IN HIGHER EDUCATION: ASSESSMENT IN THE SERVICE OF EDUCATIONAL GOALS

Arthur W. Chickering
George Mason University

The title for my chapter covers a lot of territory. I will try to address it in a way that sets the stage for the various contributions to follow. To assess personal qualities and human development in the service of educational goals means confronting at least three complex challenges. First, we need to articulate clear institutional goals, to specify the personal qualities and dimensions of human development we aim to foster. Second, we need to be clear about institutional policies and practices that encourage or inhibit those outcomes. Third, we need to identify, or create, instruments and methods for assessing progress -- or regress -- on the desired outcomes.

CLEAR GOALS

Research evidence, dating back to Newcomb's (1943) studies of Bennington College, indicates that clear and consistent institutional objectives make significant contributions to student development. In their comprehensive 1991 review of the literature, *How College Affects Students*, Pascarella and Terenzini say,

> the effects of specific within-college programs, conditions, or experiences
> consistently appear to be smaller than the overall net effect of college....
> Furthermore, while the impact of any single sub-environment may be
> small or modest, the cumulative effect of all sub-environments -- if they
> are mutually supportive -- can be substantial. Thus, instead of singular,
> large, specially designed, and campus-wide programs to achieve a

> particular institutional goal, efforts might more profitably focus on ways to embed the pursuit of that goal in *all* appropriate institutional activities. … In short, rather than seeking large levers to pull in order to promote change on a large scale, it may well be more effective to pull more small levers more often. (p. 655)

Unfortunately, in the 1980's Boyer (1987) found a pervasive absence of clear and consistent objectives. He states that,

> during our study we found divisions on campus, conflicting priorities and competing interests that diminish the intellectual and social quality of the undergraduate experiences and restrict the capacity of the college effectively to serve its students. At most colleges and universities we visited, these special points of tension appeared with such regularity and seemed so consistently to sap the vitality of the baccalaureate experience that we have made them the focus of this report. (p. 2)

At most institutions administrators, faculty, and students are all caught in the machinery. The main thing is to keep it running smoothly. Squirt oil where it squeaks. Comfort becomes the prime criterion. For administrators, the goal is smooth functioning, a shiny image, and solid financial resources. For professors, it is minimal teaching and maximum time for professional advancement and personal interests; lectures that can become books and articles; and, access for students defined as 2 office hours a week. While for students the goal is freedom to study as much or as little as they wish; adequate time for work and socializing; and, good grades with minimal effort.

As Boyer (1987) emphasizes:

> Scrambling for students and driven by marketplace demands, many undergraduate colleges have lost their sense of mission. They are confused about their mission and how to impart shared values on which the vitality of both higher education and society depends. The disciplines have fragmented themselves into smaller and smaller pieces, and undergraduates find it difficult to see patterns in their courses or to relate what they learn to life. (p. 3)

Of course it is not the simple statement of objectives that has an impact. Every college catalog has those. They need to be taken seriously. When taken seriously they help create educationally powerful environments three ways:

First, policies, programs and practices tend toward greater internal consistency. When faculty members sitting on ubiquitous committees make decisions in terms of commonly shared and explicit institutional objectives then the various parts fit together with greater coherence and integration. The educational impact of one element less frequently runs counter to another.

Second, clear objectives help students make more explicit their own reasons for attending the college and their own purposes while there. This improved self-selection, clarity of purpose, and the strengthened motivation which results, improves retention and degree completion.

Third, it's important to be explicit about objectives because they contain within them strong value commitments. No institution is without such commitments. Often they are absorbed unwittingly by students as matters not to be questioned. At some institutions, for example, the success ethic, rugged individualism, personal achievement, self denial, conservative morality, and future time orientation are among the dominant values assumed; at other institutions, such values as sociability, a relativistic moral attitude, conformity, or a hedonistic present-time orientation are assumed. Inexplicit objectives leave these values to unconscious learning — free from conscious control and modification. But when objectives are explicit, and when the attendant values are overtly expressed, they can be subjected to examination, disagreement and challenge. That kind of learning makes values more conscious and integrates them with other components of personality and behavior.

A critical issue here is the gap between our espoused purposes or values, and our values in use. As Alexander Astin (1993) has said,

> Most institutions operate according to two sets of values. We have the formal or official institutional goals and values which are usually stated in our charter, mission statement, or catalog... The other set of values ... really drives our policies. These are the values that underlie decisions such as how to allocate resources, how we hire and reward faculty and administrators, how and why we admit students, the way we establish our curriculum, the choice of pedagogical techniques, the establishment of new programs, procedures and so on... I believe we create enormous problems ... when there are inconsistencies, and there are very serious ones, between our explicit and implicit values, or if you prefer, our words and our deeds. (p. 15)

Our first, and most important task then — and it can be a daunting one — is to agree on shared purposes and to close the gap between our espoused values and our values in use. We must do no less than create institutional policies and practices internally consistent with the objectives and values we espouse. We must create an *institution of integrity*.

This task is relatively easy in a small private college, where clear objectives, shared values, and self-selection by students, faculty members, and administrators create strong institutional cohesiveness. It is much more difficult in large, complex, public institutions. But the implication for those of us in such public institutions is not to throw in the towel. Instead we need to be thoughtful about the "unit of analysis," the organizational entity where we try to agree on those shared objectives. It is probably impossible to do that across the diverse schools, colleges, departments, and other units which characterize most public institutions.

We do better to be less ambitious, to take a sub-unit or sub-culture and address that. Pascarella and Terenzini (1991) report significant differences in *departmental* impact on students in comprehensive universities. Thus, it is possible to create departmental cultures, norms, and values around shared purposes within large, bland, amorphous institutions that have distinctive consequences for students. At one institution perhaps the department is the best level to address. Or perhaps the College of Arts and Sciences, or the Business School, or Nursing, Education, Engineering, are of such a scale that cohesiveness and integrity concerning clear objectives can be achieved.

So my first point is that clear and internally consistent institutional objectives, stated in terms of desired outcomes for student learning and personal development, are critically important for educational effectiveness. And more to the point for this volume, because without such objectives there is no solid framework for assessment.

PERSONAL QUALITIES, CAREER SUCCESS, AND HUMAN DEVELOPMENT

Assertions concerning the personal qualities higher education should foster have been around for a long time. One of the earliest, and best, comes from Cardinal Newman's (1973/1852) *The Idea of a University*. He said,

> A University...aims at raising the intellectual tone of society, at cultivating the public mind, at purifying the national taste, at supplying true principles to popular enthusiasm and fixed aims to popular aspiration, at facilitating the exercise of political power, and refining the intercourse of private life. It gives a man a clear conscious view of his own opinions and judgements, a truth in developing them, an eloquence in expressing them, and a force in urging them. It teaches him to see things as they are, to go right to the point, to disentangle a skein of thought, to detect what is sophisticated, and to discard what is irrelevant. It prepares him to fill any post with credit, and to master any subject with facility, it shows him how to accommodate himself to others, how to influence them, how to come to an understanding with them. He is at home in any society, he has common ground with every class, he knows when to speak and when to be silent; he is able to converse, he is able to listen; he can ask a question pertinently and gain a lesson seasonably when he has nothing to impart himself....He is a pleasant companion and a comrade you can depend upon.... He has a repose of mind which lives in itself, while it lives in the world and which has resources for its happiness at home when it cannot go abroad. [We forgive the sexist language. Unfortunately, sensitivity to gender issues was not a high priority back in 1852.]

Take that eloquent paragraph apart and you have several key objectives for liberal education.

- Communications skills—"an eloquence in expressing them, and a force in urging them."

- Critical thinking skills— "to see things as they are, to go right to the point, to disentangle a skein of thought, to detect what is sophisticated, and to discard what is irrelevant."

- Interpersonal competence, respect for others, empathy—"how to accommodate himself to others, how to influence them, how to come to an understanding with them, how to bear with them."

- Preparation for work and learning how to learn—"to fill any post with credit and to master any subject with facility."

- Cultural sophistication and cross-cultural understanding—"he is at home in any society, he has a common ground with every class."

- Capacity for intimacy—"a pleasant companion and a comrade you can depend on."

- Clarity of values and integrity—"a clear conscious view of his own opinions and judgments, a truth in developing them."

- A basic sense of identity—"a repose of mind which lives in itself while it lives in the world."

That's a good list. Many of our institutions aim for similar outcomes. Today we might add some others, like computer literacy, computational skills, developing artistic talents.

Career Success

There is an interesting congruence between Newman's aims and the personal qualities required for a successful career. A growing body of research has identified the skills, abilities, and personal characteristics required for effective careers. The basic findings have been remarkably consistent during the past 20 years. A study in the 1970s, by George Klemp and his colleagues, examined a variety of career areas, including human services, military services, small businesses, police work, sales, civil service, and industry management, among others. What did they find?

> Our most consistent -- though unexpected -- finding is that the amount of knowledge one acquires of a content area is generally unrelated to superior

performance in an occupation and is often unrelated even to marginally acceptable performance. Certainly many occupations require a minimum level of knowledge ... for the satisfactory discharge of work related duties, but even more occupations require only that the individual be willing and able to learn new things .... In fact, it is neither the acquisition of knowledge nor the use of knowledge that distinguishes the outstanding performer, but rather the cognitive skills that are developed and exercised by the process of acquiring and using knowledge. These cognitive skills constitute the first factor of occupational success. (p. 103)

What cognitive skills are most important to success at work (Klemp, 1977, p. 104)?

1. "Information processing skills related to learning, recall and forgetting."

2. "Conceptualizing skills that enable individuals to bring order to the informational chaos that surrounds them. Such skills go beyond an ability to analyze...they involve an ability to synthesize information from a prior analysis."

3. "The ability to understand many sides of a controversial issue. [Persons with this skill can resolve informational conflicts better than persons without it. Persons who don't have this skill] typically resolve dissonance by denying the validity of other points of view and are ill equipped to mediate disputes or to understand what their positions have in common with others."

4. "The ability to learn from experience...to translate observations into a theory that can be used to generate behavioral alternatives."

The second major factor for success at work involves interpersonal skills (Klemp, 1977, pp. 105-106).

1. Non-verbal communication — "Fluency and precision in speaking and writing are important...but often it is the nonverbal component of communication, both in sending and receiving information, that has the greater impact."

2. Accurate empathy — the ability to diagnose a human concern and to *respond appropriately* to the needs of the other. "There are three aspects to this skill. One is a positive regard for others....The second aspect involves giving another person assistance, whether asked for or not, that enables the person to be effective. The third aspect involves...ability to control impulsive feelings of hostility or

anger that, when unleashed on another person, makes that person feel powerless and ineffective."

But cognitive and interpersonal skills by themselves do not guarantee superior performance. The third critical factor is motivation. Klemp (1977) says:

> This variable describes a person who habitually thinks in terms of causes and outcomes as opposed to one who sees the self as an ineffective victim of events that have an unknown cause....Our own analysis of complex managerial jobs...has shown that a person who takes a *proactive* stance, who initiates action and works to dissolve blocks to progress, will, with few exceptions, have the advantage over a person who is *reactive*, who does not seek new opportunities, but sees the world as a series of insurmountable obstacles. (pp. 107-108)

Twenty years later Sheckley, Lamdin, and Keeton (1992), in *Employability in a High Performance Economy*, shared "a consensus on necessary skills" based on commonalities among five different groups: (i) the American Society for Training and Development, (ii) the Commission on the Skills of the American Workforce, (iii) American College Testing "Work Keys," (iv) the U.S. Secretary of Labor's Commission on Achieving Necessary Skills (SCANS), and (v) German vocational education. Here's their list:

Knowing how to learn

Basic academic skills: reading, writing, & computation

Communications

Cognitive skills

Personal and career development skills

Interpersonal skills and effectiveness in groups

Organizational effectiveness and leadership

They make a critical observation about these workplace skills:

> Perhaps the most salient fact about all of these skills is that they are transferable. That is, they apply to a number of different job groups and functions....The generic nature of these skills has important implications for employability training. To teach narrowly specific skills is to ensure that its lifespan is finite, dependent on changes in technology, changes in the way companies choose to structure work, and changes in the employees' circumstances and career goals. To teach a transferable skill is to ensure its usefulness in an ever expanding number of jobs and life situations. Employability skills are truly "life skills." To achieve

maximum flexibility and mobility the workforce must have these broad-based transferable skills. (Sheckley et al., p. 114)

To me it's fascinating to find such agreement among Newman, Klemp, and Sheckley et al., across 150 years, despite the dramatic changes in the world of work since the industrial revolution. And it is especially gratifying to note the congruence between the personal qualities required for effective work and our long cherished liberal education outcomes. Perhaps it is not surprising that these personal qualities are intimately associated with more general dimensions of human development.

Human Development

How do our desired outcomes for liberal education, and the skills and personal characteristics required for effective careers, correspond with what we know about major dimensions of human development? I anchor my observations concerning human development in three conceptual frameworks: Jane Loevinger's (1976) work on ego development, Perry's (1970) work on intellectual and ethical development, and the work of Belenky, Clinchy, Goldberger, and Tarule (1986) in *Women's Ways of Knowing*. These three bodies of research and theory are generally consistent with many others, among whom are Baxter-Magolda, Erikson, Gilligan, Kegan, and Kohlberg.

These theorists see human development as a series of stages, each of which builds upon and incorporates the earlier stages. Each person moves along this continuum. In any population only a minority reach the "higher" stages. It is worth noting that these developmental sequences are toward the values enshrined in our Constitution and toward civic virtues espoused alike by liberals and conservatives, Democrats and Republicans.

Table 1 juxtaposes the stage labels used by Loevinger, Perry, and Belenky et al. It is followed by Tables 1a, 1b, and 1c that provide more details about each theorist.

Jane Loevinger's (1976) research and theory concerning ego development provides one of the most comprehensive formulations currently available. "Ego development" is a good way to approach the issue because it is a "master trait" whose different structures heavily influence our perceptions, our thinking and our behavior.

Loevinger posits a basic sequence of four developmental structures: impulse control and character development, interpersonal style, conscious preoccupations, and cognitive style. Her developmental sequence begins with the "Presocial" and "Symbiotic" stages associated with infancy and childhood. The five major stages associated with adolescence and adulthood are "Impulsive," "Conformist," "Conscientious," "Autonomous," and "Integrated." Persons at the Impulsive stage are, as the label suggests, strongly governed by their impulses and by fear of

TABLE 1. STAGES OF HUMAN DEVELOPMENT

Loevinger	Perry	Belenky et al.
Self-protective/Opportunistic	Dualism	Silence
Conformist	Dualism Multiplicity	Received and Subjective Knowledge
Conscientious	Relativism	Procedural Knowledge Separate Knowledge
Autonomous	Relativism	Procedural Knowledge Connected Knowing
Integrated	Commitment in Relativism	Constructed Knowledge

retaliation. They tend to be dependent and exploitative.   They are preoccupied with sexual and aggressive feelings and tend toward stereotyping in the way they think.   "Self-protective" persons fear being caught and are wary, opportunistic, manipulative and exploitative. They are preoccupied with gaining advantage and controlling others. Conformists are oriented toward external rules, belonging, and being nice.   Appearances and social acceptability are important.   They tend to think simplistically, having recourse to stereotypes and cliches.

Conscientious persons behave in terms of self-evaluated standards, with long term goals and ideals.   They tend to be self-critical, intense and responsible in relations with others as well as concerned about adequate communication. They are preoccupied with self-respect, achievement, and accurate self-expression. Their thinking is characterized by conceptual complexity.   The Autonomous stage adds coping with conflicting inner needs, toleration, respect for the autonomy of others, and recognition of interdependence. Persons at this stage tend to integrate physiological and psychological causes for feelings and behavior, and are concerned with self-fulfillment and how they function in relation to the larger social context.   They are conceptually complex and have high tolerance for ambiguity.   Integrated persons have reconciled inner conflicts, renounced the unattainable and cherish individuality.

If you think about it you will note that the higher stages of Loevinger's developmental structures integrate areas of development which include the major kinds of competence and personal characteristics addressed by Newman, Klemp, and Sheckley et al.   The developmental sequences labeled "Conscious Preoccupations" and "Cognitive Style" describe in more detail the kinds of changes necessary to achieve high level communication skills, critical thinking

TABLE 1a. SOME MILESTONES OF EGO DEVELOPMENT

Loevinger

Stage	Impulse control, character development	Interpersonal Style	Conscious preoccupations	Cognitive style
Presocial		Autistic		
Symbiotic		Symbiotic	Self versus nonself	
Impulsive	Impulsive, fear of retaliation	Receiving, dependent, exploitative	Bodily feelings, especially sexual and aggressive	Stereotyping, conceptual confusion
Self-protective	Fear of being caught, externalizing blame, opportunist	Wary, manipulative, exploitative	Self-protection, trouble, wishes, things, advantage, control	
Conformist	Conformity to external rules, shame, guilt for breaking rules	Belonging, superficial niceness	Appearance, social acceptability, banal feelings, behavior	Conceptual simplicity, stereotypes, clichés
Conscientious-conformist	Differentiation of norms, goals	Aware of self in relation to group, helping	Adjustment, problems, reasons, opportunities (vague)	Multiplicity
Conscientious	Self-evaluated standards, self-criticism, guilt for consequences, long-term goals and ideals	Intensive, responsible, mutual, concern for communi-cation	Differential feelings, motives for behavior, self-respect, achievement, traits, expression	Conceptual complexity, idea of patterning
Individualistic	*Add*: Respect for individuality	*Add:* Dependence as an emotional problem	*Add:* Develop-ment, social problems, differentiation of inner life from outer	*Add:* Distinction of process and outcome
Autonomous	*Add:* Coping with conflicting inner needs, toleration	*Add:* Respect for autonomy, interdepend-ence	Vividly conveyed feelings, integration of physiological and psychological, psychological causation of behavior, role conception, self-fulfillment, self in social context	Increased conceptual complexity, complex patterns, toleration for ambiguity, broad scope, objectivity
Integrated	*Add:* Reconciling inner conflicts, renunciation of unattainable	*Add:* Cherishing of individuality	*Add:* Identity	

Note: Add means in addition to the description applying to the previous level.
Source: Loevinger, 1976, pp. 24-25. Reprinted by permission.

TABLE 1b. FORMS OF INTELLECTUAL AND ETHICAL DEVELOPMENT

Perry

Dualism (Positions 1 and 2)	Multiplicity (Positions 3 and 4)	Relativism (Positions 5 and 6)	Commitment in Relativism (Positions 7, 8, and 9)
• Knowledge exists absolutely • "Right Answers" are known by authorities • Tasks that require thinking about options or many points of view are confusing. • Legitimacy of alternate perspectives is not yet acknowledged. • Judgments are stated as though they are self-evident • Diversity of opinion or uncertainty among Authorities is viewed as inadequacy on their part, or an exercise "so we can learn to find The Answer for ourselves."	• Students accept diversity and uncertainty as legitimate but still temporary in areas where Authority "hasn't found The Answer yet." • Questions now can legitimately have multiple answers. • Students assume that Authorities grade on "good expression" but remain puzzled as to standards. • Those who hold different beliefs are no longer seen as simply "wrong." • All opinions are equally valid outside of the Authority's realm where right-wrong still prevails. • Students are unable to adequately evaluate points of view, and question the legitimacy of doing so.	• All knowledge (including authority's) now is viewed as contextual and relativistic. • Dualistic right-wrong thinking exists only within certain contexts. • Students differentiate between an unconsidered belief and a considered judgment. • Authorities are no longer resisted, but can be valued for their expertise. • Their judgments, too, can be evaluated. • Differing perspectives are now not merely acknowledged but seen as pieces of a larger whole. • Personal Commitments are seen as ways to orient oneself in a relativistic world (vs. unconsidered commitment to simple belief in certainty).	• Students have a growing realization that they need to find their own choices, based on multiple "truths." • They move "off the fence" and begin to align choices with personal themes. • Active affirmation of themselves and their responsibilities in a pluralistic world clarifies identity. • Personal commitments in such areas as marriage, religion, and career are made from relativistic frame of reference.

TABLE 1c. WOMEN'S WAYS OF KNOWING:
THE DEVELOPMENT OF SELF, VOICE, AND MIND

Belenky, Clinchy, Goldberger, and Tarule

Silence

Represents an extreme denial of self and dependence on authority for direction. Ways of knowing limited to the present, to the actual, to the concrete and specific, to behaviors actually enacted. Authorities are all powerful, through might but not through expertise. Blind obedience is important for keeping out of trouble and ensuring survival. Knowing "why" is neither possible nor important.

Received Knowledge

Learn by listening. Words are central. The ideas and ideals heard in the words of others are concrete and dualistic. Things are right or wrong, true or false, good or bad, black or white. There is only one right answer to each question. All other answers or contrary views are automatically wrong. Authorities, not friends, sources of truth. Learning is receiving, retaining, and returning the words of authorities.

Subjective Knowledge

Truth is personal, private, subjectively known or intuited. I is dualistic in assuming that there are right answers. The fountain of truth has shifted, now residing within the person, and can negate answers the outside world supplies. It becomes a source of inner strength, an important adaptation in the service of self-protection, self-assertion, and self-definition. Freedom from social convention and definition represents a move toward greater autonomy and independence.

Procedural Knowledge

    Separate Knowing. Oriented toward impersonal rules. Morality based on impersonal procedures for establishing justice. Truth emerges through impersonal procedures. Listening to reason, objectivity. Purpose is to arrive at sound judgment.

    Connected Knowing. Oriented toward relationship. Morality based on care. Truth emerges through care. Access to other's knowledge and personal experiences; empathy. Purpose is not to judge but to understand.

Constructed Knowledge

Truth is a process in which the knower participates. Knowledge is relative to one's frame of reference. Challenged, not daunted, by contradiction and conflict. True experts appreciate complexity and are humble about their knowledge. Want to develop a voice of their own to communicate their understandings of life's complexity ability, information processing and conceptualizing skills, and the ability to understand many sides of a complex issue.

The sequences labeled "Impulse Control", "Character Development," and "Interpersonal Style," describe the changes necessary for cross-cultural understanding, respect, empathy, positive regard for others, giving assistance, and controlling impulsive feelings. The sense of self in a social and historical context, clarity of values and integrity, the capacity to define oneself as an actor, to exercise initiative and to be proactive, all depend on reaching at least the Conscientious stage. These qualities gain increased solidity and strength at the Autonomous and Integrated stages.

The basic point here, then, is that there is strong internal consistency among (1) the personal qualities which typically characterize the aims of liberal education, (2) the competencies and characteristics required for successful careers, and (3) basic ingredients of human development.

HIGHER EDUCATION

The entries in Table 2, Adult Development and Higher Education, suggest how some of our most fundamental orientations toward knowledge and educational practices reinforce particular stages or can encourage stage change. We see that motives for learning, orientations toward knowledge, and educational practices are systematically related to different levels of development. Motives expand as our development grows from a concern to satisfy immediate needs, through gaining social acceptance, obtaining credentials and meeting social responsibilities, to deepening self-understanding and to increased capacity to shape our own futures.

Our view of knowledge changes from acquiring facts and objective "truths," to "know how" about problem solving, and then to personally generated insights, including enjoying rather than fearing paradoxes. We move from valuing knowledge as a means to concrete ends and for social approval, to a means for achieving our own standards of excellence for our own self-development and transformation. Our assumptions about sources of knowledge expand from precepts received from external authorities, to conclusions based on rational inquiry, and then to personally generated insights and judgments. Concurrently our learning processes shift from imitation, to discovering "correct answers" through scientific inquiry and logical analysis, to seeking new experiences, to developing new paradigms, and to creating new dialectics of thought and action.

Unfortunately the dominant educational practices of most colleges and universities fit only the simpler stages of development. They are almost exclusively oriented toward the Self-protective/Opportunistic and Conformist levels of ego development, the Dualism and Multiplicity levels of Perry, and the Received and Subjective Knowledge levels of Belenky et al. They put a premium on memorizing. They treat knowledge like a commodity, a collection of discrete items, packaged in standard-sized boxes, sold by the Carnegie unit, which students accumulate to exchange for a degree at commencement.

Take any ten institutions at random. How many curriculums, courses, classes, and examinations help students build knowledge from personal experiences and personally generated syntheses and paradigms, rather than treating truth as objectively real, given by authority, or "discovered" by logical or scientific analyses? How many teachers not only help students acquire basic concepts, competence, and knowledge, but also help them apply that learning through responsible action, or help students to make better sense of the world and of themselves? How many students, consequently, see learning as acquiring information and competence to obtain recognition, get a better job, fill a role, rather than as a process of becoming and self-transformation?

Recurrent research has demonstrated that 80-90% of our teaching is lecturing and exams. This kind of teaching best fits the Self-protective/Opportunistic, the Dualistic, and the Received and Subjective Knowledge levels of development. The key dynamic is the comfortable fit between (1) the student's disposition to identify with persons in authority, to accept their definitions of right and wrong, and to avoid punishment by deferring to their power, and (2) the teacher's easy assertion of authority, emphasis on dispensing information or skills for students to master, and use of exams to punish wrong answers and reward right ones.

Most Socratic dialogue or teacher-led discussions best fit the Conformist stage of ego development along with Perry's Dualism and Multiplicity, as well as the Received and Subjective Knowledge levels. The discussions provide rich information about the teacher's views, encouraging students to shape their own responses accordingly, and to receive immediate rewards for sound contributions.

Contract learning, when it is not heavily teacher dominated, is applicable to more advanced levels of development. (I am *not* talking about "contract grading" where a student agrees to do additional work, usually specified by the teacher, in exchange for a higher grade.) Here the objectives, learning activities, products, as well as the methods and criteria for evaluation are mutually determined. Students, depending on their sophistication concerning the subject matter and appropriate resources, and depending on their general competence and self-development, can assume varying levels of self-determination and self-evaluation.

Of course, contract learning can be highly teacher controlled and authoritarian, not only in terms of the learning activities, products and evaluation, but also concerning the purposes judged acceptable. And skilled teachers can use lectures and exams as well as seminars and group discussions in ways that challenge autonomous students, encourage commitment in relativism, and foster constructed knowing. The relationships suggested in Table 2 rest on studies of typical teaching practices. They would not apply to those exceptional teachers we occasionally experience.

Different teaching practices are typically associated with different types of student-faculty relationships. The professor as authority, information transmitter, carrying sole responsibility for evaluation, best fits the Self Protective/Opportunistic and Conformist stages of ego development and the associated stages in the Perry and Belenky et al. schemes. The teacher as mentor and resource — who maintains a collegial relation where the student carries significant responsibility both for defining objectives and for subsequent implementation, who helps students clarify objectives, identify appropriate materials and educational experiences, plan a course of action, and evaluate progress — is behaving in ways consistent with the higher stages.

As we recognized earlier, all aspects of institutional life have to pull together if human development is to be encouraged. New student orientation, extra- or co-curricular activities, institutional governance, administrative styles, as well as promotional materials and other publications all send messages about what is expected, and what is valued — about life and the role of learning. This "hidden curriculum" that underlies our more formal curriculum, even though unrecognized and undiscussed, will reinforce one or another stage of development. At most institutions the dominant messages indicate that the institution aims to keep students interested in learning, to provide predetermined information, and to certify that students have at least put in the seat time and performed sufficiently well to accumulate the necessary credits. But an institution can send quite different messages which suggest that its functions aim to raise key questions and pose important dilemmas; to confront significant social issues, discontinuities, and paradoxes; and, to create contexts for rich and challenging personal experiences leading to self-generated and self-validated insights, values, and moral behaviors.

Thus, Table 2 suggests a way to think about relationships among human development, educational practices, student-faculty relationships and institutional purposes and functions. The difficulty, of course, is that we have students at all levels of development. Thus, the challenge is to help students at each stage move to higher levels. We cannot simply pitch our curricula, teaching, and relationships with students at the highest levels. We need to create alternatives which serve students at all levels so we are responsive to the full range of developmental potentials.

For example, few institutions can or should operate exclusively through contract learning. But most of us can more frequently teach in ways that challenge dualistic thinking, that expose unfettered Relativism or Subjective Knowing, and that foster principled Autonomy, Integrity, and Commitments in Relativism. To do so, however, we faculty members, together with our administrative and student services colleagues, must learn to be authoritative without being authoritarian, to build collaborative and collegial relationships as resource persons for students, to identify and create developmentally powerful encounters and experiences, as well as to help students plan, carry out, and evaluate their own learning.

TABLE 2. ADULT DEVELOPMENT AND HIGHER EDUCATION

Loevinger	Perry	Belenky et al	Motive for Education	View of Knowledge	Uses of Knowledge	Sources of Knowledge
1. Self-protective Opportunistic	Dualism	Silence	Instrumental; satisfy immediate needs	A possession that helps one get desired ends; ritualistic actions that yield solutions	Education to get; means to concrete ends; used by self to obtain effects in the world	From external authority; from asking how to get things
2. Conformist	Dualism Multiplicity	Received and Subjective Knowledge	Impress significant others; gain social acceptance; obtain credentials and recognition	Objective truth given by authority; general information required for social roles	Education to be: social approval, appearance, status used by self to achieve according to expectations and standards of significant others	From external authority; from asking what others expect and how to do it
3. Conscientious	Relativism	Procedural Knowledge Separate Knowing	Achieve competence re competitive or normative standards; increase capacity to meet social responsibilities	"Know how": personal skills in problem solving; divergent views resolved by rational processes	Education to do: competence in work and social role; used to achieve internalized standards of excellence and to serve society	Personal integration of information based on rational inquiry; from setting goals; from asking what is needed, how things work, and why
4. Autonomous	Relativism	Procedural Knowledge Connected Knowing				
5. Integrated	Commitment in Relativism	Constructed Knowledge	Deepen understanding of self, world, and life cycle; develop increasing capacity to manage own destiny	Personally generated insight about self and nature of life; subjective and dialectical; paradox appreciated	Education to become: self-knowledge; self-development; used to transform self and the world	Personal experience and reflection; personally generated paradigms, insights, judgments

TABLE 2. ADULT DEVELOPMENT AND HIGHER EDUCATION (continued)

Loevinger Perry Belenky et al	Learning Processes	Teaching Practices	Student/Faculty Relationships	Source of Evaluation	Institutional Function
1	Imitation; acquire information, competence, as given by authority	Lecture-examination system	Teacher is authority, transmitter, judge; student is receiver, judged	By teacher only	Arouse attention and maintain interest; show how things should be done
2		Teacher-led dialogue or discussion. Open, "leaderless" "learner-centered" discussion	Teacher is a "model" for student identification	By teacher only	Provide predetermined information and training programs; certify skills and knowledge
				By teacher and peers	
3	Discover correct answers through scientific method and logical analyses; multiple views recognized but congruence and simplicity sought	Programmed learning; correspondence study; televised instruction	"Teacher" is abstraction behind system; student is recipient	By system	Provide structured programs that offer concrete skills and information, opportunities for rational analysis, and practice, all of which can be evaluated and certified
4	Seek new experiences; reorganize past conceptions on the basis of new experiences; develop new paradigms; create new dialectics	Contract learning with objectives, time activities, and evaluation negotiated between student and teacher at the outset and held throughout	Teacher is resource contributing to planning and evaluation; student defines purposes	By teacher, peers, system, and self, with teacher the final judge	Ask key questions; pose key dilemmas; confront significant discontinuities and paradoxes; foster personal experience and personally generated insights
5		Contract learning with objectives, time, activities, and evaluation defined generally by the student and modified with experience	Teacher has collegial relationship with student; student defines purposes and criteria for evaluation	By teacher, peers, system, and self, with self as the final judge	

ASSESSMENT ISSUES, INSTRUMENTS, AND METHODS

Basically, I would like to address three obvious distinctions about the purposes of assessment which often seem to be forgotten or ignored. They have important implications for planning, instruments, methods, and dissemination. We must distinguish among (i) assessment to inform decisions concerning general policies and practices, (ii) assessment to inform decisions concerning local institutional policies and practices, and (iii) assessment to inform decisions concerning contextually specific sub-groups or individuals. Each will be discussed briefly in the following three sections.

Decisions to Inform General Policies and Practices

This level is illustrated by the data and actuarial statistics used by insurance companies, or by epidemiological research, or by studies of dietary and life style behaviors related to health and longevity. These large scale studies, often longitudinal, inform a wide range of public policy decisions. The closest analogues for higher education are the findings generated by the National Center for Educational Statistics and by Astin's long standing Cooperative Institutional Research Program (CIRP).

Studies like these are typically centrally planned by relevant experts. The instruments and methods of choice are survey research or analyses of existing data involving large numbers from diverse representative populations. Preferred analyses are various types of multivariate statistics which identify the reductions in variance associated with different combinations of variables. The findings suggest general norms as benchmarks for evaluating policy and practice decisions. Dissemination occurs first to appropriate political, institutional, and corporate leaders. Depending on the issue it may be important to carry out campaigns to increase general public awareness and to encourage widespread changes in general behaviors.

This kind of assessment, as Astin's reports over the years have demonstrated, can be immensely useful to enhance general understandings and for broad policy decisions, but it is not typically very useful for decisions at the local or institutional level. Astin's "involvement theory," anchored in the CIRP findings, is a good example. It is at a level of abstraction which cuts across all types of institutions. Widely disseminated, it has given visibility and legitimacy to a basic concept many find useful. But local applications will depend on particular institutional strengths and weaknesses not readily identified by this kind of assessment, even for the institutions who participate in the program.

Decisions to Inform Local Institutional Policies and Practices

Many people forget that *Involvement in Learning*, that fine, influential report, gave us a solid set of recommendations concerning assessment and feedback. Three of them are particularly pertinent to this type of institutional assessment:

> "Faculty and academic deans should design and implement a systematic program to assess the knowledge, capacities, and skills developed in students by academic and co-curricular programs."

> "In changing current systems of assessment, academic administrators and faculty should ensure that the instruments and methods used are appropriate for (1) the knowledge, capacities and skills addressed, and (2) the stated objectives of undergraduate education at their institutions."

> "Faculty should participate in the development, adoption, administration, and scoring of the instruments and procedures used in student assessment and, in the process, be trained in the ways of using assessment as a teaching tool."

Note the recurrent emphasis on faculty and administrative participation in design and implementation as well as in developing and adopting instruments and methods. That's because these folks are the ultimate users of the results, the ultimate audience for "dissemination." They have to own the content and process from the beginning. Note also the importance of tailoring assessment to the particular institutional objectives so they are pertinent to valued local outcomes.

Here the methodological choices reach for an appropriate balance among quantitative and qualitative studies; surveys and tests, standardized or local, are usefully complemented by focus groups and interviews; and, unobtrusive measures using locally available data may be especially useful. Much more attention is directed toward particular interactions among student experiences and behaviors, and desired outcomes. Specific criteria may be based on local objectives and aspirations in addition to norm-referenced comparisons with similar institutions.

Here it is also critical to recognize that "dissemination" must go beyond simple distribution of printed reports. Face to face meetings, workshops, professional development programs, and institutional change initiatives are the vehicles by which an institution profits from the assessments undertaken.

Decisions Concerning Contextually Specific Subgroups or Individuals

This level of assessment has become critical for many U.S. colleges and universities where students are dispersed across subcultures diverse in gender, age, ethnicity, and national origin. In addition, our increased sophistication concerning the importance of learning style and developmental stage differences further complicates the diversity issue. There is increasing experimentation and sophistication concerning interactions among teaching practices, gender, learning styles, developmental stages, and other dimensions of individual difference. But we do not have a lot of assessment experience responsive to this diversity.

I remember vividly meeting in the Henry Chauncey Conference Center at ETS in 1973 with about thirty institutional representatives and ETS staff. The gathering was created to discuss the assessment of experiential learning and I was representing Empire State. Soon after the meeting, twelve institutions were invited to form the Council for the Assessment of Experiential Learning (CAEL) in which Warren Willingham played so significant a role. At that initial meeting I was concerned that whatever approaches to assessment we developed, they respond to the wide ranging individual differences among Empire State adult learners. I was trying, not very successfully, to communicate this concern. Winton Manning rescued me by saying, "Oh, you are talking about trait-treatment interactions." I said, "Yes, that's it."

CAEL subsequently developed its portfolio assessment process which responds well to student diversity and to those trait-treatment interactions. That method is now being explored and adapted by the American Association for Higher Education (AAHE) in its efforts to find ways to help faculty represent and document high quality teaching. But it is very labor intensive. Although it works well for individuals, it does not lend itself so well to institutional assessment for particular sub-groups. So, assessing contextually specific subgroups and individuals remains a major challenge. And I have no good solutions.

But whatever methods and strategies we develop to assess contextually specific sub-groups and individuals, I predict that they will be more qualitative than quantitative. They will be more participatory and collaborative than top-down. They will be more frequently criterion-referenced and less frequently norm-referenced. But beyond those general observations I do not really know what particular combination of strategies might work well. I must leave that to the assessment experts.

My basic point here is that we must distinguish more clearly among these three types of assessment and recognize their different implications for planning, instrumentation, methods, and dissemination. And for me, it is especially important that we learn to address the third level of contextually specific subgroups and individuals so our assessment activities respect diversity and reinforce our pluralistic democracy, rather than ignoring our varied subcultural differences and working against such pluralism.

In conclusion let me simply recognize how critical it is that our assessment methods and strategies become sufficiently sophisticated to meet the needs of our rapidly expanding knowledge and information society. Credentials, certificates, quality assurance concerning educational outcomes, helpful feedback in the service of self-directed learning, sound representation, and appraisal of the personal qualities required for successful careers, effective citizenship, and a good life will be critical for the 21st Century.

REFERENCES

Astin, A. (1993). *Promoting social responsibility: A challenge for Higher Education.* Proceedings from Institute on College Student Values, Tallahassee, Florida.

Belenky, M. F., Clinchy, B. M., Goldberger, N. R., & Tarule, J. M. (1986). *Women's ways of knowing.* New York: Basic Books.

Boyer, E. L. (1987). *College: The undergraduate experience of America.* Princeton, NJ: Carnegie Foundation for the Advancement of Teaching.

Klemp, G. O., Jr. (1977). *Three factors of success.* In Dyckman W. Vermilye, (Ed.), *Relating education and work.* San Francisco: Jossey-Bass.

Loevinger, J. (1976). *Ego development.* San Francisco: Jossey-Bass.

Newcomb, T. M. (1943). *Personality and social change: Attitude formation in a student community.* New York: Holt.

Newman, J. H. Cardinal. (1973). *The idea of a university.* Westminster, MD: Christian classics. (original work published 1852).

Pascarella, E. T., & Terenzini, P. T. (1991). *How college affects students: Findings and insights from twenty years of research.* San Francisco: Jossey-Bass.

Perry, W. G. (1970). *Forms of intellectual and ethical development in the college years: A scheme.* Troy, MO: Holt, Rhinehart & Winston.

Sheckley, B. G., Lamdin, L., & Keeton, M (1992). Employability in a high performance economy. *Educational Record, 73*(4), 27-31.

3

ASSESSMENT TO IMPROVE COLLEGE INSTRUCTION

K. Patricia Cross
University of California, Berkeley

Once upon a time when both Warren and I were young, I was asked to review Warren's book on *Success in College* (Willingham, 1985), along with three other books speaking to the general theme of "Making College Students Successful" (Cross, 1985). I commented at the time that Warren's book stood out as the most scholarly of the four. By characterizing his work as "scholarly," I meant that he proceeded in an orderly and analytic way to build new knowledge on the foundations of what was already known about the success of students in college. Many researchers today do a pretty good job of writing about their own little corner of the research domain, but then they leave their pieces of new information scattered about the landscape, hoping perhaps that someday someone may be able to stack them to build a significant piece of knowledge. Warren is typically generous and scholarly as he contributes his work to the building of knowledge.

Using Warren's characteristic approach to scholarship as my model, I want to begin this chapter by recognizing some of the past work that has gone into research on college teaching. Effective teaching is one of the most important handles we have on helping students to become successful learners. And it becomes even more important as increasing numbers of students enter college without adequate habits or skills for learning.

Some of the work on college teaching attempts to describe the characteristics of good college teachers. The descriptions range from global essays, to extensive lists of behavioral characteristics, to a reduction to the parsimonious, basic dimensions of good teaching. The global images are perhaps best captured by essayists. Joseph Epstein's (1981) book, *Masters: Portraits of Great Teachers*, for example, is a collection of essays written by former students of some exceptional teachers. While I am struck by the rich variety in both authors and teachers,

Epstein points to some commonalties among these memorable teachers. "What all the great teachers have in common is love of their subject, an obvious satisfaction in arousing this love in their students, and an ability to convince them that what they are being taught is deadly serious." (p. xii).

Joseph Lowman (1984), after reviewing the research on great teachers, comes to a similar conclusion. He contends that excellence in teaching can be described by two major dimensions of expertise—intellectual skills and interpersonal skills. Excellent teachers, he says, are outstanding on one of these dimensions and at least competent on the other. That's something to think about. Could one become a great teacher by possessing *either* a great love of subject matter or a great love of students, heeding Lowman's caution, of course, that one could not be a complete klutz in the other domain? That seems to capture what teaching is all about; it is interacting with students to engage them in the intellectual work of learning. Memorable learning experiences for most of us have probably come either from the intellectual excitement of an idea or from the emotional rapport with a teacher who cared a lot and motivated us to do our very best—or in the best of all possible worlds, from teachers who excelled in both intellectual excitement and interpersonal rapport.

But these broad, somewhat idealized, portraits of exceptional and inspirational teachers are not always helpful to more average teachers trying to improve their teaching. For them there is the work of researchers who develop comprehensive lists of the behavioral characteristics of good teachers—in the hope, perhaps, that if we know more concretely what good teachers do, we can emulate those behaviors. Data on the characteristics of good teachers are collected in several ways, usually by asking people to describe an "ideal" or "best" teacher, or by the use of student rating scales to differentiate "good" from "poor" teachers.

An impressive synthesis of this work was done by Kenneth Feldman (1988), who located 31 studies in which students and faculty from the same institutions had been asked to rate the various components of effective teaching. In a meta-analysis across all 31 studies, he was able to rank the characteristics of good teachers with pretty good agreement among the raters. The top ten characteristics are these: The teacher: 1) communicates at a level appropriate to the level of the group, 2) is well prepared for class, 3) is knowledgeable about the subject matter, 4) stimulates interest, 5) is enthusiastic, 6) explains things clearly, 7) is available and helpful, 8) respects students, 9) is concerned about students' learning, and 10) is fair. The only characteristic that faculty put in the top ten that students did not was the ability of the teacher to challenge students intellectually, which was rated 6th by faculty and 17th by students. There is nothing very surprising about this list of virtues. Any teacher who has all of those characteristics—or even most of them —is quite likely to be a good, maybe even excellent, teacher.

Other investigators have tried to synthesize the voluminous research on teacher characteristics by reducing it to the most basic dimensions. Factor analyses of the items typically found in rating scales show that four generic characteristics can pretty well cover the characteristics of good teachers across the disciplines. Those four traits, under which all other traits can be clustered are: 1) Skill, which represents all those characteristics having to do with the ability to communicate in an interesting way, 2) Rapport, which involves empathy, interaction with and concern for students, 3) Structure, which concerns class organization and presentation of course materials, and 4) Load, which refers to workload and instructor demands (Kulik & McKeachie, 1975).

By this time, a great deal of research has been done on the characteristics of good college teachers, in part because of growing pressures to evaluate teaching. Most of the characteristics that distinguish "good" teachers from "poor" have found their way into student rating scales, and researchers have continued to study the validity of student rating scales. At latest count, there were more than 1,300 studies of the validity of student evaluations of teachers (Cashin, 1990). And the conclusions from that research are consistent enough, and the pressures from society strong enough, that the great majority of colleges in the United States now use some form of student evaluations of instruction. The question now is, how useful are the ratings in improving instruction?

The research to date suggests that teachers, especially poor teachers whose self-perception of their teaching is better than their ratings, do change as a result of feedback (Centra, 1973; Murray, 1985) Much remains to be done, however, in improving feedback procedures. One observer of the administrative uses of student ratings writes:

> Evaluation results (if faculty get them back) are returned via some...impersonal, albeit efficient method. Generally, results come back to faculty via the mail.... They come with varying amounts of statistical cybernetics to decipher and varying degrees of helpful instructions....One we know lists all sixty faculty members by the last four digits of their social security numbers and then rank orders them from top to bottom by their overall rating of effectiveness. To be last on such a list is devastating. Being tenth from the bottom is hardly encouraging. And to what end?...If the data do not help them identify specific areas in need of alteration, and if no opportunities to discuss the results are provided, faculty may be motivated to become defensive, not better teachers. (Gleason-Weimer, 1987, p. 9).

There is some evidence to suggest that feedback deserves more attention than we in higher education have been giving it. Peter Cohen (1980) located 22 research studies comparing student ratings of instruction under conditions of feedback to teachers and no feedback. In a meta-analysis, synthesizing the results of these studies, he found that the feedback group received higher end-of-term global ratings in 20 of the 22 comparisons. If the feedback was augmented by consultation with a consultant on teaching improvement, however, the average instructor raised his or her ratings from the 50th to the 74th percentile by the end of the semester. Thus relatively small changes made by individual instructors add up to very substantial improvement, we should think, for the institution. It would be hard to think of a grand policy decision that would bring about that amount of change in so brief a period of time.

Granted, the improvement was in students' perceptions of instruction, but students "do a pretty good job of distinguishing teachers on the basis of how much they have learned" according to one researcher who found a correlation of .43 in a meta-analysis of 41 studies looking at the relationship between student ratings and student achievement (Cohen, 1981, p. 305).   While not everyone is so positive about the validity of student ratings (Dowell & Neal, 1982), most of those advising caution in their use do so, not on grounds that teachers cannot get useful feedback from students, but that administrators should be cautious about depending on student evaluation in promotion and tenure decisions.   As the pressures for teaching effectiveness increase, folks are inventing a number of interesting and useful ways to evaluate and reward good teaching (See, for example, Edgerton, 1994).

Despite this generally favorable report on the use of student ratings to improve instruction, much remains to be done in involving college and university faculty in the improvement of instruction.   My colleague Tom Angelo and I have been working for the past decade on methods that will engage college teachers in self-assessment of the effectiveness of teaching and learning in their own classrooms. We call this Classroom Assessment.   The advantages of the active involvement of teachers in assessing their own effectiveness are several:

First, the focus of Classroom Assessment is on student learning rather than on faculty performance.   Rather than students judging the performance of their teachers—which has a ring of audacity about it to many college faculty—teacher and students together are assessing what students are learning in that classroom. Classroom Assessment serves a pedagogical as well as an assessment function. Through Classroom Assessment, students are monitoring their own learning as well as providing information to the instructor about the impact of the teaching on their learning.

A second advantage of Classroom Assessment lies in the shift of emphasis from studying the characteristics of teach*ers* to looking at the process of teach*ing*. This enables us to consider context.   Teaching is highly context-specific.   What works in some classrooms won't work in others.   Thus, studying the dynamic process of teacher-student interaction in a particular context will tell us more than studying the static, and sometimes unalterable, characteristics of teachers (Bloom, 1980).

Finally, college teachers need better feedback on their teaching, and Classroom Assessment can provide immediate information while the lesson is still fresh in the minds of both teacher and students and while there is still time to take corrective action.

As a group, today's college teachers are not very well prepared for their profession of teaching.   Fresh from graduate school and armed with voluminous and intricate knowledge of their specialty, they stand before a freshman class with little understanding of how students learn.   The ultimate purpose of research on teaching is to help teachers understand how teaching causes learning.   Neverthe-less, we speak of teaching *and* learning as though they were on parallel tracks.   But it is the intersection of teaching and learning that should interest us. We should be talking about teaching *for* learning or what teachers can do to *cause* learning. That kind of language, however, makes a lot of college teachers very nervous.

"Causing" learning is not a comfortable concept for many of us in higher education. Throughout much of the history of higher education, we have devoted a lot of effort and money to discover how to *select* students who will be successful in the learning environments that we offer. Now, the question for the great majority of colleges is not how to select students who will be successful, but rather how to make successful those who come. And it is an agonizing and urgent question for many teachers, especially those in open-admissions colleges. A major purpose of Classroom Assessment is to help teachers make the connection between their teaching and student learning.

With those needs in mind, Tom Angelo and I set out to develop some practical Classroom Assessment Techniques (CATS) that could be used by college faculty members without training in assessment or the research methods of the social sciences. Our purpose was not to use assessment to provide information for use by others in evaluating performance, but rather to provide information to teachers and students about the effectiveness of teaching and learning in a given classroom. We hypothesized that if the purpose of assessment is to improve the quality of under-graduate learning, then the following premises should prevail:

1. The assessment must involve directly those who are actually en-gaged in teaching and learning, namely teachers and students.

2. If assessment is to make a difference, it must address the ques-tions that are of interest to teachers. Specifically, teachers must formulate their own assessment questions and designs to provide the type of information that will inform their teaching.

3. Feedback from assessment to the people who can do something about it—namely teachers and students—must be timely and ac-curate.

Collecting what we could find from the literature and from our experience in talking with teachers, we compiled a book of 50 CATS that range in difficulty from extremely simple to complex. The 50 CATs are grouped into three large clusters—one on assessing "Course-Related Knowledge and Skills," one on assessing "Learner Attitudes, Values and Self-Awareness," and one on assessing "Learner Reactions to Instruction" (Angelo & Cross, 1993).

Fortunately, there exists a succinct synthesis of the research on effective student learning over the past several decades. Shortly after *A Nation at Risk* (National Commission on Excellence in Education, 1983) appeared in the mid-80s, calling for major educational reform, a group of distinguished researchers in higher education responded by writing a reform report for higher education entitled, *Involvement in Learning* (Study Group on the Conditions of Excellence in American Higher Education, 1984). Building heavily on the work of Alexander Astin, they concluded that there are three "critical conditions for excellence" in undergraduate education. They identified those conditions as (1) holding high expectations for student performance, (2) encouraging active student involvement in learning, and (3) providing useful assessment and feedback.

Since the primary purpose of Classroom Assessment is to provide useful feedback to both teacher and students, let us start with those "critical conditions for excellence." It is fairly obvious that learners need assessment and feedback. Good teachers spend a lot of time grading papers, making comments and corrections to let students know how they are doing and how they can do better. But teachers themselves get very little assessment and feedback on their teaching. Student evaluations at the end of the semester can be helpful, but they give very little information about the contextual nature of any particular lesson. By the time the evaluations are due, teachers as well as students have forgotten the particulars of any lesson. Both teacher and students need to be able to monitor the effectiveness of their teaching or learning immediately, while it is in process.

For those of you who are not familiar with Classroom Assessment, let me give a concrete example of Classroom Assessment's most famous CAT -- the Minute Paper, invented by a physics professor at Berkeley. The Minute Paper is a very simple device, that provides immediate feedback to the instructor on what students are learning and, equally important, it incorporates pedagogical principles that are important to students' learning. It works like this: Shortly before the end of a class period, the instructor asks students to write brief answers to two questions: (1) What is the most important thing that you learned in class today? and (2) What is the main, unanswered question you leave class with today?

In his first report on the Harvard Assessment Seminars, Light (1990) states that early on in the Seminars, he asked faculty members what single change would most improve their current teaching.

> Two ideas swamped all others. One is the importance of enhancing students' awareness of "the big picture," the "big point of it all," and not just the details of a particular topic. The second is the importance of helpful and regular feedback *from students* so a professor can make mid course corrections. (p. 35)

The Minute Paper seems to address both of these desires. It asks students to reflect on the "big picture"—the most important idea—of a specific class session, and it provides feedback to the instructor on how students are experiencing the class.

Pedagogically, we know that little is learned without the students' active involvement in making ideas and information their own. Some students just never stop to reflect, to put it all together, and draw some synthesis about what they have learned from a given class session. Class ends; they close their notebooks, assuming that whatever they have written will be useful for the exam when they get around to thinking about it, and are off to the next class. Other students just can't seem to distinguish between central and peripheral ideas. Their Minute Papers consist of a trivial sentence or two about whatever was said just prior to the request for the Minute Paper.

The Minute Paper asks all students in the class to reflect on what they have learned, to synthesize and articulate it in a few brief sentences, to commit that learning to writing, and to think actively about what they did not understand. Thus, even if the instructor failed to learn something important about students' responses to the teaching of that class session, the Minute Paper would still be worthwhile as a pedagogical technique.

But teachers do learn a great deal from the Minute Papers. Light (1990) comments in his report that "This extraordinarily simple idea [of Minute Papers] is catching on throughout Harvard. Some experienced professors comment that it is the best example of high payoff for a tiny investment they have ever seen" (p. 36).

I use the Minute Paper in my own graduate classes, and I never cease to be amazed at how revealing answers to these simple questions are. In the worst of all possible cases, I find that I'm not quite sure what the major message is myself, and students have discovered that. More often, I find an interpretation that surprises me or some confusion about an issue that can be rather easily cleared up in the next class period.

The second critically important condition for excellence in undergraduate education is active involvement in learning. We hear a lot today about the necessity for active involvement on the part of learners. But active involvement is not a new idea. Charles Gragg, the inspired teacher at the Harvard Business School 50 years ago, put it eloquently when he wrote these words:

> No one can learn in any basic sense from another except by subjecting what that other has to offer to a process of creative thinking; that is unless the learner is actively and imaginatively receptive, he will emerge from the experience with nothing more than a catalog of facts and other people's notions." (Gragg, 1940)

Classroom Assessment involves both teachers and students in learning. One of the reasons for the popularity of Classroom Assessment with college teachers, I think, is that it is a creative activity, directed and applied by teachers to satisfy their own intellectual curiosity about their work. Classroom Assessment Techniques, as they have grown and evolved over the years, offer an opportunity for various levels of teacher involvement.

This is illustrated by the experience of a writing teacher who modified the Minute Paper to get some idea of what students were learning from the small-group work sessions that she used to engage students in critiquing one another's papers. She asked students to answer these two questions when they had finished their small-group work session: 1) What specific suggestions did members of your group offer to you that are likely to help you improve your draft essay? and 2) What suggestions did you offer to others that are likely to help them improve their draft essays?

The good news is that she found that most students mentioned things they had learned from others that they thought would improve their papers. The bad news is that only 3 out of 24 students could think of something they had offered that might have been helpful to the other students in their group!

At this point, the teacher had several different options about the level of her involvement in teaching students how to make the small-group sessions more productive. She might let the CAT do the pedagogical work of reminding students that they are expected to contribute as well as to benefit from the work of the group sessions. For students, just having to respond to the question about benefits and contributions is a gentle reminder of the two-sided obligation of collaborative learning. At a somewhat higher level of involvement, the teacher might spend a little time in class discussion, eliciting suggestions from students about how the group work might be made more productive. Or she might decide to get more heavily involved yet by devising some learning exercises that teach students to critique each other's papers helpfully.

In any case, this illustrates an important use of CATs beyond assessment and feedback. CATs can be used to involve students in monitoring their own learning. One of the major conclusions from the research on cognition over the past 20 years is that students who monitor their own learning are more effective learners than those who do not. Good learners are aware of themselves as learners; they are able to watch themselves in the process of learning, and therefore able to direct and control their use of learning strategies.

Classroom teachers can help students become self-regulated learners through a variety of rather simple Classroom Assessment Techniques. For example, a CAT labeled "Punctuated Lectures" calls for stopping the class occasionally to ask students to reflect on what they were doing during the lecture and how their behavior, while listening, helped or hindered their understanding. They are then asked to write down any insights about their own learning that they have gained and give feedback to the teacher in brief anonymous notes. This form of peda-gogical assessment not only teaches students to become more aware of how they are using their learning time; it also informs the teacher about distractions in the environment. A similar assessment technique called "Productive Study-Time Logs" assesses the effective use of study time. It asks students to keep brief records of how much time they spend studying for a particular class, when they study, and how productively they study.

The third condition for excellence identified by the authors of *Involvement in Learning* is "holding high expectations for student performance." What teachers expect of students often determines what students expect of themselves. Holding high expectations for students, by its very nature, has to be geared to the perform-ance of individuals. It is not a normative or competitive matter. A teacher cannot constructively hold high expectations for a student by hoping that the student will do better than someone else. Rather the expectation must be based on the premise that individuals will improve their own performance. Classroom Assessments are, by definition, non-competitive, non-graded, and usually anonymous. Students are engaged in trying to become more aware of their own learning, and CATs help students to assess themselves.

It is also true, of course, that in using Classroom Assessment Techniques, teachers are setting an example of holding high expectations for their own performance as teachers. As a matter of fact, one of the advantages of Classroom Assessment that is mentioned most frequently by teachers, is the bonding that is formed between students and teacher when teachers are demonstrating their own interest in using assessment for self-improvement. While I have been both gratified, and frankly surprised, by the enthusiasm of college teachers for Classroom Assessment, CAT is not without its critics.

Some ask, can't teachers fool themselves, evaluating their teaching by making and using CATs that tell them what they want to hear? Yes, of course. But our experience is that teachers who use CATs are too hard on themselves rather than too easy. They tend to want to find out what is *wrong* with their teaching rather than what is *right* about it. We have also found that while we thought that one of the big advantages of Classroom Assessment was that teachers could do it in the privacy of their own classrooms, teachers tell us that a major advantage is that Classroom Assessment promotes discussion about teaching. Most teachers seem to want to share their data and its interpretation with their peers. Anything that encourages faculty to develop a campus culture "where faculty talk together about teaching, inquire into its effects, and take collective responsibility for its quality" (Hutchings, 1993, p. v) may be a step in the right direction.

Other critics ask, isn't Classroom Assessment a bit simplistic? Doesn't the improvement of learning involve far more than an individual classroom and individual lessons? Yes, of course. But classrooms are the building blocks that we have chosen for education, and if we cannot find out what goes on in the classroom, and how it can be improved, then it isn't very likely that we can improve the quality of education.

Doesn't Classroom Assessment take time away from teaching? Ah, that is the most common complaint of teachers. How can we cover the material, they ask, if we take time away from teaching it? Actually, it makes no difference how much material the teacher is covering if students aren't getting it. The point of Classroom Assessment is to find out how much of the material covered students are learning. Moreover, Classroom Assessment, used well, *is* using class time to engage students in learning.

Since Classroom Assessment is, in many respects, a child of the larger institutional assessment movement, it shares the family problem of the tension between assessment for accountability imposed from without and self-assessment undertaken for purposes of improvement. Peter Ewell warns that, ". . .once started, assessment in some form *is going to happen*." (Ewell, 1991, p.17, emphasis in original). I believe that the appropriate form of assessment in a healthy profession is self-assessment, and both students and teachers should be doing it.

REFERENCES

Angelo, T. A., & Cross, K. P. (1993). *Classroom assessment techniques: a handbook for college teachers*, Second Edition. San Francisco: Jossey-Bass.

Bloom, B. (1980). The new direction in educational research: alterable variables. *Phi Delta Kappan* (Feb.), 382-385.

Cashin, W. E. (1990). Assessing teaching effectiveness. In P. Seldin (Eds.), *How Administrators Can Improve Teaching*. San Francisco: Jossey Bass.

Centra, J. A. (1973). Effectiveness of student feedback in modifying college instruction. *Journal of Educational Psychology, 65*, 395-401.

Cohen, P. A. (1980). Effectiveness of student rating feedback for improving college instruction: A meta-analysis of findings. *Research in Higher Education*, 13(4), 321-342.

Cohen, P.A. (1981). Student ratings of instruction and student achievement: A meta-analysis of multisection validity studies. *Review of Educational Research, 51*, 281-309.

Cross, K. P. (1985). Making students successful: The search for solutions continues. *Change*, November/December, 48-51.

Dowell, D. A., & Neal, J. A. (1982). A selective review of the validity of student ratings of teaching. *Journal of Higher Education, 53*, 51-62.

Edgerton, R. (1994). A national market for excellence in teaching. *Change*, September/October, *26*(5), 4-5.

Epstein, J. (Ed.). (1981). *Masters: Portraits of great teachers*. New York: Basic.

Ewell, P. (1991). Assessment and public accountability: Back to the future. *Change*, 23(6), 12-17.

Feldman, K. A. (1988). Effective college teaching from the students' and facultys' views: matched or mismatched priorities? *Research in Higher Education, 28*, 291-344.

Gleason-Weimer, M. (1987). Translating evaluation reports into teaching improvement. *AAHE Bulletin* (April), 8-11.

Gragg, C. I. (1940). Teachers also must learn. *Harvard Educational Review, 10*, 30-47.

Hutchings, P. (1993). *Using cases to improve college teaching*. Washington, D.C.: American Association for Higher Education.

Kulik, J. A., & McKeachie, W. J. (1975). The evaluation of teachers in higher education. In F. N. Karlinger (Ed.), *Review of research in education*. Itasca, Illinois: F.E. Peacock.

Light, R. J. (1990). *The Harvard assessment seminars*. Cambridge, MA: Harvard University.

Lowman, J. (1984). *Mastering the techniques of teaching.* San Francisco: Jossey-Bass.

Murray, H. G. (1985). Classroom teaching behaviors related to college teaching effectiveness. In J. G. Donald & A. M. Sullivan (Eds.), *Using research to improve teaching. New Directions for Teaching and Teaming,* No. 23. San Francisco: Jossey-Bass.

National Commission on Excellence in Education (1983). *A nation at risk.* Washington, D.C.: U. S. Department of Education.

Study Group on the Conditions of Excellence in American Higher Education. (1984). *Involvement in Learning.* Washington, D.C.: Department of Education, National Institute of Education.

Willingham, W. (1985). *Success in college.* New York: The College Board.

4

ASSESSING AND CREDENTIALING LEARNING FROM PRIOR EXPERIENCE

Morris Keeton
University of Maryland

Some twenty years ago, Warren Willingham made a breakthrough early in the CAEL (Cooperative Assessment of Experiential Learning) Project (1974-1977) that was essential to its success and that had broader implications and applications that even today are far from fully realized. Reliability of assessment, he pointed out, does not require standardized tests and large numbers of examinees being compared on the same measures. It can be assured by way of processes that generate interrater agreement at appropriate levels. Validity of assessment, he added, does not allow examinees' knowledge to be judged on different grounds than their claims. He defined the crucial criteria for valid and reliable assessment in his *Principles of Good Practice in Assessing Experiential Learning* (1977). I assume that any sensible psychometrician already understood these ideas, but it was Warren Willingham who brought out the implications for measuring learning that had occurred outside of college precincts.

The implications and applications of the observation about reliability of assessment extend far beyond their use in assessing an entering college student's knowledge and other capabilities. The observation meant that it is feasible to provide reliable individualized assessment of learning derived from any source on a mass scale. I return to the importance of this Willingham insight later.

First, let us take note of Willingham's additional less heralded contributions and to some closely related matters that received less attention than they may have deserved. Sound assessment must be not only reliable, but also valid, Willingham reminded us. Validity being a matter of whether one is assessing what is intended, he pointed out that the strong preference of academics to judge students by what the instructors teach could mean invalid assessment if they rate the knowledge and competence claims of students in terms of what is covered in course syllabi and assigned textbooks. Both of Willingham's two key points, which are at the very foundations of psychometric standards, have been honored more in the breach than the observance in course grading, but this second point more than the first. While the majority of institutions of higher education that recognize prior learning for credit do so in terms of documenting fulfillment of the requirements in their courses, it is my impression that a growing proportion seek to honor the student's own claims as the basis for evaluation so long as they fall within the broad disciplinary or professional field of study in which credit is sought.

OVERSIGHTS AND BLEMISHES

You will remember Gerard Manley Hopkins' praise for speckled beauties. CAEL has not been a beauty without freckles and blemishes. What, for one thing, was this phrase "experiential learning" in its name? It was not really experiential learning that the CAEL Project was assessing: It was learning acquired prior to enrollment in college or after matriculation but without benefit of the college's instructional efforts. (Some institutions wait until even later to assess "prior learning.") We started, in a word, with a misnomer for ourselves.

Experiential learning, as Pam Tate and I defined it in the first of the Jossey-Bass books in the New Directions in Experiential Learning Series (Keeton & Tate, 1978), is that in which the learner is in direct touch with what is being studied or, in the case of skills and capabilities, that in which the learner engages in hands-on practice of the desired skill or capability. A great deal of what students present as prior learning is, to the contrary, learned via reading about things, hearing lectures, engaging in discussion about the subject, or in other nonexperiential ways.

This first glitch was no blemish on CAEL, merely a misnaming. But a second misfire has been a true blemish, and no fault of Warren Willingham's. Most users of CAEL's work think of its primary contribution as "portfolio assessment." It was not portfolios that Willingham was helping us assess, but the learning supposedly attested in the portfolios. The portfolio is a compilation of evidence of learning. Some students present a poor selection of evidence and have actually achieved more significant learning than their evidence communicates persuasively. Other students, in contrast, are con-artists, who put together a gorgeous portfolio meriting a prize for contemporary art, but their achievements in college-level learning may be of less laudatory dimensions. We should speak of portfolio-assisted assessment of students' learning, not of assessing portfolios.

A third problem, also a blemish and not to be placed at Warren Willingham's door, is the uneven degree of attention devoted to the assessment of sponsored experiential learning. In this case we are truly talking of learning by experience; that is, learning in internships, practica, medical residencies, apprenticeships, and service-learning pursued under the aegis of a college or university. The CAEL Project devoted almost equal attention to the assessment of both prior and sponsored learning. Indeed, there were probably more publications devoted to sponsored learning than to prior learning, and the Principles carefully treated every relevant policy as applied in each of those modes. But the more radical idea was that of recognizing learning that was not preplanned and overseen by a college representative, so both the utility of CAEL's work and its notoriety were seen by user institutions as lying predominantly in prior-learning assessment. Through their practice and limited responses to CAEL's preachings on sponsored learning, the user institutions indicated that it was less necessary to worry about assessing what was learned in internships under college aegis than in employment outside of college oversight.

A fourth set of concerns has been endemic: inadequate implementation of the principles enunciated by CAEL. Where Willingham recommended using at least two assessors (necessary for having congruence of rater judgments), institutions use only one. Where *The Compendium of Assessment Techniques* recommended cross-checking to obtain convergent evidence by more than one of six major techniques, colleges make do with only one and systemically neglect product and performance assessment. Where documentation letters are to spell out the level of proficiency exhibited in performance, too many of them are testimonials to the dedication and congeniality of the learner in a job. Where the *Principles* (Willingham, 1977) emphasize that every assessor should have undergone training, most institutions omit or skimp on this investment.

A fifth speckle on the CAEL beauty is hard to evaluate as to whether it is a beauty spot or a blemish: the balance between theory and practice as the focus of assessment. The reason this matter is hard to evaluate is that the higher education system is systemically at fault in its overemphasis upon theory divorced from its implications in practice. Most adults, the expression goes, are experience-rich and theory-poor (also history- and jargon-poor, I would add); whereas most college courses are theory-rich and experience-poor. There are exceptions: The learning of a foreign language is largely done experientially. That is, the students with the help of a proficient speaker actually practice speaking, listening, writing, and reading the language being learned. In genuinely inquiring science laboratories, as distinguished from those engaged in cookbook lab work, a student can experience the processes of scientific inquiry. But these are not the rule. Even in some professional or preprofessional degree programs, internships may be looked upon as inappropriate and as a waste of time taken away from covering the subject (the American Association of Collegiate Schools of Business frowned upon use of internships until quite recently).

CAEL has been, with respect to this issue, an uncertain beacon. It would ideally insist that a high quality postsecondary education combines theory and practice in a way that enhances each, and that it expects a student to understand the distinctive language and history of the major field of study. But it should also insist that proficiency in practice should not be confused with fluency in theory. Even acknowledging that one must in some sense understand an idea if one applies it effectively, it does not follow that one can articulate that idea and use it to predict and explain as a master of theory should be able to do.

The worst blemish of all has been the misuse of CAEL's advocacy for equitable treatment of adults by degree mills and their genre, who give away undeserved credit and degrees. The American Council on Education and CAEL have collaborated over the years in fighting abuses, as have the institutional accrediting bodies. But there continue to be significant instances of overcrediting of extra collegiate learning, negligence in adherence to the principles of good practice, and misleading advertising that raises false hopes and thus entraps unwary consumers into the hands of education providers who serve them badly.

So much for blemishes. Urban Whitaker has spelled out exhaustively what he calls "malpractices" in the assessment of learning. (See *Assessing Learning: Standards, Principles, and Procedures*, CAEL, 1989.)

CAEL'S CONTRIBUTIONS.

So Warren Willingham set CAEL off on the right foot. Not only did he assure CAEL's grounding in sound psychometric principles, he managed a 3-year program of activities that set a productivity record in the quality and volume of its work. Under his supervision some 54 publications were generated between March, 1974 and June, 1977. A number of these were not just articles, but carefully crafted handbooks of direct utility in the application of the goals and policies of CAEL. Others reported institutional models for implementing assessment programs. A further set consisted of training guides and materials for the development of faculty assessors and program administrators. While this work of intellectual development and dissemination was going on, Willingham oversaw (under John Valley's leadership with Diana Bamford-Rees' faithful execution) the creation of what turned out to be an ongoing organization to sustain, advocate, and promote the ideas and practices being generated through the research and development side of the project.

The principal contributions of CAEL to higher education since 1977 can be summarized as follows:

1. Legitimating experiential learning and its assessment in America higher education;
2. helping to increase access to American higher education, especially for working adults;
3. contributing to the press for clarification of college outcomes and standards;
4. increasing recognition of extra collegiate providers of education;
5. pushing for reform in higher education in assessment-related ways:
    a. exerting pressure to widen access to higher education by using alternative measures of potential for college studies,
    b. pressing for user-friendliness on the part of colleges and universities to their changing populations in respect to gender, ethnicity, age, and part-time status,

    c.   pressure for more learner-centered institutions of higher education,

    d.   pressing for greater flexibility in curricula and for education that draws on students' experiences,

    e.   driving toward clarification of learning outcomes of regular courses and of degree programs as a basis for clarification of standards for evaluating extra-course learning, and

    f.   introduction of portfolio-assisted assessment in courses or with respect to across-the-curriculum degree objectives;

6.   contributing to a growing emphasis on employability of the workforce and on the need for higher education for the economic health of households and of economies;

7.   building the commitment to lifelong learning; and,

8.   spreading the CAEL messages to other countries.

As the implications of CAEL's legitimation of experiential learning and its assessment grew clearer, there was resistance even within the CAEL Board of Trustees to each major move to pursue those implications. For example, when CAEL began work on Project LEARN (seeking learner-responsive institutions of higher education and later implementing "joint ventures" for employee growth and development programs), significant minority voices among trustees worried that CAEL should keep its focus more directly on assessment of learning. The sense of the Board, however, has continued to be that infusing higher education with sound assessment of experiential learning is not an end in itself nor a sufficient end, but is a means toward a greater vision of the potential services of higher education to an ever more diverse clientele.

Some Historical Notes

I've been asked to set Willingham's and CAEL's contributions in a larger historical context. The most scholarly work done with this aim is Zelda Gamson's *Higher Education and the Real World—The Story of CAEL* (1989). Her thesis is that three movements converged to make the emergence of something like CAEL likely: movements in assessment, adult learning, and nontraditional education.

The first of these movements—in assessment—saw a series of innovations leading up to CAEL, then others arising from CAEL and other forces interacting with each other. The pre-CAEL events include

1.   the introduction of aptitude testing by the College Board as an aid to college admissions (c. 1900),

2.   the creation of the General Educational Development Tests around the time of World War II,

3.   the rating for college equivalency of voluntary education and training activities by American Council on Education teams,

4. pioneer programs of testing for college placement and advising in American colleges as early as the 1940s,
5. the development of CLEP (College Level Equivalency Program) examinations and the Advanced Placement Program, and
6. work on occupational skills assessment by business and state agencies.

In the adult education movement many flowers have blossomed — dozens if not thousands. Most adult education in the American colonies occurred in churches. It was not until the 1840s that Horace Mann led the movement for the "common school" for children. Yet the Chatauqua was already under way shortly after the Civil War. Diverse steps led to the growth of noncredit continuing education, given institutional expression by the 1920s and later through the NUCEA (National University Continuing Education Association), ACHE (Association for Continuing Higher Education),and AACTE (American Association for Continuing Teacher Education). An enormous nationwide literacy movement has emerged, beginning with efforts to assist immigrants to cope with American English in the 19th century and growing still in the 1990s. Education for adults has moved from literacy and leisure pursuits (the classic basket weaving) to certification and recertification for professional and occupational pursuits, to postdoctoral studies to keep abreast of growing knowledge and changing technologies.

Workers have moved from apprenticeships—most common in the years of dominance by crafts and their unions—to formal education for professionals and paraprofessionals, to self-consciously managed on-the-job learning. Employers' views of their responsibilities for education have moved from job-specific employer-provided training to the employee growth and development programs of the 1980s and following, and may now be entering a time of jointly-planned, managed, and evaluated degree and nondegree programs offered by colleges and employers in partnership. These strands in the ever-broadening provisions for adult learning were, except for the last two, well toward maturity in their development when the Carnegie Commission on the Non-Traditional Student did its work in 1971 to 1973 and announced the need for a way to recognize the learning that individuals had done outside of formal higher education, a need to which CAEL provided a direct response.

The third movement noted by Gamson as converging in CAEL was the trend toward nontraditional provisions within formal higher education, sometimes expressed with a focus on the nontraditional student, sometimes on the nontraditional provider of education. Providers of cooperative education (alternating work and study, or concurrent work and study) marked critical incidents in 1879, 1911 (University of Cincinnati), 1920 (Antioch College), and 1959 (Wilson study of cooperative education institutions). Apprenticeships as well as medical internships and residencies have long been with us, but such arrangements have spread to additional callings as more explicit attention has been given to the role of hands-on experience in the development of competent practice. Already emerging in the early 1970s were external degree programs that permitted more and more students to attain degrees without the use of a residential or commuter campus. Beginning in the 1950s and 1960s and more in the early 1970s, new colleges for adults enjoyed a brief surge. Since the mid-1980s electronic networks have become increasingly common, gradually entering directly into collegiate usage, and just now leading to a stampede toward what is called, with varied definitions, "the virtual university." CAEL is a product of the interplay of these movements and has been, since its founding, a player in their further development.

Beginning in 1991, CAEL, the National Society for Experiential Education (NSEE), and ICEL (the International Consortium or Experiential Learning) succeeded in convening "A Global Conversation on Experiential Learning" that was attended by 1576 registrants, the largest such assemblage in the history of what we know as the experiential learning movement. Twenty-nine countries were represented at the conference, with substantial delegations from Great Britain, South Africa, Canada, Australia, New Zealand, and, of course, the host United States.

Notable in CAEL's work since 1989 has been Pam Tate's leadership of the effort to apply both the assessment and the experiential learning agenda of CAEL to the need for continuous development of a productive and prosperous American workforce. She has worked with governors and their staffs, labor leaders, and corporate executives to develop policies and programs at the state level that heighten workers' skills, enhance productivity, and support the states' economic development. She has worked with the Department of Labor, industry associations, regional agencies, and legislators on the development of federal policies and programs paralleling developments in labor and corporate policies that would foster employability in the economy. While the CAEL effort has been nonpartisan throughout, this one depends heavily upon secular trends as well as upon other partners and contributions which are necessary for the tiny CAEL to contribute to a long-term result.

A Try for Perspective

It is all too easy for one who is immersed as advocate and activist in the experiential learning movement to see its accomplishments in exaggerated proportion. To counteract that affliction, it may be useful to cite some comparative data that put the movement in somewhat different perspective.

First, consider the assessment of high-school equivalency by means of the assessment of experiential learning at the postsecondary level. In 1980, 13% of all awards of high-school level achievement were made on the basis of GED examinations. Since that time the American Council on Education has developed an alternative way to assess the usable capabilities to be expected of high-school equivalency. Yet, in comparison, at its highest measured level the proportion of credit awards (not degrees) at the postsecondary level was less than 1/2 of 1% of the credits awarded.

Various factors militate against the use of assessment at the postsecondary level to an extent comparable to that at the secondary level. One is the fact that credentials and curricula are more numerous and diverse at the postsecondary than at the secondary level. Thus the sheer apparatus that would be required to standardize and mass deliver assessment for postsecondary awards is awesome by comparison. Simply as a technical challenge, this one is decisive.

Politically, the task of developing consensus to recognize and use the new technologies of assessment for credentialing are even more daunting. Sheckley (1988) found that less than 10% of the departments in colleges professing to provide prior-learning assessment services were actually doing so. This pattern of departmental autonomy is a further barricade against universalizing prior learning assessment services. In budget squeezes such as higher education is experiencing in the mid-1990s, such things as faculty training for assessment tasks are among the first to be sacrificed.

Yet there are a few highly successful institutions that function mainly by assessing and credentialing learning: Regents College of SUNY, Thomas Edison College of New Jersey, and a few graduate institutions such as The Union Institute and the Fielding Institute. These institutions do use workshops, study centers, and other face-to-face assists but essentially base the degree award on demonstrations of knowledge and competence rather than on course completions or residency periods. However, the change that might bring reliable and valid assessment to the center of the processes of credit accumulation and degree awarding is the development of the virtual university. Teachers will come to know students in the virtual university via electronically transmitted messages and pictures (including images of the students). While students may come to a university site for proctored examinations, it is likely indeed to be performance assessment and product assessment rather than process-completion that will increasingly be the preferred basis for credentialing.

In light of this prospect, how much more important is the start that was made in 1974 toward awarding credit for demonstrated knowledge and capabilities, using processes of valid and reliable assessment by qualified experts directly examining the evidence of learning!

As a second check on excessive enthusiasm about the seeds and fruits of CAEL, one might examine the proportion of adult learning that occurs in nonformal education and, by implication, the significance of a development that seeks to promote recognition of that learning by colleges and universities. The work of Tough and his associates and disciples since the late 1970s has continued to suggest that as much as 80% of adult learning takes place nonformally. This datum does not include casual learning, unintentional learning, or even planned learning that requires less than some 500 hours of effort within a year. If the learning being credentialed by CAEL-recommended processes is less than 1/2 of 1% of college credits, and college credits are for less than a third of the nonformal learning that adults do, it would seem that this is not a very weighty enterprise, now or in prospect.

Of the nonformal learning that adults do, far and away the greatest proportion is probably in the workplace. While many students using prior learning assessment services claim credit for learning achieved in the work-place, there is almost no systematic collaboration (CAEL generates some) between employers and colleges in helping employees to seek recognition of workplace learning. Nor is there much support for more efficient plans to exploit the opportunities of worksite learning to advance workers' occupational and professional qualifications, not to speak of their general qualifications for life, work, and leisure. If, in light of the extreme time pressures and conflicts among duties that adults endure, a systematic institutionally-driven effort were made to foster efficiency in learning among working adults via partnerships between employers and colleges, one might expect the growth in assessment-based certification of learning to increase substantially.

And third, how beautiful is small? Many of us are familiar with the popular stories about how much beauty there is in smallness. Apply this thought to the evaluation of the utility of prior learning assessment for the relatively few individuals who today are enjoying its benefits. There is hardly an educator engaging in this work who cannot regale us with inspiring story after inspiring story about the impact of a credit award upon the self-esteem, the motivation, the realization of career aspirations, the promotions in responsibility, pay, and rank that have come to that educator's students. These are benefits that the recipients tell us would never have come otherwise. Is it sufficient, then, to be among these blessed few?

Concluding Note

It is my earnest hope that two of the changes for which CAEL labored will ultimately pervade educational practice throughout the world: 1) the basing of educational credentials upon validly and reliably evaluated learning, regardless of its source; and 2) the enrichment of instruction by an astute interplay of the use of history, theory, and hands-on experience in the eliciting of learning. If these causes can continue to make progress, what greater honor than to have played the part Warren Willingham played in their advancement?

REFERENCES

Gamson, Z. F. (1989). *Higher education and the real world: the story of CAEL.* Wolfeboro, NH: Longwood Academic.

Keeton, M. T., & Tate, P. J. (1978). *New directions for experiential learning: Learning by experience —what, why, how.* San Francisco: Jossey-Bass.

Sheckley, B. G. (1988). *Policies and practices for awarding credit based on learning acquired in non-collegiate settings: Results of a national survey.* Unpublished manuscript submitted to the U.S. Department of Defense, Defense Activity for Non-Traditional Educational Support (DANTES).

Tough, A. (1979). *The adult's learning projects: A fresh approach to theory and practice in adult learning* (2nd ed). Toronto: Ontario Institute for Studies in Education.

Whittaker, U. (1989). *Assessing learning: Standards, principles, and procedures.* Philadelphia, PA: Council for the Advancement of Experiential Learning (CAEL).

Willingham, W. W. (1977). *Principles of good practice in assessing experiential learning.* Columbia, MD: Council for the Advancement of Experiential Learning (CAEL).

5

COMMENTARY
FEEDBACK AND REFLECTION IN FACILITATING FURTHER LEARNING

Wilbert J. McKeachie
University of Michigan

Like Patricia Cross, I've used Minute Papers for many years—ever since Wilson first discovered their use by a Berkeley Physics Professor. But I usually allow more than a minute for a Minute Paper and I plan to use these pages for two Minute Papers stimulated primarily by the previous chapters by Cross and Keeton as well as by Chickering. I will begin by a statement of one important thing I learned from Cross and Keeton, and then comment on these points, adding two questions that I hope we will continue to think about.

The two main points I want to emphasize are not exactly *new* to me, but these chapters expanded and clarified my thinking and also led to the questions I shall raise as the second part of my Minute Papers.

1. (From Cross) An assessment device, such as the Minute Paper, should be educational for both students and teachers.
2. (From Keeton) If we are to facilitate life-long learning, we need to integrate theory, practice, and assessment. This implies that we need to teach students to be aware of their own learning, to think about what an experience has taught them, to think about how it can be transferred to other situations (theory), and to assess not only what they have learned but also how they can build on that learning. As Chickering said, it is this ability to build on prior learning that should define success.

Now let me expand a bit on these points. According to Cross, "Some students just never stop to reflect, to put it all together, and draw some synthesis about what they have learned from a given class session. Class ends; they close their notebooks, assuming that whatever they have written will be useful for the exam when they get around to thinking about it, and then they're off to the next class."

This is true not only of *classroom* learning but also of *out-of-classroom* experiences. Last weekend I spent 20 hours reading and commenting on the journals of the 26 students taking my Honors Introductory Psychology course. Part of the journal is supposed to be reflections on reading beyond the assignments, whatever they find that's relevant--journal articles, the *Scientific American*, the *New York Times*, books, even pop-psychology paperbacks or articles. But part of this journal is also supposed to be reflections on their own observations and experiences as related to the topics we have been discussing. What pleases me is that in *this* round of reading the journals I found students saying "I find that I'm noticing a lot of things that I never paid attention to before."

Ellen Langer's (1989) book, *Mindfulness*, extends this notion of self-awareness and self-assessment to a variety of areas of life. Of course there are limits. As I noted in the margins as I reviewed Cross's chapter, it is not always functional to be self-aware and self-monitoring. If we use too much of our mental capacity thinking about what we're learning, or thinking about what we're thinking, we may not have enough capacity left to do the task we are attempting. But by and large, our inadequacies are on the side of *mindlessness* rather than an excess of *mindfulness.*

We college teachers are often mindless; we fail to apply what we teach to our own behavior. I once spoke to a meeting of New England college and university presidents about the importance of the notion that faculty members should understand basic principles of learning. At the end of my talk, Vic Butterfield, President of Wesleyan University, popped up and said, "Bill, if these principles of learning are so important, why aren't psychologists better teachers?" That took me aback, and all I could say was, "Why aren't chemists better cooks?"

Cross described students who close their notebooks after class and never stop to reflect. How many of us teachers must cringe as we think of the times when we have gathered together our notes and walked out of class without further reflection. The greatest asset of the *Classroom Assessment Techniques* by Tom Angelo and Pat Cross (1993) is that they stimulate both teachers and students to think.

But thinking about feedback is not enough. We sometimes assume that feedback is always good -- that providing feedback will inevitably lead to improved performance. Unfortunately, like most psychological generalizations, we have to add, "it depends...." Feedback often results in improvement, but all too often it does not.

Conditions of Feedback that Result in Improvement

What are the conditions under which feedback leads to improvement?

1. Feedback needs to convey information that is understood by the recipient. Sometimes feedback comes in language that isn't comprehended; for example, a table of frequencies, means, quartiles, and percentiles on student ratings -- what Gleason-Weimer (1987) called "statistical cybernetics." Sometimes there is so much information that we develop "mental dazzle"—a delightful metaphor used by the Hungarian-Swedish psychologist David Katz to describe one's feeling of having too much information to even *try* to assimilate.
2. Feedback is not helpful if one does not know what to do to improve. Harry Murray at Western Ontario has demonstrated that in student ratings of faculty specific behavioral items are more likely to result in improvement than very general statements such as, "The teacher is knowledgeable."
3. Feedback is more likely to be helpful if it can be generalized. This sounds as if it contradicts the previous point; but we come back to Morris Keeton's emphasis upon the importance of theory as well as practice. We need both. One of the reasons consultants are more helpful than simple self-assessments with student feedback is that a consultant may not only be able to offer specific suggestions, but also to relate the specific problem to a concept or theory that suggests a strategy or strategies that can be applied in other situations.
4. Feedback is more helpful if it not only facilitates learning a helpful concept, theory, or strategy but also helps the individual develop skills or strategies that will facilitate *further learning*.
5. Feedback may help if we are motivated to improve. If you simply run a linear correlation, it looks as if the poorer teachers benefit more from feedback of student ratings than the better ones (partly because the better ones don't have as much room for improvement). But if you look at the data more carefully you are likely to find that the relationship is curvilinear; those who improve most from feedback are those with moderate ratings. Teachers who receive poor ratings tend not to improve (Pambookian, 1974).

How can we account for this paradoxical finding? From my experience in counseling teaching assistants and faculty with low ratings, the problem is that teachers with low ratings are already approaching the classroom with high levels of anxiety and some awareness that the students do not like them. Getting bad ratings certainly does not increase one's confidence and enthusiasm. In fact, in such cases the ratings are often dismissed as indicating that it is not appropriate for students to rate teaching. The teacher then retreats to methods of teaching that avoid interaction with students, often arguing that their role is primarily that of scholar and it is up to the students whether or not they learn what the teacher knows. My role as a consultant is to give hope, to suggest possible strategies to try, to encourage simple changes that may make a difference, to help the discouraged teachers note signs of progress, and to help them begin to appreciate and love their students.

While my examples have been drawn from the student rating literature, they fit with laboratory research as well, and they apply to Classroom Assessment Techniques as well as to other feedback devices.

Questions

That's a sample of what Cross and Keeton stimulated. I've interacted with each of them many times over the past 30-odd years and I always come away with new ideas. But what of my *questions* for the minute paper?

For Cross--I like the emphasis upon *causing* learning as contrasted with selecting students (although I would use the word "facilitating" rather than "causing"). As Cross suggested, this means that we need to get students to think about their own learning. But reflection should not only assess what has been learned but also how one can continue to develop skills and capacities for further learning. In *The Bell Curve*, Herrnstein and Murray (1994) concede that intelligence can be raised but argue that it's too expensive to help the less intelligent develop these skills; I argue that it all depends on how one values effective human beings as compared with new devices for Star Wars or an extra yacht for a speculator in the stock market. My question is (finally) "If we are to enhance both access and success, how can we build upon Classroom Assessment and other advances to go beyond learning a specific topic to facilitate development of skills in learning and thinking to be used in non-formal learning situations?"

And my question for Keeton--His paper deals mostly with cognitive and performance assessment; yet I know from listening to him through the years that he believes as I do that among the most important educational outcomes are such characteristics as zest for further learning, a sense of community, qualities that contribute to good citizenship, attitudes, values--a whole array of non-cognitive outcomes. How can we develop these? How can we assess them?

REFERENCES

Angelo, T. A., & Cross, K. P. (1993). *Classroom assessment techniques: A Handbook for college teachers* (2nd ed.). San Francisco: Jossey-Bass.

Gleason-Weimer, M. (1987). Translating evaluation reports into teaching improvement. *AAHE Bulletin* (April), 8-11.

Herrnstein, R., & Murray, C. (1994). *The bell curve: Intelligence and class structure in American life.* New York: Free Press.

Langer, Ellen J. (1989). *Mindfulness.* Reading, MA: Addison-Wesley.

Murray, H. (1986). Effective teaching behaviours in the college classroom. In J. C. Smart (Ed.), *Higher education: Handbook of theory and research*, (Vol. 8, pp. 135-172). New York: Agathon Press.

Pambookian, H. S. (1974). Initial level of student evaluation of instruction as a source of influence on instructor change after feedback. *Journal of Educational Psychology, 66*, 52-56.

Willingham, W. W. (1977). *Principles of good practice in assessing experiential learning.* Princeton, NJ: Council for the Advancement of Experiential Learning.

6

COMMENTARY
CHARACTERISTICS OF ASSESSMENT IN SUPPORT OF STUDENT ACCESS AND SUCCESS

Sister Joel Read
Alverno College

Chapters 3 and 4 have focused on assessment to improve instruction and assessing learning derived from students' experiences—each as a way to enhance student access and success in higher education. I should like to comment on them by way of indirection. I want to use selected characteristics of assessment to illustrate how assessment could enhance a student's, as well as *many* students', access and success in higher education.

I want to use these characteristics to illustrate what we, as educators, must at least consider in using assessment to enhance both access and success for students entering and working through higher education. I believe, if we are to enhance students' access and success, we need to go beyond improving instruction, which tends to leave the reigning paradigm in place, and/or assessing learning from students' experiences. Both are important but, as the philosophers say, not sufficient.

Almost 20 years ago, Alverno College and the Fund for Improvement of Postsecondary Education (FIPSE) co-hosted a conference on "Issues in Outcome-Oriented Liberal Education." Warren Willingham was both a participant and a presenter. As a presenter on "Assessment: State of the Art," Warren's approach was based on some important characteristics of assessment that I will discuss shortly. Using various ETS tests which embodied one or several of these characteristics, Warren helped participants to understand each characteristic more fully through seeing that characteristic within a concrete exemplification, such as the Test of Scientific Thinking or an AP Studio Art Test.

Given the overarching theme of this volume and the specific subject of Part II "Enhancing Student Access and Success in Higher Education," assessment characteristics from Warren's 1976 address provide a good organizing principle for this chapter.

> 1. Validity—Assessment should always measure what is
> *intended* to be measured.

While there may be no consensus on the content that constitutes a higher education, I think it is safe to say that there is a degree of consensus as to the assumptions of what a student must be capable of doing to be able to tackle whatever constitutes higher education at a given institution. Generalizing across the various types of institutions, we may say what is still intact is some form of general education and something called a major.

Therefore, a student must at least be capable of comprehensive reading at a certain level; must possess an ability to analyze and generalize, as well as an ability to think abstractly, concretely, reflectively, experimentally; and, to question, to evaluate, to apply knowledge. The student must also be able to communicate in written, oral, and numerical modes.

I suggest that, if the learner is to be able to access what constitutes higher education in any given institution, the learner and the institution need to be very clear as to the beginning point. Following this first characteristic, whatever assessment is used for access to an institution should measure what access means and is required at that given institution.

The assessment should, therefore, be diagnostic. It does not follow that the institution will necessarily grant access to the learner. But it can give the learner feedback that may assist the learner, perhaps for the first time, to access her or his own learning process. This can be a defining moment for a learner--even for an advanced learner--and send the learner off on a very real quest for lifelong learning.

> 2. Reliability—Assessment should be *consistent*
> within reasonable limits.

As related to enhancing student access and success, what might it mean to require that assessment be consistent within reasonable limits?

Picking up on my descriptions of what the first characteristic of validity might mean in regard to student access and success, then this second characteristic of reliability would mean that assessment as it occurs, not only in connection with entrance but across the curriculum, should be *consistent* in continuously diagnosing a student's progress in her or his development of those abilities that are essential for learning.

Assessment would certify, or at least indicate, the level of achievement within an ability—that is, level of developmental achievement. As the student progresses through general education and his or her major, those assessments—anticipating a later assessment characteristic evoked by the nature of the content and its function in professional life—would assess the relevant developing abilities within and through that content.

Consistency, or this second characteristic of reliability, is critical for the beginning, developing, and advanced learner. If through the initial assessment, the students begin to get a picture of what must be developed in order to master content (which means mastery of the methods by which different disciplines create their knowledge), and if the development of those abilities is incorporated into the design of classroom activities, course assignments, and the assessments that students encounter across their undergraduate career, then both access and success are being addressed at a given institution. Consistency across the curriculum both in instruction and assessment is a necessity.

Otherwise, what chance of success do ill-prepared students have, those having no insight into their educational deficits, much less any inkling about how such deficits can be overcome or the time it will take to do so? For students with these handicaps, carefully crafted feedback can be an "aha" experience. It can be a first approach toward the frontiers of their own minds and an entry into becoming their own primary teacher. For the quick-witted who are not yet sustained learners—who are perhaps superficial and grade driven—consistent diagnostic feedback can also be the beginning of a transition toward the full use of their powers.

3. Educative value—Wherever possible, the assessment itself
should have educational benefit for the student.

This third assessment characteristic of educative value has already been evidenced in the discussion of the previous two characteristics. If student learners have come to grasp how their minds function as well as what is required by way of the various methods used to access and understand the information that constitutes the disciplines and the professions, certainly those students have had their access and success enhanced.

But the benefit to the student goes beyond this. While this characteristic as stated presumes a discrete instance—that is, specific to a particular assessment-- assessment that is intentional and consistent in design, that is part of a wholistic process that begins at entrance and works with the student across the curriculum, carries within itself an enormously freeing and motivating power.

Slowly but surely, the student learner becomes extremely proficient in self-assessment, which is certainly one of the hallmarks of the professional. Roles begin to shift; students self-instruct and submit their work to critique, as do faculty who publish and expect critique. The learners develop an understanding of effective performance as well as critical judgment, enhancing their ability to critique the work of others.

> 4. Individualized content—Whenever possible, the *content* of
>   assessment should be fitted to the *individual* student and
>   her or his *particular learning*.

The fourth assessment characteristic of individualized content assumes the three preceding characteristics. Unless it is assumed that the assessment is diagnostic and fair, how would it be fitted to the individual student, either by content or particular learning?

I do not believe that we are going to be able to shake loose the reigning paradigm regarding instruction for a very long time. The departments hold sway. But every department, I think it is safe to assume, wishes its majors to be successful. Indeed, if the faculty talked together about teaching, inquired into its effects, and took responsibility for its quality, they would be delighted to have students who could analyze and think critically as well as communicate effectively in whatever mode required of them.

This is altogether possible and does happen when assessment within an institution is understood as a process through which individual students learn the frontiers of their own mind, begin to care and nurture their mind, and enter into the role of junior research colleague. Assessment that produces this result is an altogether different process than a sorting process. It has been fitted to the individual from the outset, and it proceeds through the general education and the major of the student's choice.

We know that only when a student appropriates and reconstructs data does it become her or his own knowledge. To bring students to that level almost guarantees continued success as a lifelong learner. It certainly enhances their access and success in higher education. It does so because the questions are now within the learner. Though the learner's ability to think through how to respond to her or his own questions may be faulty, the inner drive offsets the problems encountered and keeps the student developing.

> 5. Appropriate structure—It is usually necessary to
>   structure open-ended assessment in order to
>   achieve essential assessment objectives.

Structure is absolutely essential to free a student to become a truly independent learner. To get to that point requires a long and arduous apprenticeship as a learner.

Because we are speaking here of higher education, we must recognize the diversity within today's student body. While there are multiple modes of knowing, structure enables both slow, developing, and swift learners to progress at their own rate. Structure, with all the branching it affords, can guide a student learner into many levels of observation and activity that can elude a beginner—particularly one who comes to higher education still very teacher dependent.

At the conference 20 years ago, what Willingham described to illustrate this fifth characteristic was a structure that a student might use for self-assessment of an internship. He enumerated some eleven steps to assist the learner to structure the experience. Let me quickly cite those steps:

- Take stock in general learning goals
- Consider the work options available
- Define the principal tasks your supervisor is likely to expect
- Describe specific learning objectives
- Design a learning plan
- Inventory basic preparations that will be helpful
- Orient yourself to the work situation
- Monitor the plan on a regular basis (use a journal)
- Amend and redesign your learning objectives
- Self-assess the learning outcomes
- Establish new learning objectives as a result

Contrast this with how internships are only too often offered on college campuses. But, even more so, place it—analogously speaking--up against the "structure" of general education or the major at any particular institution. For a learner entering the world of higher education with or without educational deficits, with or without clear-cut goals or a career choice in mind, where is the frame of reference that provides coherence or structure to the individual learner for his or her learning?

Structure as a characteristic related to assessment that enhances access and success carries a double meaning. It assumes an overall structure for assessment across the institution that, beginning with a diagnostic entrance assessment, is developmental throughout the student's years of study in whatever discipline or profession. It likewise assumes, at the level of assessment within general education and within a major area of study, that the faculty has given serious thought to what they expect their graduate to know and be able to do.

6. Appropriate process—The method of assessment
should reflect the purpose of assessment.

This characteristic is very closely allied to the fourth assessment characteristic related to individual content and to the way it is fitted to the individual student. If the purpose of assessment in general is to enhance student access and success, then the assessment method must of necessity be diagnostic, developmental, and capable of certifying or credentialing students' levels of achievement in terms of what they know and are able to do with what they know. It cannot be punitive, episodic, and simply certify levels of lack of attainment.

If education, as embedded in the root of the word itself, is to lead out or lead to something—that is, take you from where you are to where you need or want to be —then, by definition, it is a process that should be open to all and certainly meant to enhance one's chances of succeeding. Assessment is integral to instruction and is itself a powerful form of instruction because, when well designed, it facilitates development within the learner of the very abilities by which they can lay hold of information, make it their own, and use it.

We are back to our first characteristic—assessment should always measure what is intended to be measured. If our topic is enhancing student access and success in higher education, are we not talking about enhancing that most fundamental ability--the ability to learn in all its facets--that must be brought to its highest degree of development?

We are learners before we become scholars. The best scholars are the great learners. Sophisticated assessment coupled with instruction or nonformal learning —as may well be the case when the virtual university arrives—is one way to move more students to higher levels of achievement than through what we have practiced to date.

As Willingham's final assessment characteristic concluded: "The method of assessment should reflect the purpose of assessment." ETS proclaimed under the late Gregory Anrig, and I'm sure still does—*Testing in The Service of Learning!* Therefore, assessment should not simply be a sorting device; rather, it should assist the access and success of the learner in higher education by being both diagnostic and developmental.

PART III

EXPANDING ADMISSIONS TESTING

In this last decade of the 20th century, a number of powerful forces are operating that portend radical change in the content and form of admissions testing. Some of these forces—such as the standards-based education reform movement and its paladin or principal instrument, performance assessment—are aimed at transforming the nature of elementary and secondary education. If what students know and can do, as well as the ways in which they express and display their knowledge and skill, become enhanced in this reform movement, then admissions testing will need to be similarly enhanced to provide domain-appropriate and equitable means for students to demonstrate their competence.

Other forces are aimed at transforming the nature of educational and psychological measurement by means of dramatic improvements in computer and audiovisual technology, in psychometric inferential models and construct validation, and in understanding and modeling the psychological processes underlying task performance. Each of these five forces emanating from work on standards, performance assessment, computer technology, psychometric modeling, and the psychology of cognitive and conative processes has strong implications for a new era in admissions testing. But even more striking, the confluence of these five forces at roughly the same point in time affords synergies that are likely to be more multiplicative than additive in their import for the admissions process. The ramifications of these separate forces and the power of their synergies for transforming admissions testing in the near future are the core issues examined in Part III.

In Chapter 7, Robert Linn reviews the conceptual foundation and current status of the standards-based education reform movement in the United States, with special emphasis on three essential components. These critical elements are *content standards* (i.e., what teachers should teach and students should learn in each subject area), *performance standards* (i.e., the achievement levels considered acceptable or outstanding for each content standard), and *performance assessments* (i.e., the systematic means of judging whether or not students have met the performance standards). Because content standards are being set not just at the level of specific knowledge and skill but primarily at the level of complex processes such as problem solving and the construction of knowledge, there is strong pressure to move away from traditional fixed-response or multiple-choice tests to larger constructed-response tasks involving multiple steps and integrated cognitive processing. There is also coordinate pressure to move away from normative comparisons to absolute judgments about the adequacy of student performance levels.

The simultaneous demand for changes in content standards, performance standards, and assessments has led, Linn emphasizes, to a call for closely coupled systems in which assessments are aligned with curricula or syllabi. Such alignment has several advantages such as capitalizing on the vaunted directive quality of assessment—that is, what is tested is what is taught and learned. However, Linn also stresses the potential downside of this coupling, of building assessments that teachers should teach to. He notes that this could lead to distortions of instruction and corruption of the indicator, as has occurred in other countries having high-stakes curriculum-based examinations.

With respect to college admissions, Linn points out that higher education has remained on the sidelines in the standards-based reform movement for elementary and secondary education. From one perspective, he argues that curriculum changes compatible with proposed content standards would gain considerable credibility and the reform movement considerable momentum if the associated assessments and performance standards were used in admission to higher education. However, from a counterperspective, he notes that performance standards that essentially all students are expected to meet will afford little help in making admissions decisions, especially at selective colleges. Furthermore, close ties between assessment of high-school student achievement and college entrance could run counter to the American tradition of giving students a second or third chance, as is afforded by such tests as SAT I that are not closely linked to any curriculum but instead measure developed levels of verbal and quantitative reasoning facilitative of college performance.

In Chapter 8, Hunter Breland examines some of the developments leading to renewed emphasis on performance assessment in general and the assessment of writing in particular. Some of these forces include calls for greater "authenticity" in testing, for increased "systemic validity," for more thorough grounding in cognitive psychology, and in the case of writing, for greater responsiveness to the politics of involving the English teaching profession in the assessment process. Authentic tests are those constructed to emulate samples of criterion behavior, with the hope that there will be little if any difference between the activities involved in preparing for the test and those involved in learning the skills measured by the test. Such tests, at least in principle, should exhibit so-called systemic validity or what applied linguists call "positive washback," in that the use of the test should have a beneficial influence on the ways in which the measured skills are taught and learned. Grounding assessments in cognitive psychology should lead to enhanced construct validity through theory-based test design as well as to diagnostic scoring useful in instruction. Finally, because the assessment of writing entails subjective scoring, there are scientific as well as political reasons for involving experts in the English teaching profession in the development and application of scoring rubrics.

Breland next reviews standards of quality for evaluating performance tests, especially as applied to writing assessments. Prominent among these standards are fairness and realism, which is the hallmark of authentic assessments. As applied to assessments of writing skill such as essay tests, essay-revision tests, and sentence-revision tests, Breland notes that each of these formats is realistic for some aspects of writing but that none of them captures all of the important writing processes. Hence a critical problem in the assessment of writing, as in most if not all educational assessment, is construct underrepresentation. Another problem is disentangling the effects of construct-irrelevant variance in the test. This problem becomes especially contentious when writing skill is not the prime target of the assessment but, rather, writing is the vehicle for assessing knowledge and skill in a subject-matter area.

In Chapter 9, Howard Everson recognizes that the reform movement to adopt performance-based high-school graduation standards will influence the context, content, and role of standardized tests in college admissions. However, regardless of this trend, he argues that admissions testing needs to be radically overhauled in light of new developments in cognitive psychology and model-based measurement, coupled with recent advances in computer and audiovisual technology as well as in telecommunication networks. The confluence of these disparate developments promises assessment of a broader array of knowledge and skill constructs firmly grounded in cognitive psychology, using new item types based on psychometric models supporting inferences about cognitive processing and not just performance levels as well as proficiency scaling for more informative score reporting. Furthermore, computer presentation of items permits more dynamic measures of problem solving over time, while the burgeoning growth of telecommunication networks affords the possibility of administering tests electronically, thereby improving access as well as the convenience of testing arrangements.

To accomplish this massive restructuring of admissions tests, Everson proposes a theory-based design framework and associated research agenda for moving admissions testing into the 21st century. He outlines the rationale from cognitive psychology for assessing knowledge structures as well as a broader array of cognitive abilities, and he spells out how this assessment is sustained by the new model-based psychometrics, especially latent-trait models, statistical pattern-recognition methods, and Bayesian inference networks.

In Chapters 10 and 11, Richard Snow and Fred Hargadon, respectively, offer commentary pertinent to the three previous chapters. Snow argues that both the breadth and the depth of admissions testing need to be expanded. With respect to breadth, he concentrates on the value of assessing visual-spatial abilities; idea production, especially the fluency, flexibility, and originality of ideas; and fluid reasoning, particularly reasoning in the context of knowledge and problem domains. To cope with the problem of assessing reasoning in the multiplicity of contexts needed to be fair to individuals from diverse educational backgrounds, Snow proposes the use of learning-sample tests with imaginary content. With respect to depth, Snow calls for detailed process analyses of knowledge and ability domains and of generic competencies such as writing and reading or text comprehension, so that assessments can focus on important theory-based processes rather than conglomerate total scores.

In Chapter 11, Fred Hargadon maintains that admissions officers do not so much need expanded testing as they need improved interpretation of what test scores mean relative to the context of students' educational resources and opportunities to learn. According to Hargadon, admissions officers are not just concerned with identifying high performing students but also students who will cope effectively with setbacks, capitalize on college learning resources, and grow substantially in intellect and character. This highlighting of expected student growth as a key element in admissions decisions anticipates the new accountability in higher education discussed in Part IV of this volume, wherein higher education outcomes are evaluated in terms of the value added to students' knowledge, skills, and character over and above the characteristics they entered college with.

7

IMPLICATIONS OF STANDARDS-BASED REFORM FOR ADMISSIONS TESTING

Robert L. Linn

Center for Research on Evaluation, Standards, and Student Testing.University of Colorado at Boulder

My focus here is on the standards-based educational reform movement and the implications of this movement for college admissions testing. In pursuit of this task, I will briefly describe the standards-based reform movement, its conceptual base and current status, and then turn to a discussion of its implications for admissions testing. Standards, of course, have long been a concern in college admissions. Hence, it may be worthwhile to mention this historical context before turning to the current standards-based reform movement.

STANDARDS FOR COLLEGE ADMISSIONS

In his review of the early entrance standards of American colleges, Fine (1946) begins with the following description of the examination required for entrance to Harvard College.

> In those early days the Harvard examination procedure followed the pattern: The candidate was interviewed orally by the president or the senior tutor, during which time he was rigorously examined as to his character and background. Then came questions of intellectual attainments. On this point Harvard statutes read: "When any scholar is able to read Tully (Cicero) or such like classical authors extempore and to make and speak true Latin in verse and prose at sight, and decline perfectly the paradigms of nouns and verbs in the

Greek tongue, then may he be admitted into the College, nor shall any claim admission before such qualifications." (p. 14)

The standards might have been described in today's rhetoric as high, maybe even as "world class," but rather narrow in scope of the subject areas covered. The emphasis on Greek and Latin was in keeping with the role of early colonial colleges as largely theological institutions. The decline in the stress on Greek and Latin and the addition of requirements in math or science were slow in coming. Moreover, the changes and resulting admissions procedures of different colleges were varied and rather idiosyncratic. By the late 19th century, the competing demands as described by Nicholas Butler (1925), the first Secretary of the College Board, had become a major problem for secondary schools seeking to prepare students for a variety of different colleges.

> If Cicero was prescribed, it meant in one place four orations and in another six, and not always the same four or the same six. Similar conditions existed in relation to each separate topic which appeared on the list of college admissions subjects. ... No secondary school could adjust its work and its program to the requirements of several colleges without a sort of competence as pedagogic acrobat that was rare to the point of non-existence. The situation would have been comic were it not so preposterous. (p. 2)

The chaotic situation described by Butler set the stage for the work of the famous Committee of Ten and for the formation of the College Entrance Examination Board. Standards were a central concern in the formation of the College Board. In today's terminology, the Board addressed "voluntary content standards and assessments" while leaving it to each college to determine its own "performance standards" for admission. As stated in the First Annual Report of the Secretary in 1901, the goal was to "set a fair standard based upon normal secondary school instruction; this standard to be set, and to be administered in cooperation with other colleges and schools" (CEEB, 1925b, p. 84). That is, the aim was the establishment of "uniformity of definitions, topic by topic, with a uniform test uniformly administered." Each college, however, was expected to "fix its own standards for admission" (CEEB, 1925b, p. 84).

The progress that the Board made in the establishment of standards was acknowledged in the opening paragraph of the *Twenty-Fifth Annual Report of the Secretary* (CEEB, 1925a).

> From a small beginning the Board has progressed steadily along historical and logical lines until now it is recognized quite generally as the most potent influ-

ence in America for sound standards in secondary education. ... The definitions
of the Board's requirements and specimen copies of its examination papers find
their way into every community in the United States. The deliberations of the

Board's committees and commissions are followed with interest by progressive
educators everywhere. (p. 1)

Standards have been at the heart of the work of the College Board throughout its
history. This is obvious with regard to college admissions and the award of college credit based upon Advanced Placement test results. The centrality of standards to the work of the College Board was highlighted by President Donald
Stewart at the 1993 College Board National Forum in his Annual Meeting Address
entitled *Setting Educational Standards in a Democracy: Filling the Gap.* He noted
that, "Perhaps the most important role The Board continues to play is as a voluntary standard-setting organization for the world of education, typified by its leadership in facilitating the transition from high school to college" (Stewart, 1993, p. 2).
The current press for standards-based education reform, however, poses new
challenges.

The standard-setting context has changed dramatically in the last few years.
The most notable change has been in the activity of states, the establishment of national content standards, and the involvement of the federal government. The
central actors are different. The focus is on elementary and secondary education.
Preparation for the work force in the 21st century is highlighted at least as much as
preparation for college. For the most part, the higher education community has
played only a minor role in the debate. Indeed, when mentioned by reformers,
higher education is often seen as more of an obstacle to change than as a supporter
or participant in the effort. A recent report of the National Governors' Association
(NGA) entitled *College Admission Standards and School Reform* (Houghton,
1993), for example, noted that:

school reformers have raised concerns about the need for colleges and universities to respond to the changes in curriculum, pedagogy, and assessment that are
taking place at the secondary level. In particular, the reformers say that by
clinging to conventional admission criteria, institutions of higher education are
hampering schools' efforts to implement needed changes. (p. vii)

Whether higher education is an obstacle or a participant, the standards-based reform movement in elementary and secondary education clearly could have profound implications for postsecondary education and for the transition process that
has long been a central concern of the College Board and much of the activity of
ETS. As the NGA report suggests, it is crucial that higher education be an active
participant in the dialogue about reform of the nation's education system.

STANDARDS-BASED REFORM

An *Education Week Special Report* (June 17, 1992) on the debate over standards and assessments introduced the topic with the claim that "The idea of a system of national standards and assessments is one of the most powerful and provocative to emerge from the nearly 10-year school-reform movement" (p. S1). Much has happened since that special report appeared. President Clinton was elected. Former President Bush's *America 2000* proposal (U.S. Department of Education, 1991), which had already largely fallen by the wayside before the election, was replaced by the Clinton administration's *Goals 2000*. The ink was barely dry on the newly enacted *Goals 2000: Educate America Act* (1994) when the November 1994 elections brought sweeping changes to Congress. The changed political scene in Washington put the brakes on actions called for in *Goals 2000* — halting, for example, the appointment of the National Education Standards and Improvement Council created by the Act. Indeed, the entire Act, touted as the centerpiece of the Clinton administration's education program, is fragile at best, and may be completely swept aside.

The rapid changes at the federal level reflect sharp differences of opinion about a number of key issues, such as unfunded federal mandates, the federal role in education, and opportunity-to-learn requirements, to name a few. Although there are signs of growing controversy about the standards-based reform movement in states and districts as well as at the national level, there is still wide support for many of its features. Standards and assessment continue to provide a foundation for the reform efforts in a substantial number of states.

Despite the differences in views regarding a federal role, several of the ideas of the standards-based reform movement have gained considerable support among educational, business, and political leaders. The propositions that are, perhaps, most widely endorsed are: (1) standards should encourage greater effort on the part of students and teachers, and (2) they should be "world-class." At least on a rhetorical level, there is also widespread endorsement of a third proposition that the same standards should apply to *all* students.

The reasons for buying into standards-based reform are quite varied. Some are attracted by an economic link like the one forcefully argued for in the report of the Commission on Skills of the American Workforce entitled "America's Choice: High Skills or Low Wages" (National Center on Education and the Economy, 1990). Others are persuaded that poor achievement is the result of a lack of effort and that the remedy requires the creation of a direct connection between student performance and subsequent employment as well as college entrance requirements. The proposed "Certificate of Initial Mastery," that has already been legislated by some states (e.g., Oregon) and is under consideration in others, is often justified by one or both of these propositions.

Most standards-based reform efforts include three essential components: (1) the definition of what teachers should teach and students should learn, that is, *content standards*; (2) the determination of levels of student performance that are considered acceptable or outstanding, that is, *performance standards*; and, (3) the means by which it will be decided whether or not students have met the performance standards, that is, *assessments*. Successful reform, however, requires more than content standards, assessments, and performance standards. At a minimum, implementation of the conceptions of teaching and learning embodied in content standards in each of the subject areas demands considerable professional development. Changes in curriculum, resources, school structure, and the societal support for teaching and learning are also required to provide an adequate opportunity to learn the material specified in the content standards. These other factors required to achieve the vision embodied in the standards-based reform movement are of critical importance. I'll limit my attention, however, to content standards, assessments, and performance standards.

Closely Coupled System

There are demands for change in each of these three core elements of the standards-based reform movement. As illustrated by the best known and most widely endorsed of the content standards, the *Curriculum and Evaluation Standards for School Mathematics* developed by the National Council of Teachers of Mathematics (NCTM, 1988), content standards emphasize major concepts, for example, understanding, problem solving, reasoning, and active involvement of students in the construction of knowledge. The very use of the word "assessments" rather than "tests" signals a demand for a movement away from traditional fixed-response test items to larger constructed-response tasks. Performance standards reflect a desire to move away from normative comparisons to absolute judgments about the level of performance expected of students.

Despite the emphasis on reform, there are quite familiar aspects to each of these individual standards-based reform components. Parallels to the new conceptions of learning embodied in the content standards are made evident by Linda Darling-Hammond (1993), who argued that:

> the criticisms of current education reformers — that our schools provide most children with an education that is too rigid, too passive, and too rote-oriented to produce learners who can think critically, synthesize and transform, experiment and create — are virtually identical to those of the Progressives at the turn of the century, in the 1930's and again in the 1960's. (1993, p. 755)

As Darling-Hammond suggests, even today's rallying call for a "thinking curriculum" (Resnick & Resnick, 1992) is quite consistent with John Dewey's "1900 vision of the 20th century ideal" (p. 755).

The "new" demands for performance standards and a different approach to assessment also have a familiar ring. Reflected in the demand for performance standards, for example, the search for a basis other than norms for interpreting measurement results is surely compatible with Glaser's (1963) conception of criterion-referenced measurement. And, of course, the "new" forms of assessment would seem familiar in many ways to readers of College Board tests in the early part of the century, to say nothing of our colleagues in other countries who never adopted the then "new" multiple-choice measurement technology of three-quarters of a century ago. I should hasten to add, however, that the present press for expanding the forms of assessment used, particularly the increased use of extended-response assessment tasks, has a new and more firm foundation in research on learning and cognition.

The potential influence of the standards-based reform movement comes not so much from something entirely new in any one of its components as from the tight coupling that is made among them. With a few notable exceptions such as the Advanced Placement Program and the tests of the New York State Regents, most of the external testing in this country has been largely decoupled from any particular curriculum or instructional program. The decoupling of tests from the curriculum, whether they be general achievement test batteries such as the Iowa Tests of Basic Skills or college admissions tests, is intentional, not accidental. But it has also become a topic of controversy because it is believed that though intended to be curriculum neutral, tests "shape teachers' practice" due to the fact that they are "visible and have consequences" (Resnick & Resnick, 1992, p. 55).

The standards-based reform movement eschews curriculum neutral tests and assessments. It advocates, instead, a tight coupling between what is taught and what is tested. Assessments are expected to be closely aligned with the content standards and, together with the performance standards, to determine whether students learned well the material specified in the content standards. The power of tests and assessments to shape teachers' practice is thereby converted from an unintended negative consequence to a virtue not just to be sought, but to be strengthened by increasing and making more salient the consequences of meeting performance standards.

Alignment of assessments with content standards is considered essential. The emphasis on alignment is based on the belief that measurement can have a powerful influence over what is taught. This belief is summarized in a now familiar acronym, WYTIWYG — what you test is what you get. This notion that tests shape instruction and student learning when high stakes are attached to the results is widely accepted and supported by a reasonable amount of hard evidence (e.g.,

Madaus, West, Harmon, Lomax, & Viator, 1992; Shepard, 1990; Smith, 1991; Smith & Rottenberg, 1991). If the content standards specify what we want teachers to teach and students to learn, but it is what gets tested that shapes both, then alignment of content standards and assessment is obviously of critical importance. Assuming that examinations with consequences motivate student effort, then the exams need to be focusing that effort in the direction specified in the content standards. This point was made clearly by Smith, O'Day, and Cohen (1990): "The first and central lesson is this: If exams are used to motivate students to be more serious about their studies, then examinations' content must be closely tied to the curriculum frameworks that are used to teach students" (p. 41).

Proponents of performance standards and performance-based assessments not only accept the notions of WYTIWYG and its converse, you don't get what you don't test, they embrace the concepts. The three principles presented as possible "guidelines for accountability assessments" by Resnick and Resnick (1992), for example, are: "1. You get what you assess. . . . 2. You do not get what you do not assess. . . 3. Build assessments toward which you want educators to teach" (p. 59). The third principle is the logical conclusion to reach if the first two principles are accepted and one believes, as I do, that some form of assessment for accountability purposes is almost inevitable.

It should be noted, however, that it is not clear that the third principle can be achieved without unintended negative side effects. Some of the distortions of instruction and corruption of the indicators that resulted from the high stakes uses of standardized achievement tests (e.g., Linn, Graue, & Sanders, 1990; Shepard, 1990) are not unique to that form of testing. As Messick (1994) has noted, "It is not just that some aspects of multiple-choice testing may have adverse consequences on teaching and learning, but that some aspects of all testing, even performance testing, may have adverse as well as beneficial educational consequences" (p. 22).

A concentration of effort on things judged important and therefore included in the assessments can have a desirable effect on the accomplishment of those goals. On the other hand, no assessment can be expected to adequately represent the full domain of content standards in a given discipline. As Madaus (1988) has documented, corruption of the indicator has been a long-standing problem in other countries where the form of assessment is more in keeping with the current performance-based assessment movement in this country. His example of formulaic compositions written for annual essay examinations in Ireland is only one of many examples in this regard.

Madaus (1988) has effectively made the case that when high-stakes are attached to the results of an examination "a tradition of past exams develops, which eventually de facto defines the curriculum" (p. 93). Such a tradition of past exams had already developed in this country by 1916 when the College Board introduced the

comprehensive examinations of the "New Plan." This is evident by the consterna-
tion the New Plan caused those who were already attuned to the tradition. In his
history of the first 50 years of the College Board, Fuess (1950) described the controversy.

> The idea of comprehensive examinations did at first seem revolutionary and was
> attacked as such by reactionaries. It disturbed good teachers who had been ac-
> customed to study the Board's bound volumes of old examinations and then
> "guess" what passages or problems were likely to appear on the next series.
> Some of them had developed an uncanny gift of prognostication which had
> brought them prestige, but was obviously useless in tests of the comprehensive
> type. (p. 80)

Madaus (1988) illustrates the way in which the tradition of past exams can constrain the curriculum in an extreme and dysfunctional way with an example related
to him by Benjamin Bloom based on Bloom's observation of a former student
teaching in a classroom in India. When Bloom's former student began to discuss a
broader set of implications related to the topic of the lesson, the students began to
chant "NOE, NOE," an abbreviation familiar to them and their instructor for "not
on the exam." This illustrates that, in the extreme, there are likely to be dysfunctional aspects of assessments when the stakes are high for individual students even
if it proves possible to "build assessments toward which you want educators to
teach" (Resnick & Resnick, 1992, p. 59), because the intended curriculum is always broader than any assessment.

WYTIWYG leads to several major concerns. As has already been noted, the
decoupling of tests and assessments from the content standards and curriculum is a
concern because of the influence tests and assessments have on what gets taught.
This concern is exacerbated by a widespread belief that current tests overemphasize factual knowledge and low-level procedural skills. Neither the concern about
alignment nor the concern about the level of cognitive skill and understanding demanded by tests is particularly new. Both concerns contributed to the decision to
introduce comprehensive examinations as part of the New Plan of admissions by
the College Board in 1916. The responses to the concerns about alignment and an
overemphasis on passive memorization of facts, however, led to quite different
types of changes in testing than are now being proposed in the standards-based reform movement. Indeed, the introduction of comprehensive examinations in the
New Plan was part of an effort to move away from examinations that were thought
to be too closely tied to a particular course of study and to rely too heavily on
memorization.

Fuess (1950) described this shift in examination philosophy as follows:

> During the second decade of the twentieth century momentous changes were
> taking place in the thinking of persons interested in the philosophy of examina-
> tions, especially those for admission to college. All of a sudden, like the victims
> of an epidemic, teachers began to pontificate glibly about "comprehensive ex-
> aminations" — by which they meant examinations not based mainly on the
> memorization [or] mastery of assigned subject matter, but rather designed to test
> a candidate's ability to reason independently and compare and correlate the ma-
> terial of a broad field of study. (p. 79)

As Fuess went on to note, this position was summarized a decade later by then
President of Harvard, A. Lawrence Lowell (1926) in an article that first appeared
in the *Atlantic Monthly* and that was reprinted in a volume marking the completion
of the first quarter century of the College Board, *The Work of the College Entrance Examination Board 1901-1925 (CEEB,* 1925b*)*. While acknowledging the
place of quick and accurate recall, Lowell (1926) clearly noted that there was a
need to go beyond the memorization of facts.

> But a knowledge of facts is a small part of education. We hear much today of
> teaching by problems; and rightly, because bare facts are of little value unless
> one knows how to use them. The important thing is to understand their relations
> to one another; to be able to correlate them, as the current expression goes; not
> merely to grasp and retain the relations one has been taught, but to perceive new
> relations, for no teacher can cover more than a minor fraction of the combina-
> tions actually met in the pursuit of any subject. The pupil must learn to apply
> principles to new and unexpected situations, and the extent to which he can do
> so will largely determine the degree of his future effectiveness. (p. 38, quoted
> by Fuess, 1950, pp. 79-80)

It is notable that there is a convincing parallel between Lowell's observation and
the strong message from business that it is not so much content specific knowledge
as the ability to learn and apply general principles that is needed in the workforce.

The introduction of the Scholastic Aptitude Test (SAT) a decade after the first
comprehensive examinations can be seen as a natural progression from the Old
Plan examinations that were closely tied to specific instructional materials with a
high premium on memorization to more generalized tests of reasoning ability.
Thomas S. Fiske (CEEB, 1919), the Secretary of the College Board for a quarter
of a century, foreshadowed this trend in the 1919 Annual Report of the Secretary
under the heading "Comprehensive Examinations as Intelligence Tests:"

> It should be the purpose of the College Entrance Examination Board not only to
> ascertain whether the candidates have acquired the information and methods of

> thought necessary for successful work in college, but also to determine whether they possess certain important intellectual qualities which are sometimes described as alertness, power, and endurance, although these terms would seem to indicate excellencies of the body rather than the mind. Up to the present time the Board's endeavors in this direction are exhibited most conspicuously in the comprehensive examinations. (CEEB, 1919, quoted by Fuess, 1950, p. 101)

The association of the SAT with intelligence testing and popular conceptions of intelligence as a fixed, genetically determined capacity is one of the most unfortunate of the SAT legacies. The use of these associations by critics of the SAT are quite familiar (e.g., Crouse & Trusheim, 1988; Owen, 1985). Although "scholastic aptitude" is more modest in scope than "intelligence," it still has a popular connotation of being an unmodifiable ability. Such an interpretation undermines reforms that would use tests and assessments to encourage greater effort. Concerns about such unintended connotations of the word "aptitude" led to the recent decision of the College Board to change the name of the SAT from Scholastic Aptitude Test to Scholastic Assessment Test. Clearly, continued work will be needed to disabuse people of the notion that the SAT I: Reasoning Tests measure abilities that are developed rather than fixed capacities.

The lack of a close tie of the SAT to content standards and curriculum, however, would remain as a major concern for the standards-based reform movement even if the change of name and other efforts eliminated the misinterpretation that the SAT measures a fixed capacity. As described in the 1984 *Technical Handbook* (Donlon, 1984):

> the verbal section of the SAT is so broadly constituted, and its item types so far removed from school-centered materials, that no precise counterpart exists for the test. The verbal section reflects learnings that are acquired in a variety of settings, and of these, the school system is merely one. To some extent, this is true of the mathematical section of the SAT also. (p. 5)

Important changes were made in both format and content when the SAT I: Reasoning Tests was introduced in March 1994. The revised and renamed test, however, continues to be considerably removed from any specific high school curriculum. Although for some this lack of a tight coupling is a major weakness, I believe it continues to be a strength. Moreover, I will argue that the emphasis on reasoning and problem-solving that is found in the content standards currently being advanced is ironically compatible with the SAT I: Reasoning Tests.

Conception of Learning

Although, as has been illustrated, there is much that has an old familiar ring in the standards-based reform movement, there are also some new elements. For example, I have already discussed the emphasis that is given to creating a tightly coupled system with curriculum, instruction, and assessment all neatly aligned with the content standards and the desire to encourage a belief that it is effort rather than fixed ability that matters. Another relatively new feature that has important implications for assessment concerns the conceptions of knowledge and learning that undergird much of the movement.

Lauren Resnick is one of the leading proponents of the need to base assessments on new conceptions of knowledge and learning as well as the need to shift from an emphasis on ability to an emphasis on effort. Her position on the first of these issues was concisely articulated in her statement in the previously mentioned 1992 special issue of *Education Week* on the standards-based reform movement. According to Resnick (June 17, 1992), "We've got a terrible model of what knowledge is, and what we care about, built into those tests: Collections of decontextualized and decomposed bits of knowledge that do not add up to competent thinking, to knowing a body of history or science or whatever we might care about" (p. S5). This conclusion provides part of the conceptual underpinning for the rapid acceptance of performance-based assessments and, in many instances, the wholesale rejection of multiple-choice testing.

As I have said elsewhere, "the rejection of multiple-choice testing is, in my view, a gross overreaction to some of the limitations of the multiple-choice format and to some of the misuses of standardized tests" (Linn, 1994, p. 24). The multiple-choice format has limitations, but they are nowhere near as severe as those assumed by critics. It is admittedly easier to write multiple-choice test items that require only factual recall, but the format can also require higher-order reasoning and problem-solving skills that are quite consistent with the goals of the reform. A careful analysis of the SAT I: Reasoning Tests or the GRE General Tests provides strong support for this observation. More systematic support is provided by research using think-aloud protocols and relational studies supporting the construct validity of these tests (see, for example, Donlon & Burton, 1984).

There is an unfortunate tendency in education to swing radically from one end of the pendulum to the other, discarding past practices in favor of those currently in vogue with little thought for tradeoffs. The current attacks on multiple-choice testing by some advocates of performance-based assessment are in keeping with this tendency. There are good reasons for wanting to expand the forms of assessment. We clearly have had too much reliance on a single format. Different assessment formats have different strengths and weaknesses. The gains made by avoiding the weaknesses associated with one assessment format may be swamped by losses in the associated strengths. Moreover, any new assessment format will also have limitations.

Efficiency, breadth of domain coverage, enhanced generalizability, and comparability are among the strengths of multiple-choice testing that are not easily replaced by complex performance-based assessment tasks. On the other hand, performance assessment tasks that require students to frame the problem, explore multiple solution paths, and communicate results and conclusions with a specific audience in mind may provide better models of desired instructional activities as well as tap important sources of construct-relevant variance that are poorly measured by fixed-response test items. The design of an assessment, however, need not be limited to an either-or choice between the two extreme ends of the continuum of structured to open-ended assessment. A mix of approaches is likely to yield better validity than the exclusive use of any one approach. This is true of the consequential basis of validity as well as the evidential basis of validity (Messick, 1989).

HIGHER EDUCATION

As indicated earlier, higher education has not been a major player in the standards-based reform efforts for elementary and secondary schools. Through their entrance requirements, colleges have long had a conservative influence on secondary schools and to a lesser extent on elementary schools as the result of a trickle-down effect. According to Nathan (February 15, 1995), for example, admissions requirements push high schools "toward a continuing reliance on discipline-based courses, credits and grades" (p. 30). Radical changes in curriculum frequently meet resistance from parents of college-bound youth who worry that reforms will have a negative impact on their children's performance on admissions tests.

There is little doubt that curriculum changes compatible with the content standards would gain considerable strength if the associated assessment and performance standards became the coin of the realm for admission to higher education. Schwartz (1993) has advocated a proactive role for higher education in relation to the standards-based reform movement. In his words:

> ...the most important function higher education can play in relation to standards setting is to insist, after a reasonable phase-in period, that the standards have teeth. This means, for example, that high school seniors who cannot meet national standards would not be admitted to four-year institutions and that college credit would no longer be awarded for work that is in fact precollegiate. Until colleges and employers start to base admissions and hiring decisions on student

performance, standards setting will be a hollow exercise, for students will have little incentive to work hard to meet the standards. (pp. 22-23)

Some states are taking steps to move in the direction advocated by Schwartz. The NGA report, *College Admissions Standards for School Reform* (Houghton, 1993) highlights activities in Minnesota, Nebraska, Oklahoma, Wisconsin, and Wyoming to illustrate signs of movement in this direction. Nathan (1995) cites the movement of Oregon toward "admission based on proficiency" (p. 30) as another example.

I think that it is critical for higher education to become more involved in the dialogue regarding standards-based reforms. Although it may be true that the reform effort would be enhanced by putting teeth in standards through admissions practices, there are several major complications and potential downsides that need to be weighed. First, it must be recognized that most colleges are not very selective. In fact, many of them are struggling to attract enough students. It is unlikely that colleges in this category will adopt higher entrance requirements based on new standards of student performance.

Second, colleges and universities that are highly selective will find little help in making admissions decisions from the results of performance standards that essentially all students are expected to meet or from standards that place students into one of a small number of categories, such as the proficient and advanced levels of performance now being used to report student achievement on the National Assessment of Educational Progress or the proficient and distinguished performance levels used by Kentucky. Normative comparisons are abhorred by the standards-based reform movement, but relative comparisons are inherent to competitive admissions and hiring decisions.

Third, the close coupling between high school performance and college opportunities also has potential downsides as well as potential benefits. It could hinder, for example, the American tradition of providing students with second, third, and fourth chances. A test such as the SAT I that is not closely tied to a specific course of study is "useful in helping identify the so-called late bloomer or student who, for whatever reason, did not put forth great effort in high school but who has developed high levels of verbal and mathematical reasoning" (Linn, 1994, p. 30). Systems in other countries with high-stakes, syllabus-driven college entrance examinations that reformers sometimes point to as models, also have, as Shanker (June 17, 1992) has noted "a lot in them that is repugnant to our values and commitment to second, third, and more chances" (p. S11).

Fourth, although the goal of having the same high standards for all children is appealing, it is not clear that a single set of standards is appropriate for all students at the end of high school. Of the other countries that proponents of the standards-based reform movement are fond of pointing to, none maintains the same standards for all students at the end of secondary school. Rather, as Shanker (June 17, 1992) has stated:

> our competitors' content and performance standards—and assessments—vary according to whether their students are aiming for an apprenticeship or for a technical school or hoping to go to a university; sometimes, those standards and tests also vary by what kind of technical education or university major students intend to pursue. (p. S11)

It is controversial to talk about individual differences that lead to different educational experiences and outcomes. Much of the controversy stems from the strong association of class and race with educational outcomes in a society that likes to pretend to be both classless and color-blind. We cannot solve fundamental dilemmas, however, by ignoring them or wishing them away. We need to find a way to get beyond the impasse that results from implied affirmative answers to two provocative questions posed by Shanker (June 17, 1992) in this regard:

> Has our necessary preoccupation with ending different expectations for students based on group membership — race, ethnicity, class — blinded us to the fact that different students have different strengths, weaknesses, interests, and aspirations? Are we so unwilling to talk openly about differentiated standards or so paralyzed by our history of handling them inequitably that we'd rather risk massive student failure? (p. S11)

Fifth, the adoption of performance-standards requirements could exacerbate differences between those who come from privileged backgrounds and those who come from disadvantaged backgrounds. Schwartz (1993) recognized this potential dilemma and suggested that an "implication of the school reform agenda for higher education is that as standards are raised, colleges and universities will need to find new ways to work with schools and other community institutions to ensure that large numbers of students are not left behind" (p. 23).

Finally, it must be recognized that there are "savage inequalities" (Kozol, 1991) in opportunity to learn the material specified in new content standards. As was stated in the report of the Standards Task Force of the National Council on Education Standards and Testing (1992), "if not accompanied by measures to ensure equal opportunity to learn, national *content* and *performance standards* could help widen the achievement gap between the advantaged and disadvantaged within our society" (p. E-12). That is, without a level playing field, sole reliance on achievement in content areas would be unfair to students who did not have an adequate opportunity to learn well the subject-matter material defined by the content standards.

CONCLUSION

There is much in the standards-based reform movement that is attractive. The emphasis on reasoning and problem-solving, while not all that new, is supported by research on learning and cognition. The expansion in forms of assessment and the emphasis on conveying the message that effort matters are positive features. We need to expand our approaches to assessment.

It seems clear that there is also a need for greater involvement of the higher education community in the standards-based reform effort. Such involvement is likely to lead to a desirable rethinking of college entrance requirements and the ways we obtain as well as report information about student accomplishments and preparation for college.

I hope, however, that the rethinking will lead to an expansion of information rather than a substitution of one type of information for another. Thus, I would advocate the use of multiple sources of information such as those that can be provided by a mix of high school performance records, general achievement tests, reasoning tests that are not tied to any curriculum, and a variety of course specific results such as those currently provided by the Advanced Placement Program as well as those that might be provided in the future by the College Board's Pacesetter program. It is time we went beyond a wholesale rejection of the past in favor of an untried alternative. A combination is apt to be far superior to either alone.

REFERENCES

Butler, N. M. (1925). How the College Board came to be. In College Entrance Examination Board, *The work of the College Entrance Examination Board 1901-1925* (pp. 1-6). New York: Author.

College Entrance Examination Board. (1919). *Nineteenth annual report of the Secretary*. New York: Author.

College Entrance Examination Board. (1925a). *Twenty-fifth annual report of the Secretary*. New York: Author.

College Entrance Examination Board. (1925b). *The work of the College Entrance Examination Board 1901-1925*. Boston: Ginn and Company.

Crouse, J., & Trusheim, D. (1988). *The case against the SAT*. Chicago: University of Chicago Press.

Darling-Hammond, L. (1993). Reframing the school reform agenda: Developing capacity for school transformation. *Phi Delta Kappan, 74*, 752-761.

Donlon, T. F. (1984). The admissions testing program: A historical overview. In T. F. Donlon (Ed.), *The College Board technical handbook for the Scho-*

88   Linn

lastic Aptitude Test and achievement tests (pp. 1-11). New York: College Entrance Examination Board.

Donlon, T. F., & Burton, N. W. (1984). Construct and content validity of the SAT. In T. F. Donlon (Ed.), *The College Board technical handbook for the Scholastic Aptitude Test and achievement tests* (pp. 123-140). New York: College Entrance Examination Board.

Education Week. (June 17, 1992). By all measures: The debate over standards and assessments. *Education Week Special Report*, S1-S20.

Fine, B. (1946). *Admission to American Colleges: A study of current policy and practice.* New York: Harper and Brothers.

Fuess, C. M. (1950). *The College Board: Its first fifty years.* New York: Columbia University Press.

Glaser, R. (1963). Instructional technology and the measurement of learning outcomes. *American Psychologist, 18*, 519-521.

Goals 2000: Educate America Act of 1994, Pub. L. 103-227, Sec. 1 et seq. 108 Stat. 125 (1994).

Houghton, M. J. (1993). *College admission standards and school reform: Toward a partnership in education.* Washington, DC: National Governors' Association.

Kozol, J. (1991). *Savage inequalities: Children in American schools.* New York: Crown.

Linn, R. L. (1994). The education reform agenda: Assessment, standards, and the SAT. *The College Board Review*, No. 172, Summer, 22-25, 30.

Linn, R. L., Graue, M. E., & Sanders, N. M. (1990). Comparing state and district test results to national norms: The validity of claims that "everyone is above average." *Educational Measurement: Issues and Practice, 9*(3), 5-14.

Lowell, A. L. (1926). The art of examination. College Entrance Examination Board. *The work of the College Entrance Examination Board 1901-1925* (pp. 31-43, reprinted from the January, 1926 *Atlantic Monthly*). Boston: Ginn and Company.

Madaus, G. F. (1988). The influence of testing on the curriculum. In L. N. Tanner (Ed.), *Critical issues in curriculum* (Eighty-seventh yearbook of the National Society for the Study of Education (pt. 1, pp. 83-121). Chicago: University of Chicago Press.

Madaus, G. F., West, M. M., Harmon, M. C., Lomax, R. G., & Viator, K. A. (1992). *The influence of testing on teaching math and science in grades 4-12: Executive summary.* Technical Report. Chestnut Hill, MA: Boston College, Center for the Study of Testing, Evaluation, and Educational Policy.

Messick, S. (1989). Validity. In R. L. Linn (Ed.), *Educational measurement*, (3rd ed., pp. 13-103). New York: Macmillan.

Messick, S. (1994). The interplay of evidence and consequences in the validation of performance assessments. *Educational Researcher, 23*, 13-23.

Nathan, J. (February 15, 1995). To improve high schools, change college-admissions policies. *Education Week, 14*(21), 30, 32.

National Center on Education and the Economy. (1990). *America's choice: High skills or low wages*. Rochester, NJ: Author.

National Council on Education Standards and Testing. (1992). *Raising standards for American education: A report to congress, the secretary of education, the national education goals panel, and the American people*. Washington, DC: U.S. Government Printing Office.

National Council of Teachers of Mathematics. (1988). *Curriculum and evaluation standards for school mathematics*. Reston, VA: Author.

Owen, D. (1985). *None of the above: Behind the myth of scholastic aptitude*. Boston: Houghton-Mifflin.

Resnick, L. B. (June 17, 1992). The "most promising way" of getting the education we want. In *Education Week*, By all measures: The debate over standards and assessments. *Education Week Special Report, 11*, S6-S7.

Resnick, L. B., & Resnick, D. P. (1992). Assessing the thinking curriculum: New tools for educational reform. In B. R. Gifford & M. C. O'Connor (Eds.), *Changing assessments: Alternative views of aptitude, achievement and instruction* (pp. 37-75). Boston: Kluwer Academic Publishers.

Schwartz, R. (1993). Higher education's vital role in school reform. *Education Record, 74*(3), 21-23.

Shanker, A. (June 17, 1992). Coming to terms with "world-class standards." In *Education Week*, By all measures: The debate over standards and assessments. *Education Week Special Report, 11*, S11.

Shepard, L. A. (1990). Inflated test score gains: Is the problem old norms or teaching the test? *Educational Measurement: Issues and Practice, 9*(3), 15-22.

Sizer, T. R. (June 17, 1992). Eight questions: On cost, impact, the politics of who chooses. In *Education Week*, By all measures: The debate over standards and assessments. *Education Week Special Report, 11*, S5-S6.

Smith, M. L. (1991). Put to the test: The effects of external testing on teachers. *Educational Researcher, 20*(5), 8-11.

Smith, M. L., & Rottenberg, C. (1991). Unintended consequences of external testing in elementary schools. *Educational Measurement: Issues and Practice, 10*(4), 7-11.

Smith, M. S., O'Day, J., & Cohen, D. K. (1990). National curriculum American style: Can it be done? What might it look like? *American Educator*, Winter, 10-17, 40-47.

Stewart, D. M. (1993). Setting educational standards in a democracy: Filling the gap. Annual Meeting Address, 1993 College Board Forum, New Orleans, October 30.

U.S. Department of Education. (1991). *America 2000: An education strategy*. Washington, DC: U.S. Department of Education.

8

FROM 2 TO 3 Rs: THE EXPANDING USE OF WRITING IN ADMISSIONS

Hunter M. Breland
Educational Testing Service

A look at developments in a number of admissions testing programs over the last several years makes it obvious that many changes are taking place. Computers are, of course, being used more in testing programs. But another change that is quite remarkable is the increasing use of writing assessment, and the increasing proportion of total testing time used for it. Consider the following testing programs:

- **MCAT.** The Medical College Admission Test introduced a writing skill assessment in 1991. This writing skill assessment consists of two 30-minute essays. The MCAT is an all-day test, with almost 6 hours of actual testing time, so that the writing portion represents only about one-sixth of the total testing time.

- **GMAT.** The Graduate Management Admissions Test now includes a writing assessment, introduced in 1994. Like the MCAT writing assessment, the GMAT writing assessment also consists of two 30-minute writing tasks. Since the GMAT is a 4-hour test, the writing tasks represent one-fourth of testing time. The GMAT Verbal Reasoning measure also includes a 25-minute sentence correction test in multiple-choice format.

- **GRE**. The Graduate Record Examination announced plans some time ago to introduce a writing assessment as part of the GRE. The new GRE is scheduled for introduction in 1999. Present plans suggest that this assessment would consist of at least one 45-minute essay, and possibly an additional 30-minute essay if results from field tests support that. The proportion of total testing time that will be devoted to writing will be in the one-third to one-half range, depending on the outcomes of the field tests.

- **SAT**. The SAT now includes SAT-W, a test which includes an essay assessment, first administered in 1994. SAT-W consists of two parts: a 20-minute essay and a 40-minute multiple-choice section. The multiple-choice section has questions on both sentence revision and essay revision. Since the SAT-W is administered only as part of SAT II, it does not affect testing time in SAT I.

- **LSAT**. The Law School Admission Test has included a writing sample since 1982. The LSAT Writing Sample requires 30 minutes of testing time, which represents about one-sixth of total testing time. The LSAT Writing Sample is not scored, but is included with admissions materials.

FORCES CREATING EXPANSIONS

There have been in recent years a number of books and articles published that call for new kinds of assessments in education. While one cannot be certain that these writings led to the changes in major testing programs noted above, they would appear to be related. Consider the following:

- **Authenticity**. Numerous writers have called for more "authenticity" in educational testing (e.g., Wiggins, 1993; Shepard, 1991; Moss, 1992, 1994). Related to authenticity are arguments that two key assumptions of traditional test design, that knowledge can be decomposed and decontextualized, are inappropriate (Resnick, 1990).

- **Systemic Validity**. There has been a call for more systemic, ecological, or edumetric validity in tests (N. Frederiksen, 1984; Frederiksen & Collins, 1989). The idea behind systemic validity is that tests should provide feedback into the educational system such that teaching and learning is encouraged. Systemically valid tests are described as those with at least these two characteristics:

(1) directness as opposed to indirectness, and (2) the use of subjective judgment in assigning scores. Essay tests of writing skill, when scored properly, are cited as examples of systemically valid tests.

- **Politics of Writing Assessment.** Some forces influencing more writing in admissions assessments have been articulated perhaps less than authenticity and systemic validity, but they may be even more powerful forces. One is the politics of writing assessment in the English teaching profession (see, e.g., White, 1994; White, Lutz, & Kamusikiri, 1996). Those in the English teaching profession have for many years called for more essay testing and less multiple-choice sentence-level tests of writing skill. Multiple-choice tests of writing skill have little face validity in their view, but perhaps more importantly they can be administered and scored without the involvement of experts in the English teaching profession. Essay assessments require extensive involvement of the English teaching profession.

- **Cognitive Psychology.** An important force probably influencing the expanded use of writing in admissions is the resurgence of cognitive and instructional psychology as disciplines (Bennett, 1993; Mislevy, 1993; Nichols, 1994; Snow & Lohman, 1989). Since these disciplines have become more closely associated with the testing establishment in recent years, this influence is in some senses a force from within. Related arguments are: (1) that traditional testing practices place more emphasis on statistical techniques than on the psychology of the construct being measured (Anastasi, 1967), and (2) that traditional tests often do not serve a diagnostic function useful in instruction (Nichols, 1994).

- **Fairness.** Some evidence (Klein & Bolus, 1984) indicates that women perform better on tests that include writing assessments, although some might question the value of added verbal testing for language minority students.

SOME POSSIBLE PROBLEMS WITH EXPANSIONS

Those of us who have been studying writing skill assessment for many years are of course pleased with all of the attention it is receiving of late. Nevertheless, there is some concern that the arguments being made in support of expanded writing assessment are not always as cogent as they might be. One problem is the language being used. Let us consider the word *authentic*, for example. In my Random House dictionary, authentic is defined as follows:

1. entitled to acceptance or belief because of agreement with known facts or experience; reliable; trustworthy.

2. not false or copied; genuine; real.

If authentic means reliable, then considerable confusion is generated by its use in describing essay tests (which often have questionable reliability). If we use the second definition, "not false or copied," then the implication is that the tests that more authentic tests might replace are false or copied, and that is simply not true.

To avoid this kind of confusion, it is preferable to use the language that industrial and organizational psychology uses to describe performance tests (which include essay tests). It is also important to recognize that industrial and organizational psychologists have been studying performance testing for many years and thus have much experience with its philosophy and use. Fitzpatrick and Morrison (1971) use the term *realism* to describe the degree to which performance tests represent real-life activities:

> If a performance measure is to be interpreted as relevant to "real-life" performance, it must be taken under conditions representative of the stimuli and responses that occur in real life. But each of these can be analyzed into many aspects, and most aspects . . . vary from occasion to occasion. Hence, it would be desirable for the performance measure to be taken a number of times under a wide variety of conditions. (p. 239)

In the Fitzpatrick and Morrison schema, the degree to which all aspects of a real-life activity are covered by a performance assessment is termed its *comprehensiveness*. Each aspect can also be judged with respect to the degree to which real-life activity is simulated; this is called *fidelity*. By analyzing both the comprehensiveness and fidelity of the various aspects of an assessment, one can evaluate its realism. Probably, most tests used in admissions settings will be limited in both comprehensiveness and in fidelity and thus will not be completely realistic.

The use of the term *directness* to describe an appropriate test characteristic has also been challenged. Messick (1994a) notes that the term *direct assessment* is generally inappropriate in the behavioral sciences and should not be used. Moreover, Messick notes that "a claim that a particular performance assessment is authentic and direct is tantamount to a claim of construct validity and needs to be supported by empirical evidence of construct validity."

Subjectivity is another term that has current popularity. The requirement that subjective judgment is necessary can also be questioned, because some performance tasks can be objectively scored (Messick, 1997) and others can be scored by computer algorithms (Bejar, 1991; Sebrechts, Bennett, & Rock, 1991). An assessment can be both direct and scored by judgmental procedures and still not be realistic. For example, a single 20-minute writing task on a topic the examinee has never thought about before is a common type of writing assessment, but it is clearly not realistic in the sense that it is something that people are not often required to do in real life. Such brief tests of writing are best thought of as simulations of real-life writing tasks.

TYPES OF WRITING SKILL ASSESSMENTS

In admissions, writing skill is typically assessed in three different ways, although all three are not often used in a single assessment: with essay tests, with essay or paragraph revision tests, and with sentence-revision tests. Each of these types of writing skill tests has its advantages and disadvantages.

- **Essay tests**. Essay tests can be of various types, but the typical essay test used for admissions purposes is the brief impromptu writing task. A brief statement is made or a quotation given and the examinee is asked to respond to a specific question related to the statement or quotation. Usually, 20 to 45 minutes is allowed for the response. The English teaching profession favors this kind of writing skill assessment, especially when it is scored holistically.

- **Essay–revision Tests**. The College Board has had long experience with this type of writing skill test. In the 1950s and 1960s, a test was used that was known as the "interlinear exercise." This test was administered in pencil and paper format and consisted of a brief essay which was poorly written. The examinee's task was to revise the essay by crossing out words and phrases and by inserting words and phrases between the double-spaced lines, as one might normally do when editing a piece of writing. These completed exercises were then scored by experienced English teachers using detailed scoring rubrics consisting of a page for each writing problem in the essay.

Accordingly, the scoring rubrics could be 40 to 50 pages in length, and they were costly and cumbersome to score. These tests were discontinued in the 1960s. A more recent version of the revision test is administered in multiple-choice format, and it is included as part of the new SAT-W. An advantage of the multiple-choice format is flexibility: Rather than being limited to the usual kinds of corrections, broad questions can be posed about the essay as a whole. For example, questions can be posed about the thesis, rhetorical strategy, the conclusion, transitions, audience, tone, and other global features.

•   **Sentence-revision Tests**.   Sentence-revision tests of writing skill typically test knowledge of grammar, usage, diction, idiom, and effectiveness of expression. They can also test sentence combining skills. In the early 1970s, the College Board introduced a new writing test named the Test of Standard Written English (TSWE). This was a 50-item, 30-minute sentence-level tests. A relatively easy test, the TSWE was intended primarily for use as a placement test, although it was administered along with the SAT and scores were available to college admissions officials when making admissions decisions. For those institutions who wanted a higher-level test, the English Composition Test (ECT), an achievement test, could also be required by institutions. The ECT was similar to the TSWE but more difficult. These tests were not popular with the English teaching profession, however, who argued for more essay testing (White, 1994), because the only essay testing available for admissions was in only one administration per year in the ECT. These multiple-choice tests of writing skill would not qualify as authentic or systemically valid assessments by the Frederiksen & Collins (1989) rules, since they were indirect assessments requiring no judgmental activities.

STANDARDS OF QUALITY

Since some view the expanding use of performance assessments as a threat to the traditional standards of quality in educational testing (Messick, 1994a; Mehrens, 1992; Dunbar, Koretz, & Hoover, 1991), it is useful to attempt an evaluation of the quality standards of the new writing assessments. Linn, Baker, & Dunbar (1991) outlined several evaluative criteria that might be used. Their evaluative criteria have been revised and supplemented to obtain the following list: content, generalizability, predictive validity, fairness, cognitive complexity, realism, consequences, meaningfulness, and cost & efficiency.

Content

Messick (1997) has observed that an important aspect of construct validity is a consideration of the boundaries of the construct domain to be assessed. The intent here is to insure that all important parts of the construct domain are covered. The boundaries of the construct domain might be determined through job analysis, task analysis, or curriculum analysis, for example. Fortunately, in the field of writing skill assessment, protocol analyses have been conducted and sound theories developed about what constitutes the writing process. Following detailed and extensive protocol analyses, Hayes and Flower (1980) proposed that writing consists of three major processes: planning, translating, and reviewing (see Figure 1). The planning process consists of generating, organizing, and goal-setting. The translating process consists of those activities required to produce language. Reviewing consists of reading and editing. In another model, Collins & Gentner (1980) separate writing into idea production and text production. They suggest that ideas can be captured by keeping a journal of interesting ideas, brainstorming with a group, looking in books or other source materials, getting suggestions from somebody, and trying to explain your ideas to someone else. Text production includes not only the initial writing but also editing.

   To simplify, we might say that writing consists of idea generation, drafting, reviewing, and editing. From these descriptions of what writing consists of, it clear that the construct domain of writing skill is quite large and, as a consequence, is not likely to be completely covered in any writing assessment. Writing assessments used for admissions purposes almost always fail to cover the entire construct domain of writing skills. If a brief essay is used, or even two brief essays, there is little time for idea generation and no time for review and editing. Essentially, what one does with a brief essay is to cover the initial drafting stage of writing, with only minimal time allowed for idea generation. If a revision exercise is used, neither idea generation nor drafting skills is covered. If sentence correction alone is used, only that part of review and editing having to do with sentences is covered. There is some merit, then, in using more than a single assessment type. A brief essay can cover some idea generation and drafting; a brief revision exercise can cover review and editing. Of course, the brief essay can cover idea generation only for the topic selected, and the brief revision exercise will be limited in the number of revision problems presented. Ackerman & Smith (1988), following factor analyses of both

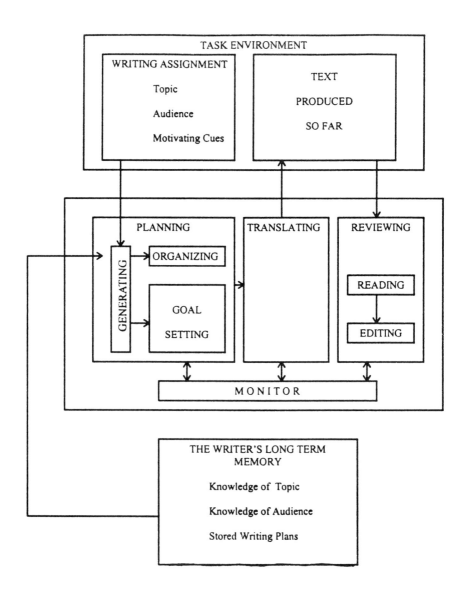

FIG. 1 Hayes & Flowers Writing Model.
From Hayes (1996). Used by permission.

essay and multiple-choice tests of writing skills, suggested that both types of tests should be used. Miller and Crocker (1990) came to a similar conclusion.

Generalizability and Reliability

The principal problem encountered by the essay test has been that of generalizability. In this paper, generalizability and reliability are treated as essentially the same, although there are some distinctions. A good review of reliability problems in essay tests is given in Dunbar, Koretz, & Hoover (1991), who have shown that essay tests of the type usually used in admissions typically have reliabilities of around .50, on average. Linn (1994) and Linn & Burton (1994) have argued that, rather than reliability, it is more useful to think about the standard error of measurement, which is derived from reliability.

Table 1 is useful in examining the reliability problem in more detail. Two sets of reliability estimates are given in Table 1, one set from Breland et al. (1987) and another set from Coffman (1966). These studies are particularly useful to contrast because there were many differences in the procedures used and they are 21 years apart in time. Despite the differences, they tell pretty much the same story: Multiple writing samples, each scored independently by several different experienced scorers, can yield respectable reliability coefficients. In the Breland et al. (1987) study, a total of six different essays, each scored by three different experienced readers, yielded a reliability of .88. In the Coffman (1966) study, five essays each scored independently by five different experienced readers yielded a reliability of .84. Such evidence is highly supportive of writing assessments for which multiple samples of a student's written work are evaluated.

For the usual admissions setting, however, Table 1 tells a different story. Commonly, essay tests used for admissions purposes are limited to a single essay scored independently by two different readers. For this situation, the Breland et al. (1987) data give an estimated reliability of .53 and the Coffman (1966) data an estimate of .42. Linn (1994) suggests that generalizability coefficients even as high as .80 can be problematical. Accordingly, the use of a single essay alone for admissions purposes is questionable. The two-essay assessments being used for the MCAT and GMAT, and proposed for the GRE, are better, but the data of Table 1 would suggest that even these relatively elaborate assessments will not result in generalizability coefficients as high as .80.

Reckase (1995) illustrates the problem in an analysis of a hypothetical writing portfolio assessment. His results show that to approximate a .80 reliability a

TABLE 1

Estimated Reliabilities for Essay Examinations

			Number of readers per essay			
Modes	Topics	Essays	1	2	3	4

From Breland et al. (1987):

Modes	Topics	Essays	1	2	3	4
1	1	1	.42	.53	.58	.63
	2	2	.59	.70	.74	.77
	3	3	.69	.77	.81	.84
2	1	2	.57	.68	.72	.76
	2	4	.73	.81	.84	.86
	3	6	.80	.86	.88	.90
3	1	3	.66	.75	.79	.82
	2	6	.80	.86	.88	.90
	3	9	.85	.90	.92	.93

From Coffman (1966):

Modes	Topics	Essays	1	2	3	4
	1	1	.26	.42	.52	.59
	2	2	.38	.55	.65	.71
	3	3	.44	.62	.71	.76
	4	4	.49	.66	.74	.79
	5	5	.52	.68	.76	.81

portfolio of five different writing samples is required. For this hypothetical portfolio, each component would need to have a reliability of at least .55 and the correlation between components would have to be at least .28. The correlational requirement means that the components cannot be too disparate. In reviewing the psychometric challenges of the Kentucky Instructional Results Information System (KIRIS), Haertel (1994) noted that the low reliability of performance assessments was generally recognized as a problem. In KIRIS, high-stakes decision making has been limited to the school level and to the pooling of data across 2 years of experience. Haertel cautions: "Any pressures to use or interpret data at the *individual* level must be resisted until such time as adequate reliability is assured" (p.71).

No generalizability studies for revision in context exercises are available, but evidence on reliability from the old judgmentally-scored "interlinear exercises" of the 1950s and 1960s indicates that 30-minute exercises of this type had reliabilities averaging about .83. Of eighteen such exercises for which we have data, only two had reliabilities less than .80 and nine had reliabilities in the .84 - .86 range (see Table 2). Two exercises of this type, requiring one hour of testing time, would probably have a reliability exceeding .90.

Sentence-level tests usually have reliabilities higher than those for essay revision exercises, and reliability can easily be increased by increasing the number of sentence-level items.

Predictive Validity

Breland et al. (1987) found that brief (45-minute) narrative or expository essays with two readings correlated .40, on average, with grades in English composition courses. Longer, take-home essays correlated more highly with grades (.49 on average). In the same study, the SAT Verbal score correlated .44 with grades, and a 30-minute multiple-choice test of sentence skills correlated .41 with grades. The incremental predictive validity of essays, beyond that possible with multiple-choice measures, was small but statistically significant. The incremental predictive validity of a 30-minute multiple-choice test of writing skill was greater than that for a single essay with two readings. Similar results for predicting grades in English composition courses in college were obtained by Breland & Gaynor, 1979; Breland & Griswold, 1982; and Breland & Duran, 1985. No predictive validity studies of revision in context exercises were found, but correlations between these exercises and essay writing performance are high. Godshalk, Swineford, & Coffman, (1966) obtained correlations of .67 and .64, respectively, between two "interlinear" exercises and their total essay score based on five essays each read five times.

Fairness

Linn, Baker, & Dunbar (1991) report that results from NAEP indicate that average scores on essay tests for Black and White students show about the same differences as do multiple-choice reading tests. And Klein (1981) showed that increased essay testing on the California Bar Exam did not reduce the differences in passing rates between White and minority groups (although it did increase passing rates for women). Nevertheless, the increasing proportion of test time devoted to writing skill assessment may work to the disadvantage of linguistic minorities. With only two R's, reading and 'rithmetic, only half of a test is primarily verbal. But with three R's, two-thirds of a test might be primarily verbal.

TABLE 2

Reliabilities for 30-Minute Editing Tasks

Title	Number of Items	Reliability
Queen Elizabeth	44	.86
The Civil War	54	.86
The South	50	.86
Popular Literature	42	.86
The Housefly	47	.85
Cowardly Americans	43	.84
Declaration of Independence	34	.84
Local Color	53	.84
Universal Spider	44	.84
Air Mail Pilot	44	.83
Valley Forge	47	.83
Columbus	47	.82
Catastrophes	46	.82
Fiction and the Devil's Work	48	.82
Spanish Armada	40	.81
Myth of the American Farmer	48	.80
Love for Dogma	43	.78
Red Cross Worker	50	.77
Averages	45	.83

Consequences

Dunbar, Koretz, & Hoover (1991) have noted that it is difficult to evaluate the consequences of the current wave of performance assessments without examining specific types of assessment and their purposes. This paper focusses on writing skill and its assessment for purposes of admission to college and graduate and professional schools. In the admissions setting, as already noted, the time available for writing skill assessment is limited. Accordingly, the assessments used are often as brief as 20 minutes and rarely longer than 1 hour.

The consequences most often discussed for performance assessments are those related to instructional systems. Will the assessment encourage teachers to teach and students to learn writing skills? There is no evidence to date that the increased use of writing in admissions is resulting in changes in the way it is taught, but perhaps there has not been time for that to occur. Linn (1994) has observed that the collection of this kind of consequential information may be difficult.

Another possible consequence of increased writing skill assessment could be feedback of diagnostic information to the instructional system. This is the goal of cognitively diagnostic assessments (CDA's) as described by Nichols (1994). The usual essay tests are not likely CDA's because, when scored holistically (the method preferred by most in the English teaching profession), very little information is provided for diagnosis. A better prospect for CDA would be either revision in context exercises or sentence-level tests of writing skills.

Messick (1994b) describes possible adverse consequences as "any negative impact on individuals or groups" resulting from any source of test invalidity. For example, "low scores should not occur because the assessment is missing something relevant to the focal construct that, if present, would have permitted the affected persons to display their competence." In other words, the construct is underrepresented. Given that writing is conceived as a complete process, if an examinee is a good writer but no essay writing is required, the construct is underrepresented. Similarly, if an examinee is good at revision, but no revision is required, the construct is underrepresented. Secondly, Messick (1994b) notes that "low scores should not occur because the measurement contains something irrelevant that interferes with the affected persons' demonstration of competence." In a writing skill assessment, construct irrelevance could possibly occur in an essay assessment with a prompt of excessive cognitive complexity. For such an assessment, the examinee may be able to write nothing, or very little, and thus be unable to demonstrate competence.

The problem of demonstrating competence in writing tests has also been noted by those in the English teaching profession. Lloyd-Jones (1982), observed that the single impromptu essay represents only "one probe into a massive competence" (p. 3) and such tests "by definition understate competence" (p. 9).

Cognitive Complexity

Linn, Baker, & Dunbar (1991) emphasized that the criteria for judging all forms of assessment need to "include attention to the processes that students are required to exercise." Although one of the promises of performance-based assessments is that they will assess higher-order thinking skills, we will not know in fact that they do so until cognitive analyses of the performance tasks have been conducted.

Snow & Lohman (1989) note that

> ...the cognitive psychology of problem solving is a central concern for educational measurement because all mental tests are, in some sense, problem-solving tasks. Hence, existing or proposed test designs ought to be evaluated as such. The methods of cognitive psychology seem particularly well suited to this purpose. (p. 265)

They describe three broad avenues in which cognitive psychology might contribute to educational measurement:

1. Cognitive analyses of existing measures can help improve understanding of the construct(s) represented by them.

2. Cognitive study of assessment domains might suggest alternative measurement strategies.

3. New theories of aptitude, learning, and achievement might result from cognitive analyses.

More specifically, cognitive analyses might indicate what types of learning may derive from performance assessments. Protocol analyses of examinees' thoughts as they approach an impromptu writing task would also be of great interest. Just what goes through the mind of a typical examinee immediately after reading the prompt for an impromptu essay test? The answer probably depends on how the prompt is written.

Realism

Of the three types of writing skill assessment discussed in this paper, the essay is usually considered to be the most realistic. What could be more real than asking an examinee to actually write something and then having the result judged by experts? Whether an essay test is realistic, that is, representative of real-world writing, however, depends on its comprehensiveness and fidelity. A single essay on a single topic cannot possibly represent all types of writing on all types of topics, so questions can be raised about the comprehensiveness of an essay assessment. Fidelity can also be questioned by asking: How close to the real thing is the assessment? If it is a 20-minute task on a topic the examinee has never thought about before, it is not very realistic because, in the real world, people are not asked to perform such tasks. Ruth & Murphy (1988) state that:

> Many observers…have noticed that much of present practice in writing assessment is incongruous with the accounts we have of the real world writing process. Current assessments often elicit an impromptu written product based upon an imposed topic within a time frame that seldom allows adequate opportunity for the natural unfolding of a process of conception, development, revision and editing. (p. 100)

The kinds of essay-writing tasks used for admissions purposes can only be simulations of real-life writing tasks.

The revision in context test has considerable comprehensiveness with respect to the aspects of writing that could be covered: Organization, rhetorical strategy, development, audience, and logical continuity can all be tested (in addition to sentence-level skills). The only part of the writing process that such tests cannot cover is the initial drafting stage. The fidelity, or the degree of realism, of revision in context exercises is also high: It represents an activity that most people who write engage in every day. Some argue, nevertheless, that revising something written by someone else is not the same as revising one's own writing. Like impromptu essays, then, revision exercises as used in admissions tests can only be simulations of the real thing.

In the Fitzpatrick & Morrison schema of fidelity and comprehensiveness, sentence-level tests would possess some degree of realism. There are some aspects of writing skill that they do not cover (e.g., organization, thesis development, rhetorical strategy, logical continuity), but they cover practically all of the aspects that have to do with sentences. These aspects are covered with reasonable fidelity, with the exception that responses are not actually constructed by the examinee. As a simulation of writing skill, sentence-level tests are not all that unrealistic, since most of us have to deal with sentences every day of our working lives.

Meaningfulness

Essay drafting, essay revision, and sentence revision all would appear to represent "meaningful problems that provide worthwhile educational experiences" (Linn, Baker, & Dunbar, 1991). Nevertheless, some data gathering on this issue would be useful.

Cost and Efficiency

With respect to cost and efficiency, essay testing is well known to have negative consequences. The most efficient writing skill assessment is sentence revision. Much information about an examinee's writing skill can be obtained very quickly. Essay revision, is more time consuming than sentence revision, but more efficient than essay drafting.

SUMMARIZATION OF EVALUATIVE CRITERIA

Table 3 gives a rough summary of standards of quality for writing skill assessment. Plus and minus signs are used to indicate how well each of the evaluation criteria are satisfied by each of the types of writing skill assessment. A question mark has been used where there is little evidence or where the situation is uncertain.

The requirements for content coverage are poorly satisfied by any one type of writing skill assessment. If the content domain is considered to be the basic elements of the writing process--consisting of idea generation, organization, drafting, reviewing, revising, and editing--it is clear that no single one of these three common types of assessment can cover the entire domain. All three in combination or, at a minimum, essay drafting and essay revision, would appear to cover the domain, however.

All three types of writing skill assessment have been shown to have reasonable reliability, but for essay assessments of the type used in admissions (one or two tasks), reliability has been shown to be below commonly acceptable levels. Although writing portfolios, used in instructional settings, have been shown to have adequate reliability, brief assessments of one or two tasks have not.

Fairness can be questioned on the grounds that an increasing use of verbal tasks of any type may work against linguistic minorities. It is difficult to specify at just what point unfairness begins, however, because the work of most students is heavily verbal and it can be argued that admissions tests should reflect the nature of the work a student will be expected to do. Nevertheless, some majors (especially graduate majors) are more verbal than others, and admissions tests with heavy verbal emphases have been questioned.

There can be no question that many essay writing tasks are of considerable cognitive complexity (thus, a double "++" in Table 3). The cognitive complexity of some kinds of prompts may be excessive, however, and threaten the boundaries of the construct domain. Essay revision tasks can also be quite complex, but whether they satisfy demands for higher-order thinking is not clear. Sentence revision is usually regarded as a low-level task, although it can be made to be quite difficult.

Although both essay drafting tasks and essay revisions tasks are realistic real-world tasks, the nature of some essay prompts can lead one to question their realism. A task that requires examinees to write on topics unknown to them, or on topics that they have not thought about recently, and then imposes a very brief time constraint cannot be a realistic representation of real-life writing tasks. It is difficult to argue that sentence revision is realistic in the sense that it represents writing, more generally. But as one aspect of essay revision, it is realistic; thus sentence revision might be considered to have fidelity for that aspect of writing, but it is not comprehensive.

While it appears to be assumed that introducing more writing into assessments will result in better instruction in writing, there is no evidence as yet that such has occurred. Consequences of this type will probably require some time to be realized.

TABLE 3
Summary Evaluation

Criteria	Essay Drafting	Essay Revision	Sentence Revision
Content	-	-	-
Generalizability	-	+	+
Predictive Validity	-	+	+
Fairness	?	?	?
Cognitive Complexity	++	?	-
Realism	?	+	-
Consequences	?	?	?
Meaningfulness	+	+	+
Cost & Efficiency	-	+	++

For meaningfulness, Table 3 assigns "+" values to all three types of writing assessment considered, since all three would appear to be meaningful educational experiences to examinees--provided that they are properly designed.

With respect to cost & efficiency, Table 3 shows sentence revision to be most positive (++), essay revision next (+), and essay drafting last (-). It is clear that essay assessments are the most costly and the least efficient because human scorers are required. With computer-delivered essay assessments, some improvements in efficiencies of essays, as well as the other two types of writing assessments, should be realized.

CONCLUSION

As admissions testing programs move forward with expanded writing assessments and with a greater proportion of testing time devoted to writing skill assessment, it is important to evaluate these assessments using a broad set of criteria. Questions concerning the fairness and consequences of these new assessments remain as well as questions concerning the degree to which they represent real-life writing tasks. And as testers strive for "authenticity" and cognitive complexity in their assessments, questions need to be asked about whether such strivings lead beyond the construct boundaries of writing skill and encroach on other abilities that may be less amenable to instruction.

All writing tests used in admissions are necessarily simulations of real-world writing tasks. Brief essay writing tasks, essay revision tasks, and sentence revision tasks all fail as realistic representations of writing as most of us know it. The design of writing assessments thus becomes an optimization procedure to determine what mix of assessment types will be most beneficial. The evidence available suggests that a balancing of drafting and revision tasks would be desirable.

REFERENCES

Ackerman, T. A., & Smith, P. L. (1988). A comparison of the information provided by essay, multiple-choice, and free-response writing tests. *Applied Psychological Measurement. 12* (2), 117-128.

Anastasi, A. (1967). Psychology, psychologists, and psychological testing. *American Psychologist, 22*, 297-306.

Bejar, I. I. (1991). A methodology for scoring open-ended architectural design problems. *Journal of Applied Psychology, 76*, 522-532.

Bennett, R. E. (1993). On the meanings of constructed response. In R. E. Bennett and W. C. Ward (Eds.), *Construction versus choice in cognitive measurement: Issues in constructed response, performance testing, and portfolio assessment* (pp. 1-27). Hillsdale, NJ: Lawrence Erlbaum Associates.

Breland, H. M., Camp, R., Jones, R. J., Rock, D., & Morris, M. (1987). *Assessing writing skill.* New York: College Entrance Examination Board.

Breland, H. M., & Duran, R. P. (1985). Assessing English composition skills in Spanish-speaking populations. *Educational and Psychological Measurement, 45*, 309-318.

Breland, H. M., & Gaynor, J. (1979). A comparison of direct and indirect assessments of writing skill. *Journal of Educational Measurement, 16*, 119-128.

Breland, H. M., & Griswold, P. A. (1982). Use of a performance test as a criterion in a differential validity study. *Journal of Educational Psychology, 74*, 713-721.

Coffman, W. E. (1966). On the validity of essay tests of achievement. *Journal of Educational Measurement, 3*, 151-156.

Collins, A., & Gentner, D. (1980). A framework for a cognitive theory of writing. In L. W. Gregg & E. R. Steinberg (Eds.), *Cognitive processes in writing* (pp. 51-72). Hillsdale, NJ: Lawrence Erlbaum Associates.

Dunbar, S. B., Koretz, D. M., & Hoover, H. D. (1991). Quality control in the development and use of performance assessments. *Applied Psychological Measurement, 4*, 289-303.

Fitzpatrick, R., & Morrison, E. J. (1971). Performance and product evaluation. In R. L. Thorndike (Ed.), *Educational measurement* (2nd ed.) (pp. 237-270). Washington, DC: American Council on Education.

Frederiksen, N. (1984). The real test bias: Influences of testing on teaching and learning. *American Psychologist, 39*, 193-202.

Frederiksen, J. R., & Collins, A. (1989). A systems approach to educational testing. *Educational Researcher, 18*(9), 27-32.

Godshalk, F. I., Swineford, F., & Coffman, W. E. (1966*). The measurement of writing ability*. New York: College Entrance Examination Board.

Haertel, E. H. (1994). Theoretical and practical implications. In T. R. Guskey (Ed.), *High stakes performance assessment: Perspectives on Kentucky's educational reform* (pp. 65-75). Thousands Oaks, CA: Corwin Press, Inc.

Hayes, J. R. (1996). A new framework for understanding cognition and affect in writing (pp. 1-27). In C. Michael Levy and Sarah Ransdell (Eds.), *The science of writing*. Mahwah, NJ: Lawrence Erlbaum Associates.

Hayes, J. R., & Flower, L. S. (1980). Identifying the organization of writing processes. In L. W. Gregg & E. R. Steinberg (Eds*.), Cognitive processes in writing* (pp. 3-30). Hillsdale, NJ: Lawrence Erlbaum Associates.

Klein, S. P. (1981). *The effect of time limits, item sequence, and question format on applicant performance on the California Bar Examination*. San Francisco: Committee of Bar Examinees of the State Bar of California and the National Conference of Bar Examinees.

Klein, S. P., & Bolus, R. (1984). *An analysis of the performance test on the July 1983 California bar examination* (PR-84-2). San Francisco: Committee of Bar Examinees of the State Bar of California.

Linn, R. L. (1994). Performance assessment: Policy promises and technical measurement standards. *Educational Researcher, 23*, (9), 4-14.

Linn, R. L, Baker, E. L., & Dunbar, S. B. (1991). Complex, performance-based assessment: Expectations and validation criteria. *Educational Researcher, 20* (8), 15-21.

Linn, R. L, & Burton. E. (1994). Performance-based assessment: Implications of task specificity. *Educational Measurement: Issues and Practice, 13* (1), 5-8, 15.

Lloyd-Jones, R. (1982). Skepticism about test scores. In D. A. McQuade & V. B. Slaughter (Eds.), *Notes from the National Testing Network in Writing*. New York: City University of New York, Instructional Resource Center.

Mehrens, W. A. (1992). Using performance assessment for accountability purposes. *Educational Measurement: Issues and Practices, 11*(1), 3-9, 20.

Messick, S. (1989). Validity. In R. Linn (Ed.), *Educational measurement*, (3rd ed., pp. 13-103). Washington, DC: American Council on Education.

Messick, S. (1994a). The interplay of evidence and consequences in the validation of performance assessments. *Educational Researcher, 23* (2), 13-23.

Messick, S. (1994b). Foundations of validity: Meaning and consequences in psychological assessment. *European Journal of Psychological Assessment, 10*(1), 1-9.

Messick, S. (1997). Alternative modes of assessment, uniform standards of validity. In M. D. Hakel (Ed.), *Beyond multiple-choice: Evaluating alternatives to traditional testing for selection* (pp. 59-74). Hillsdale, NJ: Lawrence Erlbaum Associates.

Miller, M. D., & Crocker, L. (1990). Validation methods for direct writing assessment. *Applied Measurement in Education, 3*, 285-296.

Mislevy, R. J. (1993). A framework for studying differences between multiple-choice and free-response items. In R. E. Bennett & W. C. Ward, Jr. (Eds.), *Construction versus choice in cognitive measurement: Issues in constructed response, performance testing, and portfolio assessment* (pp. 75-106). Hillsdale, NJ: Lawrence Erlbaum Associates.

Moss, P. A. (1992). Shifting conceptions of validity in educational measurement: Implications for performance assessment. *Review of Educational Research, 62*, 229-258.

Moss, P. A. (1994). Can there be validity without reliability? *Educational Researcher, 23*(2), 5-12.

Nichols, P. D. (1994). A framework for developing cognitively diagnostic assessments. *Review of Educational Research, 64*, 575-603.

Reckase, M. (1995). Portfolio assessment: A theoretical estimate of score reliability. *Educational Measurement; Issues and Practice, 14* (1), 12-14, 31.

Resnick, L. B. (1990). Tests as standards of achievement in schools. In *The uses of standardized tests in American education: Proceedings of the 1989 ETS Invitational Conference.* Princeton, NJ: Educational Testing Service.

Ruth, L. & Murphy, S. (1988). *Designing writing tasks for the assessment of writing.* Norwood, NJ: Ablex Publishing Corporation.

Sebrechts, M. M., Bennett, R. E., & Rock, D. A. (1991). Agreement between expert system and human raters' scores on complex constructed-response quantitative items. *Journal of Applied Psychology, 76*, 856-862.

Shepard, L. (1991). Psychometrician's beliefs about learning. *Educational Researcher, 20*(6), 2-16.

Snow, R. E., & Lohman, D. F. (1989). Implications of cognitive psychology for educational assessment. In R. Linn (Ed.), *Educational measurement* (3rd ed., pp. 263-331). Washington, DC: American Council on Education.

White, E. M. (1994). *Teaching and assessing writing.* San Francisco: Jossey-Bass Publishers.

White, E., Lutz, W., & Kamusikiri, S. (1996). *Assessment of writing: Politics, policies, practices.* New York: Modern Language Association of America.

Wiggins, G. (1993). Assessment: Authenticity, context, and validity. *Phi Delta Kappan, 75,* 200-214.

9

A THEORY-BASED FRAMEWORK FOR FUTURE COLLEGE ADMISSIONS TESTS

Howard T. Everson
The College Board

What will college admissions tests look like in the future? Speculating about the future, particularly in the field of educational assessment, is risky business. Nevertheless, I will attempt it by sketching the outlines of a theory-based framework for the next generation of college admissions tests, with a focus on the SAT. Emphasizing the need for broader measures of developed cognitive abilities, model-based psychometrics, and increased access to assessments through the use of computer-based testing, this framework provides a vision of what we can expect in college admissions testing over the next 10 to 20 years (Bennett, 1993, 1994; Frederiksen, Mislevy, & Bejar, 1993; Messick, 1994).

There are at least three very good reasons why the time is right to visit the issue of the future directions of college admission tests. The first is the continuing pressure from educational reformers to develop content, performance, and assessment standards for graduation from high school. These debates raise the inevitable question of how graduation standards might be made part of the college admissions process. Colleges and universities today are more and more becoming involved in the development of high school exit standards, and they are grappling with how these standards might fit in their admissions processes. If these trends continue unabated, the context, content, and role of standardized admissions tests will be influenced by the adoption of performance-based high school graduation standards.

Similarly, the technological advances characterizing today's "Information Age" will influence the content and form of college admissions tests in the future. The computer's potential for presenting test items and tasks using simulations and multi-media will move large-scale testing beyond the constraints of multiple-choice formats, providing design advantages over traditional forms of paper-and-pencil tests. Coupled with software systems that track and monitor examinee performance during testing, it is not difficult to envision more informative adaptive testing systems that, in the future, provide richer and more dynamic forms of assessment (Bennett, 1993). We see, too, with the recent growth of telecommunications networks the possibility of delivering tests electronically, thereby providing students and their families with greater access to admissions tests and more convenient testing opportunities (Bennett, 1994). Third, and perhaps most important, is the influence of cognitive and educational psychology on testing and assessment. Snow and Lohman (1989) state the case this way.

> Cognitive psychology can contribute to educational measurement in several related ways ...   First, cognitive analyses of existing measures can help improve understanding of the construct(s) represented by them ... Second, cognitive study of the target aptitudes, achievements, and content domains for which educational measures are to be built or used might suggest alternative measurement strategies and refinements of existing instruments. And third, new and improved theories of aptitude, learning, and achievement in education might be derived from cognitive psychological research. (p. 266)

To remain relevant in the educational environment(s) of the future, succeeding generations of SATs must capture the promise of advances in psychology, measurement science, and technology. Given this premise, evolving the SAT to meet this challenge calls for a framework built on the principles of cognitive theory, modern measurement science, and a commitment to technology-based design and delivery systems that foster access and equity. This theme of a theory-based framework, that is, a principled design that moves the SAT from a task-based focus to a theory-based focus, is central to our thinking and will be reiterated throughout in our discussion of what the next generation of college admissions tests might be like. Before exploring this framework in detail, it may be instructive to take a long view and trace briefly the evolution of the SAT over the course of the 20th century. This perspective aids our understanding of the educational and social role of the SAT, and places college admissions testing in a broader cultural context. With this as background, a theory-based design framework for the future SAT is proposed. The chapter closes with an outline of a generative research agenda designed to support and advance the proposed framework.

THE EVOLVING SAT

The College Board had its beginnings as an educational association in the Fall of 1900 (Angoff, 1971; Downey, 1961). From the outset, the College Board's purpose was to provide order in the transition from high school to college by creating a system of uniform college admissions examinations. Beginning in 1901, 973 students sat for achievement examinations in nine subjects--English,

French, German, Latin, Greek, history, mathematics, chemistry, and physics. By 1910, 3,731 students took the College Board's examinations. Following the successes of the U. S. Army's large-scale testing program in World War I, the design of the College Board examinations had by 1925 come under the influence of the intelligence testing movement associated with Robert M. Yerkes, Henry T. Moore, and Carl C. Brigham. Recognizing this trend in psychological and educational measurement, the College Board adopted the advice of a commission chaired by Carl Brigham and introduced the Scholastic Aptitude Test, a clear design shift away from the achievement measures that had been characteristic of previous examinations.

The first SAT, administered on June 23, 1926 to 8,040 candidates, included nine subtests: definitions, arithmetical problems, classification, artificial language, antonyms, number series, analogies, logical inference, and paragraph reading. Much like they are today, scores were reported on a scale with a mean of 500 and standard deviation of 100. Three short years later, in 1929, again with the vision and direction of Carl Brigham, the SAT was redesigned to have two separate sections, measuring verbal and mathematical aptitudes. In these early days the College Board reported verbal and mathematics scores with differential weightings depending on the college(s) receiving the examinees' scores. In 1937, the Board's Achievement Tests were first reported on a scale with a mean of 500 and standard deviation of 100, like the scale used on the SAT since 1926.

At around the same time, Ben Wood and Henry Chauncey, working in conjunction with IBM, introduced technology into the SAT with the advent of a machine-scorable format. A short time later, in June 1941, the scores on every form of the SAT were equated directly to scores on preceding forms. Thus, we see a design framework emerging for the SAT that includes merging the science of psychometrics with early data storage and computing technologies, a trend that will re-emerge as the SAT moves into the 21st century.

Reflecting changes in our conceptions of learning as well as a sensitivity to the educational reform movement of the 1980s, the SAT was redesigned in the early 1990s. Moving away from earlier notions of aptitudes as fixed abilities, the math and verbal reasoning sections were revised to tap a broader range of developed abilities in these domains. The new verbal section, for example, now includes measures of critical reading, contextualized word knowledge, and analogical reasoning. Similarly, the mathematics section stresses the application of mathematical concepts and quantitative comparisons, as well as permitting the use of calculators. The tests were renamed (and renormed) and the acronym SAT now stands for Scholastic Assessment Tests, and includes the SAT-I Reasoning Test and the SAT-II Subject Tests.

Moving from early notions of intelligence and aptitude testing based in a behaviorist paradigm, the SAT has evolved over the course of the 20th century to include a greater emphasis on developed abilities, while at the same time demonstrating a responsiveness to educational reform. Looking back, we see that as our knowledge of learning and educational measurement has changed, so, too, has the SAT. Looking ahead, we can anticipate that as advances in these areas continue, they will propel change in the SAT in the 21st century.

A THEORY-BASED DESIGN FRAMEWORK

There is little doubt that the educational reform movement will play itself out in important ways in the transition from high school to college. As high school graduation standards are established and assessments are created to measure them, college and university admissions criteria are likely to shift and change accordingly. Maintaining the SAT's relevance to the college admissions process-- whether, for example, it continues with an emphasis on verbal and mathematical reasoning or whether it is modified to become a more standards-based measure--will depend in large measure on the framework that guides the changes to the test. The central thesis of this chapter is that by employing a theory-based framework we have the opportunity to re-create the SAT and introduce a new generation of college admissions tests--that is, tests that measure a broader array of developed abilities (including both reasoning and achievement measures). As Mislevy (1996b) noted recently , "models, principles, and conceptual frameworks are practicable tools-- not for discovering singular truth, but for structuring our discourse about students, so that we may better support their learning" (p. 32). Thus, coupled with model-based measurement approaches and computing technologies, a theory-based focus ensures that the SAT will be more aligned with reforms in teaching and learning, that it will remain relevant in the transition from high school to college, and define the cutting edge in the large-scale assessment arena.

Developed abilities in verbal comprehension and mathematical reasoning, for example, may be assessed in the future with test items and tasks that are based on stronger theoretical foundations of domain-specific knowledge, problem solving strategies, and metacognitive skills and heuristics relevant to performance. Indeed, the potential exists for building assessments that provide cognitive profiles of developed abilities in both the verbal and mathematical domains (and, for that matter, in subject-specific domains) that should prove useful for selection and placement. As Lane (1991) and others (Glaser, 1989; Mitchell, 1989) have noted, researchers working on the border between cognitive psychology and educational measurement have developed methods for assessing students' knowledge structures in a number of domains, including science, mathematics, reading comprehension, critical thinking, and analytical reasoning. In related efforts, a number of salient cognitive dimensions have been suggested by Glaser, Lesgold, and Lajoie (1985) that include knowledge organization and structure, problem representation, mental models, the efficiency of procedures, automaticity of performance, and metacognition. This work, no doubt, will influence test design.

Continuing with this example, recent work in the general area of self-regulated learning and problem solving (Tobias & Everson, in press; Weinstein, 1995) provides strong evidence to suggest that for students to be successful in college they need to become strategic learners. According to this view, strategic learners are able to take responsibility for their own learning by setting realistic learning goals and using knowledge about themselves as learners as part of their approach to learning. Strategic learners also use executive control processes (i.e., metacognitive skills and abilities of planning, monitoring, and modifying their learning strategies and goals) to achieve their educational objectives. Thus, what has emerged is a view of domain expertise that appears to require combining declarative and procedural knowledge with effective strategies for learning within a domain. Faceted tasks that measure aspects of metacognition and strategic learning are candidates for inclusion in future assessments, particularly in specialized achievement domains where metacognitive abilities may develop and manifest themselves differentially. Collectively, we see the possibility that work in these areas of cognitive psychology and assessment can be leveraged to enrich our understanding of student learning. These efforts, in turn, will translate into new constructs, new item types, and, ultimately, new forms of assessment.

Measuring Cognitive Abilities

The information processing view of the human mind embodied in modern cognitive science has become dominant in psychology and education in the latter half of the 20th century. In general, cognitive psychology attempts to study thinking and intelligence in terms of the mental (i.e., cognitive) representations and processes that are presumed to underlie observable behavior (Sternberg, 1984). Messick (1984a) captured the essence of the theoretical import of cognitive psychology for educational testing when he wrote:

> Educational achievement refers to what an individual knows and can do in a specified subject area. At issue is not merely the amount of knowledge accumulated but its organization or structure as a functional system for productive thinking, problem solving, and creative invention in the subject area as well as for further learning. The individual's structure of knowledge is a critical aspect of educational achievement because it facilitates or hinders what he or she can do in the subject area. What a person can do in an area includes a variety of area-specific skills, such as extracting a square root or parsing a sentence or balancing a chemical equation, but also broader cognitive abilities that cut across subject areas, such as comprehension, memory retention and retrieval, reasoning, analysis and restructuring, evaluation or judgment, and fluency. These broader cognitive abilities contribute to the assembly and structuring of knowledge, to the continual reassembly and restructuring of cumulating knowledge, to the accessing and

retrieval of knowledge, and to its use in problem representation
and solution...Because cognitive abilities play a central role in
both the acquisition and organization functions of educational
achievement, their influence can hardly be suppressed or
ignored in educational achievement testing that assesses
knowledge structures.

A person's structure of knowledge in a subject area includes
not only declarative knowledge about substance (or information
about what) but also procedural knowledge about methods (or
information about how) and strategic knowledge about
alternatives for goal setting and planning (or information about
which, when, and possibly why). (pp. 155-156)

Like others working in this area of psychology, Messick's view of educational
achievement stresses knowledge structures as both a product of earlier learning as
well as a vehicle for subsequent learning. It follows, then, that if our assessments
can be designed to reveal precise weaknesses in an examinee's knowledge base,
specific instructional prescriptions can be proffered. This capability would
increase the SAT's utility and relevance to educational reform. Again, Messick
(1984a), draws an important distinction for test design.

Cognitive abilities are not the same as subject-matter
achievement, even those representing generalized school-related
learnings...Thus, the coordinate measurement of cognitive
abilities as well as subject-matter achievement may contribute to
the comprehensive diagnosis of academic difficulties...
Cognitive abilities are independent of subject matter but they are
by no means content-free; rather, they cut across content areas.
In some instances, they may be specialized by types of content
such as verbal, numerical, or figural, but at higher orders they
represent more general functions such as memory or fluency.
(p. 163)

What we are learning is that cognitive psychology's potential for contributing to
test design is significant. The areas where a principled application of cognitive
psychology to test design would be appropriate include: (1) constructing tests to
include contents that reflect measures of information processing, information
search, problem solving, and comprehension monitoring, among others; (2)
validating tests with reference to the higher order cognitive planning, monitoring,
and control that underlie competent performance; (3) interpreting test performance
based on the cognitive processes (as opposed to psychometric factors) that underlie
performance on reasoning measures; and (4) modifying tests to clarify the
assumptions about speed versus power and the role of stress and anxiety as
cognitive interference factors (Hunt, 1986; Messick, 1984b; Sternberg, 1984).

In all, these brief examples suggest that test design in the future, including test specifications and frameworks, ought to be informed by the growing knowledge base in cognitive psychology, as that research contributes to our understanding of human thinking and reasoning. As cognitive analyses reveal the structure of competence in broad domains such as verbal comprehension and quantitative reasoning, as well as in narrower, specialized achievement domains, these theory-based descriptions can provide a sound basis for disciplined test design. Moreover, the application of cognitive theory, in turn, will allow us to draw interpretations and inferences from test performance that have sound theoretical underpinnings and more direct implications for teaching and learning.

Model-Based Measurement

Early development work in admissions testing was based largely on classical measurement, on what Snow and Lohman (1989) have called the educational psychometric measurement approach. The dominant goal of this approach to measurement is to estimate an examinee's position on a scale that measures a latent variable(s). This classical model was developed largely to permit inferences about how much knowledge, aptitude, or ability an individual possesses. In the case of the SAT, the latent variable space is assumed to include both verbal and mathematical reasoning. In general, the standard test-theory model is useful for inferences related to selection and classification. It is much less helpful for making instructional decisions or for diagnosing learning or achievement deficiencies--an oftstated measurement goal of many new assessments (The Commission on New Possibilities, 1990).

With the emergence of a cognitive perspective, however, the emphasis shifts from tests and assessments stressing how much a student has learned, or where he or she ranks on a continuum of achievement, to a focus on the importance of how knowledge is organized and how students reorganize that knowledge to represent and solve problems. That is, it begins to tell us more about what students know. Indeed, this theoretical shift underscores the need for measurement models that distinguish learners in terms of their knowledge states, cognitive process abilities, and strategies for solving problems.

Snow and Lohman (1993) make the case eloquently for principled design and model based measurement.

> The possibility now exists to bring new concepts and measures of aptitude, learning, development, and achievement, together with instructional innovations, to create truly diagnostic and adaptive systems. But we must learn how to use the new psychometric, substantive, and technological advances in concert to do it right. This is the main challenge for the 1990s.
> (p. 1)

In response to the challenge articulated by Snow and Lohman, a number of new and promising psychometric approaches with a decidedly cognitive flavor are being developed. These include, for example, latent-trait models (Embretson, 1985; Samejima, 1995), statistical pattern classification methods (Sheehan, 1996; Tatsuoka, 1985; 1990), and causal probabilistic networks (Mislevy, 1995). As we noted earlier, these approaches do not aim simply to rank students along a dimension of proficiency. But rather these models, albeit in somewhat different ways, attempt to build on detailed task analyses, presumed production rules, and representations of knowledge structures, to create cognitively sound assessments (Nichols, 1994; Nichols, Chipman, & Brennan, 1995).

A number of these more modern measurement models are extensions to item-response theoretic (IRT) models (Hambleton & Swaminathan, 1984; Lord & Novick, 1968). Others extend IRT work further and build on multidimensional latent-trait IRT models introduced by Samejima (1988), Reckase (1985), and Embretson (1985). Still others, like those growing out of the work on Bayesian inference networks (Mislevy, 1995), represent attempts to capitalize on pattern recognition methods and conditional probability estimation techniques for gathering evidence and supporting inferences about examinee performance. Many of these newer models attempt to provide descriptions of the students' knowledge or ability structures, as well as the cognitive processes presumed to underlie performance on single test items or tasks, or sets of tasks. Thus, if successfully developed and adapted, they hold promise not only for tests like the SAT, but also for dynamically linking assessment and instruction (Everson, 1995). A brief sampling of these approaches may provide a sense of their utility in this theory-based framework.

Latent-Trait Models. This class of models is appropriate for mapping student performance to an underlying (latent) ability, often referred to as a latent trait. Variations on these models are being developed which attempt to model the use of solution strategies in problem solving contexts (Mislevy &Verhelst, 1990), while others attempt to model shifts in examinee strategies (Gitomer & Yamamoto, 1991) as they work through a series of test items. The development of latent-trait models has advanced in recent years and models are now available for use with nominal, continuous, and graded response problems. More important, these models are often developed specifically for use in situations where cognitive information is sought. Samejima (1983, 1988, 1995) and Embretson (1985, 1994, 1996), for example, have developed multidimensional latent trait models for assessing the cognitive processes underlying performance on paragraph comprehension and spatial ability tasks. Other cognitively motivated models, including the Hierarchically Ordered Skills Test (HOST) model (Gitomer & Rock, 1993) and the HYBRID model (Yamamoto, 1987; Yamamoto & Gitomer, 1993), have potential applications in large-scale assessment programs. Although different in their measurement approaches, these models all have promise for further explicating students' levels of understanding as they move through relatively well defined content domains. For a more thorough discussion of these measurement models, the reader is referred to work by Bennett and Ward, (1993); Frederiksen, Glaser, Lesgold, and Shafto, (1990); and Frederiksen, Mislevy, and Bejar, (1993).

Statistical Pattern Recognition Methods. Typically, score reports from educational tests provide summary information on the number of correct responses by each student, sometimes using raw scores but more often than not by reporting scaled scores. Often, these score reports fall short when it comes to providing information about specific cognitive skills. In an effort to accurately characterize examinees in terms of the cognitive attributes associated with performance and to enhance our ability to report scores in more meaningful ways, a number of researchers (see, for example, Sheehan & Mislevy, 1994; Sheehan, 1996; and Tatsuoka, 1990, 1993) are currently working to apply statistical pattern recognition methods and cluster analysis techniques to large-scale testing data. This is in an attempt to develop proficiency scaling methods that would provide score users--examinees, teachers, schools, and colleges--with instructionally relevant diagnostic information.

Pursuing this line of research, Tatsuoka and her colleagues (1983, 1985, 1993) have developed a methodology known as rule space that provides cognitive diagnoses and classifications. The rule-space method is based on a statistical pattern recognition approach that classifies individuals into a number of cognitively meaningful groups established through careful task analysis of a domain. Building on IRT methods, Tatsuoka's rule-space model formulates a knowledge-state classification space and uses Bayes' decision rules (Nunnally & Bemstein, 1994) to minimize classification errors. The resulting classification spaces are directly related to various knowledge states, and forms of misconceptions or "bugs" in cognitive abilities are inferred. This methodology has been applied with some success in the domains of basic mathematics (Tatsuoka & Tatsuoka, 1992), algebra (Birenbaum, Kelly, & Tatsuoka, 1992), architecture (Katz, Martinez, Sheehan, & Tatsuoka, 1993), and document literacy (Sheehan, Tatsuoka, & Lewis, 1993).

In a parallel approach, Sheehan (1996) has been working with a tree-based regression method that may be applicable to tests, such as the SAT, that have been designed for use with broad-based ability groups. Sheehan's recent work in the area of reading comprehension suggests that tree-based regression methods may be useful for identifying the combinations or clusters of cognitive skills that underlie performance on complex tasks. In the future we can expect more refined instantiations of this approach to be applied to computer-based adaptive testing systems, where item- or task-selection algorithms will include not only rich information about the task but also more distinct and discernible characterizations of the students' proficiencies.

Bayesian Inference Networks. As we see from the work of both Sheehan (1996) and Tatsuoka (1985), with the statistical tools available now it is possible to design and implement pattern recognition networks in large and complex systems of student response variables, the types of databases typical of large-scale testing programs such as the SAT. The extent of their utility, however, may well rest on how much confidence we can have in the sets of inferences drawn from these statistical pattern recognition methods (Mislevy, 1993, 1995). Bayesian inference networks or, alternatively, causal probability networks, may strengthen the systems' ability to draw reasonably sound inferences about the students' knowledge states.

In general, Bayesian networks are complex sets of interdependent variables that provide a statistical framework for reasoning under conditions of uncertainty (Martin & VanLehn, 1995; Mislevy, 1995; Pearl, 1988). These inference networks have been implemented with some success in a variety of fields, including medical diagnosis (Lauritzen & Spiegelhalter, 1988), physics (Martin & VanLehn, 1995), troubleshooting (Gitomer, Steinberg, & Mislevy, 1995), and proportional reasoning (Belan & Mislevy, 1996). In each instance the inference problem is the same: The system or network must reason abductively from a set of observations--that is, combinations of known task parameters and response variables gathered in a theory-driven framework--to a model of student performance. Thus, in theory, inference networks are able to build upon cognitive task analyses and statistical pattern recognition methods, extend them to draw inferences about the probabilistic structure of the student's knowledge state, and then update those "beliefs" as the examinee moves through a set of assessment tasks.

Together, these relatively new psychometric models all take the important step of attempting to integrate cognitive psychology and model-based measurement. Indeed, they can all be viewed as forms of intelligent assessment (Bennett, 1993) and as efforts that synthesize methods and techniques from three vital research areas: artificial intelligence and expert systems, modern psychometrics, and cognitive psychology. To be useful in a theory-based test design framework a number of issues will have to be resolved. More work, for example, is needed on the painstaking task analyses that foreshadow cognitive model development in various reasoning and achievement domains. Just how fine-grained should these models be? What kinds of assessment tasks will be needed to capture the cognitive complexity we seek? In addition, issues of utility, reliability, and validity will also require further research. As measurement science and computer technologies advance so, too, will our ability to gather and incorporate evidence from other cognitively rich constructs--such as metacognitive abilities, problem solving, prior knowledge, and response mode preferences. These various forms and combinations of evidence could be incorporated into a theory-based, inferential framework for assessment using the modern measurement approaches discussed above.

A Future of Networked Assessments

Personal computers are everywhere, and more and more they exist as addresses or nodes on a network. As computing technology has transformed itself--and the worlds of business, science, and education change along with it-- computer uses have moved from numerical calculators, to data processing machines, to interacting networks of intelligent information retrieval, control, and delivery systems. In a new world of networks and webs we can easily imagine a future where the best schools, teachers, and courses will be available to all students (Jones, 1994; Penzias, 1995; Stewart & Everson, 1994). In theory, access, equity, and excellence are achievable. This scenario suggests that tests and assessments designed with a singular focus on selection may become largely unnecessary.

In some sense the future is already here. Distance learning opportunities are becoming more widely available. Computer-based adaptive tests, that is, assessments in which the examinee is presented with different test questions or tasks matched to his or her ability or skill levels, are in widespread use with the College Board's Computerized Placement Tests and ETS's Graduate Record Examination. In these instances and others, computers construct the tests, present the items adaptively, score the responses, and generate reports and analyses. The potential of computer-based testing can be pushed further, and more intelligent forms of assessment are possible, even likely. Bennett (1993) framed the future of intelligent assessment this way.

> Intelligent assessment is conceived of as an integration of three research lines each dealing with cognitive performance from a different perspective: Constructed-response testing, artificial intelligence, and model-based measurement. These tasks will be scored by automated routines that emulate the behavior of an expert, providing a rating on a partial credit scale for summative purposes as well as a qualitative description designed to impart instructionally useful information. The driving mechanisms underlying these tasks and their scoring are cognitively grounded measurement models that may dictate what the characteristics of items should be, which items from a large pool should be administered, how item responses should be combined to make more general inferences, and how uncertainty should be handled. (p. 99)

As Bennett suggests, the convergence of computer-based testing with advanced networks makes possible new forms of college admissions tests, having, for example, more complex items and tasks, seamless branching across content areas and domains, and modular components. This merging of theory and technology also makes likely the introduction of new test delivery systems, remote scoring of constructed responses, and more powerful means for summarizing and communicating performance. Again, these advances in information technologies, no doubt, will provide platforms for the next generation of college admissions tests.

A RESEARCH AGENDA FOR GETTING THERE

An ambitious program of research will be required if we are to transform college admissions testing in ways that make them useful not only for selection and prediction, but also for placement and diagnosis. The research and development agenda outlined below provides some general direction in four areas: (1) developing new measurement constructs that go beyond verbal and mathematical reasoning (e.g., spatial reasoning, critical thinking, problem solving, and metacognition); (2) designing new item types and response formats; (3) developing psychometric models for multidimensional scales and cognitive diagnosis; and, (4) communicating examinee performances in ways that inform teaching and learning. A brief overview of each of these directions follows.

New Measures

If the next generation of college admissions tests are to provide information that is richer diagnostically, then cognitive design principles will further our understanding of how content, knowledge structures, and processing abilities interact and manifest themselves in various subject-matter domains.   The organization of domain knowledge for use in new forms of assessment must become better informed by the findings of cognitive research.   This line of research will offer some general conceptions to help shape problem representation both across and within a number of domains. It can shed light, for example, on the elements and structures that constitute expertise, as well as the task factors that affect performance. Within the framework proposed here, constructs measuring conceptual knowledge, cognitive processing speed, working memory, problem solving, and procedural and strategic knowledge are all candidates for further research.

New Item Types

To achieve the complex and multidimensional textures of the tasks that are likely to emerge from cognitive theories of domain knowledge, item types and tasks that go beyond the four or five-option multiple-choice format are needed. It is not likely that traditional item characteristics, such as item difficulty or person ability, will be of much use for assessments that are theory-based. As Embretson (1996) suggests... "applying cognitive principles to the design of test items requires analyzing how item stimulus content influences the cognitive processes, strategies, and knowledge structures that are involved in item solving" (p. 29). Schema theory approaches (Marshall, 1995) may be helpful in guiding research in this area. Moreover, research in this area should lead to capabilities that permit the use of a variety of constructed-response formats that would enable the evaluation of a broad range of written and mathematical expressions and the graded scoring of extended problem solutions. It is not difficult to imagine that computer-based simulations and item types that capitalize on multimedia have a good deal of potential for the future. As we noted earlier, computer-based testing offers opportunities for standardizing item creation and presentation, while at the same time providing the flexibility to track and monitor examinee progress through complex response modes or solution paths. The research needed to conceptualize and construct item types of these sorts will draw on the knowledge of the domain and the degree to which its structure and problem-solving processes are known.

Model-based Measurement

As was pointed out earlier, the principled design framework envisioned for the next generation will incorporate model-based measurements, in some instances to improve test efficiency and in others to broaden the range and depth of information that can be elicited from test performance. Computerized adaptive testing (CAT) represents the most commonly used model for enhancing conventional measurement and will have a continuing significant role in future assessments. Further work in this area is required for applications involving a mixture of dichotomous and graded scoring, ones that yield multidimensional performance, and those employing achievement tests with small item pools, calibration samples, and complex content specifications. Computerized mastery testing--suitable for classification and placement testing--might also be useful for some applications in the next generation of SATs. And as noted earlier, new models arising from a cognitive framework will be needed especially to deal with assessments embedded in and contributing to teaching and learning. Multidimensional latent trait models, confirmatory factor analytic techniques, and Bayesian inference networks are all candidates for reconceptualizing many of the measurement problems raised by the cognitive perspective. Work on these measurement models is currently underway and needs to be continued.

Enhanced Score Reporting

This capability is closely related to diagnostic testing and aims to improve reports of student performance to test takers and others, including admissions officers, instructional designers, and placement personnel. More research work will be needed to be assured that proficiency statements and enhanced score reports are useful to a broad range of consumers. Theory-based proficiency scaling, as we noted earlier, is technically feasible and promising. However, creating descriptions of proficiencies that will be useful and acceptable to students and eachers has proved difficult. Additional research is required to better communicate this information and to craft reports that serve a variety of purposes.

CONCLUSION

We are at an exciting time in educational measurement. The sketch presented in this chapter holds out the promise of creating a strong theoretical foundation for the next generation of the SATs . This design framework suggests that we need to shift our views of testing and assessment to create large-scale assessments that address the many, and often competing, demands and driving forces in education and society. With this unique opportunity before us, I am reminded of a comment Warren Willingham made in a paper he presented nearly a decade ago when speculating about the prospects of broadening our measures in the admissions process. Willingham wrote in 1986:

> To some skeptics, 'additional measures' may sound like trouble--lax practices, vague subjectivity, loss of direction. It is not idle worry. Such dangers will arise if expediency becomes acceptable or if 'flexibility' comes to dominate assessment for entry to coveted jobs and scarce educational resources. The challenge is to maintain an effective balance among measures that offer different strengths and safeguards (p. 127).

As the first century of large-scale ability and aptitude testing draws to a close, we find ourselves challenged to move in the next millennium to a principled design framework that will ensure the development of large-scale tests and assessments that address society's need to develop human capital. We need to keep Willingham's sage advice in mind as we proceed.

REFERENCES

Angoff, W. H. (1971). *The College Board Admissions Testing Program: A technical report on research and development activities relating to the Scholastic Aptitude Test and Achievement Tests.* NY: College Entrance Examination Board.

Belan, A., & Mislevy, R. J. (1996). Probability-based inference in a domain of proportional reasoning tasks. *Journal of Educational Measurement*, 33(1), 3-27.

Bennett, R. E. (1993). Toward intelligent assessment: An integration of constructed-response testing, artificial intelligence, and model-based measurement. In N. Frederiksen, R. J. Mislevy, & I. Bejar (Eds.), *Test theory for a new generation of tests* (pp. 99-124). Hillsdale, NJ: Lawrence Erlbaum Associates.

Bennett, R. E. (1994, October). *The role of technology in creating assessments that increase participation in post-compulsory education.* Paper presented at the annual meeting of the International Association for Educational Assessment, Montreal, Canada.

Bennett, R. E. & Ward, W. C. (Eds.), (1993). *Construction versus choice in cognitive measurement: Issues in constructed response, performance testing, and portfolio assessment.* Hillsdale, NJ: Lawrence Erlbaum Associates.

Birenbaum, M., Kelly, A. E., & Tatsuoka, K. (1992). *Diagnosing knowledge states in algebra using the rule space model.* (ETS Report No. 92-57-ONR). Princeton, NJ: Educational Testing Service.

Birenbaum, M. & Tatsuoka, K. K. (1987). Open-ended versus multiple-choice response formats--It does make a difference for diagnostic purposes. *Applied Psychological Measurement, 11*, 329-341.

Commission on New Possibilities for the Admissions Testing Program. (1990). *Beyond prediction.* NY: College Entrance Examination Board.

Downey, M. T. (1961). *Carl Campbell Brigham: Scientist and educator.* Princeton, NJ: Educational Testing Service.

Embretson, S. E. (1985). Multicomponent latent trait models for test design. In S.E. Embretson (Ed.), *Test design: Developments in psychology and psychometrics* (pp. 195- 218). Orlando, FL: Academic Press.

Embretson, S. E. (1994). Applications of cognitive design systems to test development. In C. Reynolds (Ed.), *Advances in cognitive assessment: An interdisciplinary perspective* (pp. 107-135). NY: Plenum.

Embretson, S. E. (1996). Cognitive design principles and the successful performer: A study on spatial ability. *Journal of Educational Measurement, 33*(1), 29-39.

Everson, H. T. (1995). Modeling the student in intelligent tutoring systems: The promise of a new psychometrics. *Instructional Science, 23*, 433-452.

Frederiksen, N., Glaser, R. L., Lesgold, A. M., & Shafto, M. G. (Eds.) (1990). *Diagnostic monitoring of skill and knowledge acquisition.* Hillsdale, NJ: Erlbaum.

Frederiksen, N., Mislevy, R. J., & Bejar, I. I. (Eds.) (1993). *Test theory for a new generation of tests.* Hillsdale, NJ: Lawrence Erlbaum Associates.

Gitomer, D. H., Steinberg, L. S., & Mislevy, R. J. (1995). Diagnostic assessment of troubleshooting skill in an intelligent tutoring system. In P. Nichols, S. Chipman and R. Brennan (Eds.), *Cognitively diagnostic assessment* (pp. 73-101). Hillsdale, NJ: Lawrence Erlbaum Associates.

Gitomer, D.H., & Rock. D. (1993). Addressing process variables in test analysis. In N. Frederiksen, R. J. Mislevy, & I. Bejar (Eds.), *Test theory for a new generation of tests* (pp. 243-268). Hillsdale, NJ: Lawrence Erlbaum Associates.

Gitomer, D. H., & Yamamoto, K. (1991). Performance modeling that integrates latent trait and latent class theory. *Journal of Educational Measurement, 28*, 173-189.

Glaser, R. (1989). Expertise and learning: How do we think about instructional processes now that we have discovered knowledge structures? In D. Klahr & K. Kotovsky (Eds.), *Complex information processing: The impact of Herbert A. Simon* (pp. 269-282). Hillsdale, NJ: Erlbaum.

Glaser, R., Lesgold, A., & Lajoie, S. (1985). Toward a cognitive theory for the measurement of achievement. In R. R. Ronning, J. Glover, J. C. Conoley, & J. C. Witt (Eds.), *The influence of cognitive psychology on testing and measurement* (pp. 41-85). Hillsdale, NJ: Lawrence Erlbaum Associates.

Hambleton, R. K., & Swaminathan, H. (1984). *Item response theory: Principles and applications*. Boston, MA: Kluwer Academic Publishers.

Hunt, E. (1986). Cognitive research and future test design. *ETS Invitational Conference Proceedings*. Princeton, NJ: Educational Testing Service.

Jones, V. (1994). *Reflections on equity and the College Board*. Unpublished manuscript. NY: The College Board.

Katz, I. R., Martinez, M. E., Sheehan, K. M., & Tatsuoka, K. (1993). *Extending the rule space model to a semantically rich domain: Diagnostic assessment in architecture*. (ETS Report No. 93-42-ONR). Princeton, NJ: Educational Testing Service.

Lane, S. (1991). Implications of cognitive psychology for measurement and testing: Assessing students' knowledge structures. *Educational Measurement: Issues and Practice, 10*(1), 31-33.

Lauritzen, S. L., & Spiegelhalter, D. J. (1988). Local computations with probabilities on graphical structures and their application to expert systems (with discussion). *Journal of the Royal Statistical Society, Series B, 50*, 157-224.

Lohman, D. F. & Ippel, M. J. (1993). Cognitive diagnosis: From statistically-based assessment toward theory-based assessment. In N. Frederiksen, R. J. Mislevy, & I. Bejar (Eds.), *Test theory for a new generation of tests* (pp. 41-71). Hillsdale, NJ: Lawrence Erlbaum Associates.

Lord, F.M., & Novick, M.R. (1968). *Statistical theories of mental test scores*. Reading, MA: Addison-Wesley.

Marshall, S. P. (1995). *Schemas in problem solving*. Cambridge, MA: Cambridge University Press.

Martin, J. D., & VanLehn, K. (1995). A Bayesian approach to cognitive assessment. In P. Nichols, S. Chipman, & R. Brennan (Eds.), *Cognitively diagnostic assessment* (pp. 141-166). Hillsdale, NJ: Lawrence Erlbaum Associates.

Masters, G., & Mislevy, R. J. (1993). New views of student learning: Implications for educational measurement. In N. Frederiksen, R.J. Mislevy, & I. Bejar (Eds.), *Test theory for a new generation of tests*. Hillsdale, NJ: Lawrence Erlbaum Associates.

Messick, S. (1984a). Abilities and knowledge in educational achievement testing: The assessment of dynamic cognitive structures. In B. S. Plake, S. N. Elliott, J.V. Mitchell, Jr. (Eds.), *Buros-Nebraska symposium on measurement and testing. Social and technical issues in testing: Implications for test construction and usage* (pp. 155- 169). Hillsdale, NJ: Lawrence Erlbaum Associates.

Messick, S. (1984b). The psychology of educational measurement. *Journal of Educational Measurement, 21*(3), 215-237.

Messick, S. (1994). The interplay of evidence and consequences in the validation of performance assessments. *Educational Researcher, 23*(21), 13-23.

Mislevy, R. J. (1993). Foundations of a new test theory. In N. Frederiksen, R.J. Mislevy, & I. Bejar (Eds.), *Test theory for a new generation of tests* (pp. 19-40). Hillsdale, NJ: Lawrence Erlbaum Associates.

Mislevy, R. J. (1995). Probability-based inference in cognitive diagnosis. In P. Nichols, S. Chipman, & R. Brennan (Eds.), *Cognitively diagnostic assessment* (pp. 43- 71). Hillsdale, NJ: Lawrence Erlbaum Associates.

Mislevy, R. J. (1996a). *Some recent developments in assessing student learning* (Center for Performance Assessment Report No. 95-03). Princeton, NJ: Educational Testing Service.

Mislevy, R. J. (1996b). Postmodern test theory. Paper presented at the conference entitled *Transitions in work and learning: Implications for assessment*, The National Research Council Board on Testing and Assessment, Washington, DC.

Mislevy, R. J., & Verhelst, N. (1990). Modeling item responses when different subjects employ different solution strategies. *Psychometrika, 55*, 195-215.

Mislevy, R. J., Wingersky, M. S., Irvine, S. H., & Dann, P. L. (1991). Resolving mixtures of strategies in spatial visualization tasks. *British Journal of Mathematical and Statistical Psychology, 44*, 265-288.

Mitchell, K. J. (1989). New concepts in large-scale achievement testing: Implications for construct and incremental validity. In R. F. Dillon & J.W. Pellegrino (Eds.), *Testing: Theoretical and applied perspectives* (pp. 132-145). NY: Praeger.

National Council of Teachers of Mathematics (1989). *Curriculum and evaluation standards for school mathematics*. Reston, VA: National Council of Teachers of Mathematics.

Nichols, P. D. (1994). A framework for developing cognitively diagnostic assessments. *Review of Educational Research, 64*(4). 576-603.

Nichols, P. D., Chipman, S., & Brennan, R. (Eds.) (1995). *Cognitively diagnostic assessment*. Hillsdale, NJ: Erlbaum.

Nunnally, J. C., & Bernstein, I. H. (1994). *Psychometric theory*. NY: McGraw-Hill.

Pearl, J. (1988). *Probabilistic reasoning in intelligent systems: Networks of plausible inference*. San Mateo, CA: Morgan Kaufmann.

Penzias, A. (1995). *Harmony: Business, Technology, and life after paperwork*. NY: Harper Collins.

Reckase, M. D. (1985). The difficulty of test items that measure more than one ability. *Applied Psychological Measurement, 9*, 401-412.

Rogers, T. B. (1995). *The psychological testing enterprise*. Pacific Grove, CA: Brooks Cole.

Samejima, F. (1983). *A latent trait model for differential strategies in cognitive processes* (Office of Naval Research Rep. No. 83-1) Knoxville: University of Tennessee, Department of Psychology.

Samejima, F. (1988). *Advancement of latent trait theory*. (Office of Naval Research Rep. No. N00014-81-C-0569). Knoxville: University of Tennessee, Department of Psychology.

Samejima, F. (1995). A cognitive diagnosis method using latent trait models: Competency space approach and its relationship with DiBello and Stout's unified cognitive psychometric diagnosis model. In P. Nichols, S. Chipman, & R. Brennan (Eds.), *Cognitively diagnostic assessment* (pp. 391-410). Hillsdale, NJ: Lawrence Erlbaum Associates.

Sheehan, K. M. (1996). *A tree-based approach to proficiency scaling*. Unpublished manuscript, Educational Testing Service, Princeton, NJ.

Sheehan, K. M., & Mislevy, R. J. (1994). *A tree-based analysis of items from an assessment of basic mathematical skills*. (ETS Report No. 94-14). Princeton, NJ: Educational Testing Service.

Sheehan, K. M., Tatsuoka, K. K., & Lewis, C. (1993). *A diagnostic classification model for document processing skills*. (ETS Report No. 93-39-ONR). Princeton, NJ: Educational Testing Service.

Snow, R. E., & Lohman, D. F. (1989). Implications of cognitive psychology for educational measurement. In R.L. Linn (Ed.), *Educational Measurement* (3rd ed., pp. 263-332). New York: Macmillan.

Sternberg, R. (1984). What cognitive psychology can (and cannot) do for test development. In B. S. Plake, S. N. Elliott, & J. V. Mitchell, Jr. (Eds.), *Buros-Nebraska symposium on measurement and testing. Social and technical issues in testing: Implications for test construction and usage* (pp. 39-60). Hillsdale, NJ: Lawrence Erlbaum Associates.

Stewart, D. M., & Everson, H. T. (1994). Educational assessment and national standards: The equity imperative. In M. Nettles (Ed.), *Equity and assessment* (pp. 263-272). Boston, MA: Kluwer Academic Press.

Tatsuoka, K. K. (1983). Rule space: An approach for dealing with misconceptions based on item response theory. *Journal of Educational Measurement, 20* (4). 345-354.

Tatsuoka, K. K. (1985). A probabilistic model for diagnosing misconceptions in the pattern classification approach. *Journal of Educational Statistics, 12*(1), 55-73.

Tatsuoka, K. K. (1990). Toward an integration of item-response theory and cognitive error diagnoses . In N. Frederiksen , R. L. Glaser, A. M . Lesgold, & M. G. Shafto (Eds.), *Diagnostic monitoring of skill and knowledge acquisition* (pp. 453-488). Hillsdale, NJ: Erlbaum Associates.

Tatsuoka, K. K. (1993). Item construction and psychometric models appropriate for constructed responses. In R.E. Bennett & W.C. Ward (Eds.), *Construction versus choice in cognitive measurement: Issues in constructed response, performance testing, and portfolio assessment* (pp. 107-134). Hillsdale, NJ: Lawrence Erlbaum Associates.

Tatsuoka, K. K., & Tatsuoka, M. M. (1983). Bug distribution and statistical pattern classification. *Psychometrika, 2*, 193-206.

Tatsuoka, K. K., & Tatsuoka, M. M. (1992). *A psychometrically sound cognitive diagnostic model: Effect of remediation as empirical validity.* (ETS Report No. 92- 38ONR). Princeton, NJ: Educational Testing Service.

Tobias, S. & Everson, H. (in press). Assessing metacognitive word knowledge. In G. Schraw (Ed.), *Issues in metacognitive research and assessment.* Omaha, NE: Buros Institute.

VanLehn, K. (1988). Student modeling. In M.C. Polson & J.J. Richardson (Eds.), *Foundations of intelligent tutoring systems* (pp. 55-78). Hillsdale, NJ: Lawrence Erlbaum Associates.

Villano, M. (in press). *Probabilistic student models: Bayesian belief networks and knowledge space theory.* Proceedings of the Second International Conference on Intelligent Tutoring Systems. NY: Springer-Verlag, Lecture Notes in Computer Science.

Ward, W. C. (1986). Measurement research that will change test design for the future. *ETS Invitational Conference Proceedings.* Princeton, NJ: Educational Testing Service.

Weinstein, C. E. (1995). Innate ability versus acquired ability: A student dilemma. *Innovation Abstracts*, XVII, No. 3. Austin, TX: National Institute for Staff and Organizational Development.

Willingham, W. W. (1986). Multiple measures, multiple objectives in college admissions. *Measures in the college admissions process: A College Board colloquium* (pp. 123-128). NY: The College Entrance Examination Board.

Yamamoto, K. (1987). *A model that combines IRT and latent class models.* Unpublished doctoral dissertation. University of Illinois, Champaign-Urbana.

Yamamoto, K., & Gitomer, D. H. (1993). Application of a HYBRID model to a test of cognitive skill representation. In N. Frederiksen, R.J. Mislevy, & I. Bejar (Eds.), *Test theory for a new generation of tests* (pp. 275-296). Hillsdale, NJ: Lawrence Erlbaum Associates.

10

COMMENTARY
EXPANDING THE BREADTH AND DEPTH OF ADMISSIONS TESTING

Richard E. Snow
Stanford University

This commentary focusses on the two contributions, by Hunter Breland and by Howard Everson, on research aimed at expanding admissions testing. In Chapter 8, Breland gave us a comprehensive survey of writing assessment covering the types of tests, the pros and cons of each, the evaluation standards and needed research, and a good sense of the driving forces and potentials for the future in this domain. In Chapter 9, Everson did a similar job for reasoning and knowledge assessments, with special emphasis on the potentials of computerization in these domains. I'll not review or comment in detail on their ideas here. Rather, I will elaborate on their research directions and also add some other directions I think deserving of attention in this domain.

The motivating question for this effort might be: What is missing in admissions testing today? Or, more constructively: How can we expand the breadth and the depth of admissions testing in valuable and useful directions for both individuals and institutions in higher education today? *Breadth* means expanding the spectrum of cognitive, conative, and affective aptitudes that are assessed. This emphasis argues that we ought to be promoting increased diversity in the talents and personal qualities that get considered and developed in higher education. *Depth* means gaining a deeper, richer description and understanding of the psychology of the constructs being assessed. The point here is that we ought to be pursuing construct validation in admissions testing with a renewal of both vigor and rigor.

Both breadth and depth expansions have been severely limited over the history of the development of admissions testing. As Everson's review suggests, admissions testing grew out of the practical need for prediction and was evaluated primarily on empirical grounds. The development of testing technology far outdistanced the development of relevant psychological theory through most of this century. But psychological theory has now caught up with, and outdistanced, the testing technology. So it is possible now to ask not just whether practical prediction for higher education can be improved by expanded assessment, but also whether adding to the breadth and depth of assessments can help increase the diversity of relevant aptitudes that higher education uses and seeks to develop. If aptitudes for higher education are more fully represented, they may also be more fully recognized as goals of higher education. In effect, in contrast to the history, in the present era we can turn the traditional question around. Instead of asking: "What aptitudes are practical predictors of success in present programs," we can ask, "What does psychological theory and research say we should assess as aptitudes to be developed by higher educational programs, including programs that may not now exist?" In general, and in short, it is crucially important for a society to understand the broad aptitude spectrum it has, needs, and wants given present theory and research.

BROADER ADMISSIONS TESTING

Consider the breadth issue first. We now have Carroll's (1993) hierarchical model of ability organization, based on his massive reanalysis of most of this century's correlational literature on ability tests. Table 1 provides an abbreviated listing of Carroll's results emphasizing the major group ability factors; under each of these, I list only two examples of the more differentiated abilities identified at the third, primary abilities level. At the second, major group level there are eight ability constructs: fluid-analytical reasoning (G_f), crystallized-verbal educational ability (G_c), visual-spatial-perceptual ability (G_v), auditory perception (G_a), idea production (G_i), memory (G_m), speediness (G_s), and reaction time (G_t). Given this model, we can ask two questions: Where do current admissions tests fit in the existing array of ability constructs? What major ability constructs are left out of current admissions tests?

Regarding the first question, most current tests aim at G_c or mixtures of G_c and G_f; specific knowledge tests would also be regarded as specializations of G_c. Note also that mathematical ability, writing ability, and some other constructs common to everyday educational discussion are not represented in the Carroll hierarchy. This is because such constructs are considered complex blends or mixtures of more basic abiities. Mathematical ability, for example is considered a mixture of analytic reasoning reflecting G_f, mathematical conceptual knowledge represented as part of G_c, and speedy numerical facility related to G_s (at least for most adolescents and young adults). Similarly, writing ability is seen as a mixture of basic verbal and language abilities in G_c along with knowledge of the domains and purposes of concern in particular writing performances. Of course as research on these constructs continues, as exemplified in Breland's work on writing and that of Everson on reasoning and knowledge domains, clearer understanding of the constituents of these complexes should lead to better assessments.

TABLE 1

The Hierarchical Factor Model of Cognitive Abilities
(Adapted from Carroll, 1993)

Third Order Factor	Second Order Factor	First Order Factor Examples	Brief Descriptions
G			General Intelligence
	G_f		Fluid-Analytic Intelligence/Abstract Reasoning
		IR	Inductive Reasoning
		QR	Quantitative Reasoning
	G_c		Crystallized Intelligence/Generalized Achievement
		VC	Verbal Comprehension
		RC	Reading Comprehension
	G_v		Visual-Spatial Perception
		VZ	3-D Visualization
		SR	2-D Spatial Relations
	G_a		Auditory Perception
		MD	Musical Discrimination
		SD	Sound Discrimination
	G_i		Idea Production
		OI	Originality of Ideas
		FI	Ideation Fluency
	G_m		Memory
		MS	Memory Span
		MA	Associative Memory
	G_s		General Speediness
		PS	Perceptual Speed
		NS	Numerical Facility
	G_t		Reaction Time
		RT	Choice Reaction Time
		RS	Semantic Processing Speed

Note: Carroll's (1993) factor symbols have been modified slightly here.

Regarding the second question, there are several major group factors that could be discussed as additions to the spectrum considered in admissions testing. I concentrate on three that I think deserve special attention both in their own right and as part of the reasoning, writing, and knowledge assessments addressed by the Breland and Everson chapters. These are G_v, G_i, and G_f. G_v or visual-spatial-perceptual ability, including visualization, imagery, and mechanical reasoning, is a clear candidate for inclusion in admissions testing. Historically, it has not been well measured, and the typical finding has been that it adds little to the prediction of gross criteria such as college grade–point average. But there is good evidence that this kind of ability relates to specialized achievements in such fields as architecture, dentistry, engineering, and medicine. And it can be hypothesized that many problems in mathematics and science involve visual-spatial reasoning as a process parallel to and interacting with verbal-analytic and quantitative reasoning. Given this base plus long standing anecdotal evidence on the role of visualization in scientific discovery, from Einstein and many others, it is incredible that there has been so little programmatic research on admissions testing in this domain.

Idea production (G_i) is another major group factor typically left out of consideration. In his interpretation of this factor, Carroll (1993) now emphasizes retrieval of ideas from memory, but I prefer to retain his earlier terms emphasizing fluent, flexible, and original idea production. This ability is part of what we typically think of as creative as well as critical thinking; Guilford (1967) referred to it as divergent thinking. There is scattered evidence that G_i measures relate to creative performance in science, mathematics, and architecture. G_i is also a likely part of Breland's impromptu essay test. However, it cannot be well measured by an essay test that addresses only one topic. Perhaps some writing tasks could be redesigned to require multiple idea production and elaboration. Increasing the number of independent topics in a writing assessment should increase reliability as well as the involvement of G_i. Certainly idea production is a valued function in most fields of higher education, not only those emphasizing writing.

The third ability construct deserving of further research attention is fluid reasoning (G_f). G_f as a construct is closest to and perhaps identical to G (see Gustafsson & Undheim, 1995). It is interpreted as flexible, adaptive, abstract, inferential reasoning in the face of novel learning and problem solving situations. Of course, G_f is always involved in admissions testing whenever mental tests such as the Scholastic Assessment Test (SAT), American College Test (ACT), or Graduate Record Examinations (GRE) are used because total scores on such tests give fair estimates of general mental ability or general intelligence (G). However, these estimates are biased toward G_c. Purer measures of G_f, such as Raven Matrices or the Bongard Test, might be uniquely useful in studying novelty and creativity. But the further need today is for more detailed assessment of reasoning in context -- that is, in the knowledge and problem domains where it is likely actually to be used. Everson's theory-based framework is concerned directly with this issue. The GRE Board recently had a committee chaired by Marcia Linn studying the problem. And, of course, a similar problem faces Breland's writing efforts.

The problem is: How can one create a context in which to assess reasoning or writing that is broad enough to be economical, so that it can be used for large numbers of examinees, and yet be fair to different specialites; one cannot create a different context for each subspecialty.

In this connection, I have often thought about the possibility of developing learning–sample tests using imaginary content. Such tests could be computerized to include the kinds of learning and problem-solving tasks found in college-level work. The content could be based, for example, on imaginary sciences such as Martian Fauna (Pask & Scott, 1972) and Xenograde Systems (Merrill & Stolurow, 1966), which could be made parallel to existing science domains yet completely novel as content. The original idea for such learning–sample tests was to assess how and how well high school students could learn new and challenging material. But they could serve as well as a base for assessing reasoning and writing as well as many other ablities, in simulated contexts. A whole array of such simulated domains might be designed, each constructed on principles paralleling a real domain of college study, but with imaginary content.

The criticism often heard about simulations of this sort is that they are artficial—they lack realism. In today's reform movement in educational assessment, the term "authentic" is often emphasized. I agree that realism may be important in the assessment of reasoning and writing; perhaps it is also important in the assessment of visual-spatial and idea production abilities. Breland spoke of realism in terms of fidelity and comprehensiveness. In previous times, following the ideas of Egon Brunswik (Snow, 1974), the concern was with representative design. Of course, every test is a sample of both content and process in a domain, so we want representative sampling of both. However, it is easy to overemphasize realism in the service of face validity in today's political climate. In fact, some highly valid tests are quite unrealistic—think of the Ishihara Test of color blindness or the Snellen Chart as examples. In principle, one might have visual-spatial, idea production, and even reasoning and writing tests that measure sharp distinctions within and between the target constructs without realism. The purpose of a test is to capture the distinctions that are critical to the construct of interest. And realism may at least sometimes interfere with that. I am reminded in this regard of the observation of some military psychologists I know: The best training device is often not the most realistic simulator—rather it is the device that makes performance transparent, with success and failure visible to both instructor and trainee.

Still further broadening of the aptitude spectrum in admissions tests would come through sampling of constructs from beyond the cognitive ability domain. Warren Willingham's (1985) own work has certainly emphasized personal qualities beyond the cognitive that relate to success in education. I call this the conative and affective aptitude domain. Much current work suggests candidate constructs. Everson's chapter refers to metacognitive and learning styles and strategies. There are also motivational and self-regulation strategies, and constructs that combine cognitive and conative aspects, such as deep versus surface processing, mindfulness, and action control. For admissions testing purposes, of course, questionnaire measures of such constructs are fakeable and thus limited. However, there are now computerized performance tests of some constructs and free response techniques for assessment of others that offer promising (as well as more realistic) alternatives to conventional questionnaires (see Snow, Corno, & Jackson,1995).

DEEPER ADMISSIONS TESTING

Now consider increasing depth; this is really the harder problem. To understand more deeply what is being assessed and what ought to be assessed, we need cognitive models of test performance *and* cognitive models of exemplary college learning and problem solving. We also need careful research aimed at increasing the overlap between the two, where overlap is understood to include *process* not just *content* sampling.

There are cognitive models of various kinds already in hand. Breland used the example of the Hayes-Flower (1980) model of writing. There is also the work of Collins and Gentner (1987) and Bereiter and Scardamalia (1987) on writing. Then, of course, there is much work on models of reading and text comprehension (Perfetti, 1986; Kintsch, 1988). One can imagine putting reading comprehension and writing together for in-depth analysis and assessment, perhaps in the sort of learning–sample tests described earlier.

Another line of development yields cognitive processing models of fluid reasoning. Sternberg's (1985) work on components of analogical, classification, and series–completion reasoning problems is one example. The analysis and simulation of performance on Raven Matrices problems by Carpenter, Just, and Shell (1990) is another. We still need process analyses of other item types found on SAT-Verbal, SAT-Mathematical, GRE-Analytical, and other such tests. But we also need to build deeper and broader models of adaptive, flexible problem solving in college and work situations. Here is the G_f and reasoning–in–context problem again. Of course, computerization helps the development of modeling immensely because it allows the use of dynamic and adaptive systems as tasks and provides detailed performance analysis. As Everson demonstrates in Chapter 9, computerization also allows much more fine-grained and individualized analysis of knowledge domains, not just of reasoning.

The continuing quest for depth serves construct validation but also increased usefulness. Beyond improved prediction lies the need for diagnosis--in counseling, placement, special treatment, and remediation. This is perhaps the most difficult issue. There have been advances on this front recently (see, e.g., Frederiksen, Glaser, Lesgold, & Shafto, 1990; Frederiksen, Mislevy, & Bejar, 1993; Nichols, Chipman & Brennan, 1995). The work of Mislevy (1996) and Tatsuoka (1995) is particularly noteworthy in improving our understanding of how to make assessments diagnostic. However, as I follow all this work it becomes increasingly clear how situated our concept of diagnosis needs to be. The concern is not for diagnosis of strengths and weaknesses as abstract "things in the head," but rather for diagnosis of person-situation interactions where individual aptitudes are as much a part of the situation as they are the person. In my prototheory of aptitude (Snow, 1992, 1994), individual success and failure reflect the degree to which person and situation are tuned to one another. Successful performance comes when the demands and affordances of person and situation are in harmony. To diagnose the sources of problems thus means to study disharmony in the person-situation interface, not in the person alone. And this, in turn, means the study of college instructional situations. That is a tall order for ETS, the College Board, the GRE Board, and all others in the admissions testing enterprise. But it is an appropriate order.

To conclude, let me reiterate two main points: One is the importance of promoting broader diversity of talent relevant to higher education; the other is the importance of deeper, more comprehensive construct validity in assessments in and for higher education. If we believe in these goals, then the possibilities are there in new psychological theories and new information technologies for the development of assessment in this direction.

REFERENCES

Bereiter, C., & Scardamalia, M. (1987). *The psychology of written communication.* Hillsdale, NJ: Lawrence Erlbaum Associates.

Carpenter, P. A., Just, M. A., & Shell, P. (1990). What one intelligence test measures: A theoretical account of the processing in the Raven Progressive Matrices Test. *Psychological Review, 97,* 404-431.

Carroll, J. B. (1993). *Human cognitive abilities.* New York: Cambridge University Press.

Collins, A., & Gentner, D. (1987). How people construct mental models. In D. Holland & N. Quinn (Eds.), *Cultural models in thought and language* (pp. 243-265). Cambridge, MA: Cambridge University Press.

Frederiksen, N., Glaser, R., Lesgold, A., & Shafto, M. (Eds.). (1990). *Diagnostic monitoring of skill and knowledge acquisition.* Hillsdale, NJ: Lawrence Erlbaum Associates.

Frederiksen, N., Mislevy, R., & Bejar, I. (Eds.). (1993). *Test theory for a new generation of tests.* Hillsdale, NJ: Lawrence Erlbaum Associates.

Guilford, J. P. (1967). *The nature of human intelligence.* New York, NY: McGraw-Hill.

Gustafsson, J-E., & Undheim, J. O. (1995). Individual differences in cognitive functions. In D. C. Berliner & R. C. Calfee (Eds.), *Handbook of educational psychology* (pp. 186-242). New York: Macmillan.

Hayes, J. R., & Flower, L. S. (1980). Identifying the organization of writing processes. In L. W. Gregg & E. R. Steinberg (Eds.), *Cognitive processes in writing* (pp.31-50). Hillsdale, NJ: Lawrence Erlbaum Associates.

Kintsch, W. (1988). The role of knowledge in discourse comprehension: A construction-integration model. *Psychological Review, 95,* 163-182.

Merrill, M. D., & Stolurow, L. M. (1966). Hierarchical preview versus problem-oriented review in learning an imaginary science. *American Educational Research Journal, 3,* 251-261.

Mislevy, R. J. (1996). Test theory reconceived. *Journal of Educational Measurement, 33,* 379-416.

Nichols, P. D., Chipman, S. F., & Brennan, R. L. (Eds.). (1995). *Cognitively diagnostic assessment.* Hillsdale, NJ: Lawrence Erlbaum Associates.

Pask, G., & Scott, B. C. E. (1972). Learning strategies and individual competence. *International Journal of Man-Machine Studies, 4,* 217-253.

Perfetti, C. A. (1986). *Reading ability.* New York: Oxford University Press.

Snow, R. E. (1974). Representative and quasi-representative designs for research on teaching. *Review of Educational Research, 44,* 265-292.

Snow, R. E. (1992). Aptitude theory: Yesterday, today, and tomorrow. *Educational Psychologist, 27,* 5-32.

Snow, R. E. (1994). Abilities in academic tasks. In R. J. Sternberg and R. K. Wagner (Eds.), *Mind in context: Interactionist perspectives on human intelligence* (pp. 3-37). New York: Cambridge University Press.

Snow, R. E., Corno, L., & Jackson, D. N. III. (1995). Individual differences in affective and conative functions. In D. C. Berliner & R. C. Calfee (Eds.), *Handbook of educational psychology* (pp. 243-310). New York: Macmillan.

Sternberg, R. J. (1985). *Beyond IQ: A triarchic theory of human intelligence.* Cambridge, MA: Cambridge University Press.

Tatsuoka, K. (1995). Architecture of knowledge structures and cognitive diagnosis: A statistical pattern recognition and classification approach. In P. D. Nichols, S. F., Chipman, & R. L. Brennen (Eds.), *Cognitively diagnostic assessment* (pp. 327-359). Hillsdale, NJ: Lawrence Erlbaum Associates.

Willingham, W. (1985). *Success in college.* New York: College Entrance Examinaton Board.

11

COMMENTARY
INTERPRETING SCORES IN CONTEXT TO
IDENTIFY STUDENT POTENTIAL

Fred A. Hargadon
Princeton University

I tend to be a skeptic when it comes to expanding admissions testing. As a practicing admissions officer, I have spent the last couple of months, day in and day out, reading thousands of applications with all kinds of test results attached to them and wondering how expanded testing could be useful in admissions decisions. As an instance, I am skeptical of the writing sample of the Scholastic Assessment Test (SAT), partly because it is brand new, partly because I am generally reluctant to think that we can keep measuring more and more in fewer and fewer minutes. But it also struck me that all of the college faculties I ever worked with make the assumption that we should be admitting people who can write. They are not interested in us having a broader diagnostic evaluation for those we admit who cannot write. In other words, a basic requirement in college admissions, admittedly from a narrow focus, is, "How can I distinguish those who can write potentially well enough to succeed in our curriculum from those who cannot?"

However, when I look at the writing test right now, I don't know what to do with the writing scores. I have no idea what they mean. Now that we have a writing score in the admissions process, all of a sudden we get a flood of letters from schools—usually independent schools—saying that the writing scores are all out of whack with the verbal scores and do not agree with their own assessment of the students' ability to write. The fact is that many of us who use these tests do not know how to interpret the composite score and the separate subscores for the writing sample and the multiple–choice exercises. With respect to the subscores, which we really hardly have time to look at, I do not know if it is better to admit people, if that is our choice, who are higher on the writing sample and lower on multiple choice or higher on multiple choice and lower on the writing sample. Or do we use the composite score which, I believe, is some configuration of one third for the essay or writing sample and two–thirds for the multiple choice?

Furthermore, I worry about the clinical impressions. And to show you how skeptical you get in this job if you do it long enough, I worry that we will keep creating tests until we find measures of intelligence on which everyone can score high. I am not a Neanderthal regarding multiple intelligences, but I live a life where I am always told that we are measuring the wrong thing because on some of the things we are now measuring a particular person does not do well. I get many letters from hired guns (as I call them) or educational consultants who are now writing to tell me to disregard Mary's test scores because he has personally given her a set of tests which show that the SAT–Verbal score should be 200 points higher than in fact it is.

So one of our problems is how do we evaluate tests in context? We do it now by the seat of our pants. We use terms like "they have low tests scores in Wyoming." That's because we want to admit this candidate from Wyoming who does not have very high test scores. We begin to believe ourselves that people from Wyoming are not very facile test takers. But the fact is that the importance of context is less ambiguous in the cases where we are explicitly trying to take it into account. By context I mean socioeconomic status, I mean geographic area, I mean the context of attending a school that is very marginal or does not have very many resources but where a student has done well with the resources available. One of the things I would love to know is, at what point can I tell whether a student has met his or her maximum academic height and which ones will continue to grow. That is a very important question for us when we are considering scores in context because we make decisions of the sort that say: "I'll bet on students who have done very well in a school that doesn't offer a single AP course and doesn't have a science teacher who was a science major in college. I will bet that once they get here, after a difficult period, they will do well. They will catch up." We find the test scores very useful, but they would be even more useful if we could learn how to interpret them relative to the context of educational resources and opportunity to learn.

I hope at some time we get practicing admission officers together in the 1990s with testing specialists and see what the intersection is between what the testing specialists refer to as admissions testing and what it is that admissions officers will actually be using. What they can or need to use and what they won't be able to use. To some extent, I think we have enough tests. What we don't have is a good everyday working explanation of what some of these tests mean in making decisions about individual candidates. As an admissions officer in the spring of the year, I now have numbers going through my head from 14,000 folders. In one folder I see a physics score of 650. I know that is lower than a physics score of 700 and higher than a physics score of 500. What I don't know is what are the five or six things this student knows about physics or doesn't know about physics. How can I go to a faculty member knowing the level at which we start physics at Princeton and ask, "What do you think?" I would like to know what constitutes a decent chemistry score for a student who is in the middle of first–year chemistry when he or she has to take the test. That has to have a different meaning than a chemistry score from someone who took chemistry the year before and completed the course. These are the kinds of things that we wrestle with. As another instance, we have a student who writes, "I apologize for my 400 in German. I never studied a word of German but I paid for three achievement tests." Well, we are also looking at people who took 3 years of German who didn't get that score.

On a more serious note, there is a tendency in what we do to make the rational assumption that higher is better than lower. But if we try to take context into account—to factor in where somebody is and what kind of resources they have had and so forth—we would like to know what a good physics score is under those circumstances. I am talking about physics scores because physics is a big deal where I am and also because it is the one area where high schools have a hard time finding trained teachers. So if we are trying not to cut out a segment of the population simply because they are unlucky enough to attend a school that doesn't have a physics teacher who majored in physics, what reasonably could I take into account in such cases? This is a critical problem in educational measurement, namely, how to interpret scores in context.

I am well aware, of course, as are we all, that test scores have played their biggest part in admissions before I even get the application. This is because of self-selection in the pool of students who actually apply, which ironically reduces the influence of the test in actual admissions decisions. If we start out with an applicant group of 14,000 and 10,000 have a 750 SAT–M score or better and 7,000 have a 700 math score or better, with similar credentials on the verbal side, we are drastically reducing the usefulness of the test in differentiating who can succeed from those who cannot. What we end up doing is reading through folders with very similar high credentials. My rule of thumb is that anyone admitted is not a risk, but there is quite a range of characteristics that influence admissions decisions for reasons other than academic and test credentials. Basically, all of the reasons go back to questions of personal qualities.

If you asked me today what I would like a measure of, it would be information about which candidates would make the most of the outstanding resources that we offer at Princeton. Which of these candidates, with all their fine academic credentials, will actually come and make the most of the opportunities offered by Princeton? And, by implication, by whom would the opportunities be wasted? Who among the candidates is likely to be or become intellectually engaged or engaging while an undergraduate? Who among the candidates will make the biggest contributions to their fellow students, the faculty, a seminar? What are the kinds of measures or indicators that will help us identify such individuals more definitively than we can now ascertain? What will maximize acceptance of those kinds of students?

In a book about how he built the team, Bill Walsh, the former coach of the San Francisco 49ers, wrote something that really struck a chord with us in admissions. He wrote that when he looked at prospects for the 49ers he could not care less how fast they could run a 40–yard dash on an open track with somebody holding a stop–watch. He wanted to know how fast they could run with a football through the opposition or catch a pass in heavy traffic. A lot of what we would like to know, if we could assess it, is how fast these candidates could run in the heavy traffic of a university—when they get away from home, when they get among peers many of whom are at least as bright as they are (if not brighter than has been their experience in the past), and where they are going to go through a particular phase in life, the 17 to 22 year–old phase. In short, we wish we knew more about how to measure students' character.

If anybody asks us, "Do you look for good character?" The answer is, "Yes." It has struck me as a little odd that at the end of our essay exercise we have a thing students have to sign that says, "I swear that all the above is true and my own work." The very first person who is going to sign that is the biggest liar in the world. What is that oath to somebody who is not going to be honest? But still we would like to know something about character. We would like to know something about a student's ability to respond to setbacks. The worst thing I can put on a folder is to suggest that a student is too fragile. This might be someone who has straight As and every indication of high motivation and effort who is confronted by the fact that the odds are very, very high they will not be first in their class. When I tell such students that, "Tomorrow most of you will drop into the bottom 90% for the first time in your lives," how will they respond? Or, as another instance, when we graduate the senior class, "90% of you, I hate to tell you, will be in the bottom 90%." If you tell that to a group 95% of whom may have been in the top 5% of their high school class, they'll smile and say, "Not me, fortunately." But, we would like to know how they will react to that kind of shift.

As a final point, I have made a list of areas in which more work needs to be done. For example, I am about to start a campaign in the schools to teach English as a foreign language because what really strikes one about our applicant pool is how well recently immigrated students perform on English tests relative to native English–speaking candidates. How is it that so many recently immigrated students to this country, although English might only have been their language for 3 or 4 and maybe even 6 years, manage to score so well on writing, language, English, and verbal tests—much better than many of our students who have been here since day one? Why is it that so many of these immigrant students present us with the most cogently written applications, sentence by sentence, paragraph by paragraph? It is a group that I suspect takes little advantage of coaching or anything else. Then I jokingly turn to my staff and tell them that we have to teach English to our students as a foreign language. I will leave it there, because the joke isn't funny.

PART IV

POLITICS AND PUBLIC POLICY OF HIGHER EDUCATION ASSESSMENT

Assessment of the quality of higher education has been a long-time concern within the academy as part of a curricular and pedagogical reform movement to improve undergraduate education. Because the need for reform was generally perceived as being deep-rooted and widespread, the issue of quality gradually escalated from the level of concern for local improvement to the national level of policy debate. As the context broadened beyond the local institution, higher education quality quickly became embroiled in the politics of accountability. Federal and state officials saw assessment of quality as a lever for elevating higher education accountability in times of constrained economic resources, but also as a means of channeling the academy's responsiveness to societal needs.

Once in the political arena, there was enormous pressure for the assessment of quality to become more focussed with respect to the desired outcomes of higher education that are addressed. There also needed to be some resolution of debates about value perspectives as to what constitutes excellence in higher education. For example, is excellence embodied in high quality resources (including the quality of faculty and students) or in institutional reputation or in successful talent development? Alternatively, we need some way of dealing with the pros and cons of endorsing diverse views of excellence. These considerations as to what outcomes of higher education to assess in terms of what criterion of excellence have profound implications not only for the content of quality assessment but also for the appropriate mode or form of assessment. The implications of these issues of politics and policy for higher education assessment are the topics of Part IV.

In Chapter 12, Peter Ewell traces the confluence of political and economic forces that have brought higher education to judgment in terms of a "new accountability," namely, accountability in terms of return on investment to society as a whole. As a consequence, higher education has become a much more public enterprise, with employers and the general citizenry demanding a voice in what the outcomes of higher education ought to be.

Ewell then focusses on some of these public views of desired outcomes, which turn out to be highly similar to the goals of liberal or general education from the time of Cardinal Newman to present-day college catalogues, attributes

145

akin to those delineated by Chickering in Chapter 2. However, these current public views differ from the traditional lists in two essential ways, namely, by emphasizing affective and motivational as well as cognitive aspects of competence and by insisting that knowledge and skill be demonstrable in action and not just in theory. A direct implication of this is that assessment of higher education outcomes should become more performance-based or "authentic" in embodying real-world problems, so that student performances and products can be evaluated for multiple aspects of quality (including noncognitive as well as cognitive aspects) against appropriate criteria of excellence.

In Chapter 13, Alexander Astin argues that the criterion of excellence in higher education should not depend on resources or reputation but, rather, on successful talent development. That is, higher education outcomes should be measured in terms of the *value added* to students' knowledge, skills, and character over and above the attributes they entered college with, which accords well with the new accountability in terms of return on investment.

Again, a direct implication is that higher education outcomes, including non-cognitive outcomes, should be measured in criterion-referenced and not just normative terms. By describing what students know and can do, as opposed to their rank-order relative to other students, performances can be evaluated against publicly-endorsed standards, as can measures of growth in competence. Focussing on measures of growth or value added is not only in the spirit of the new accountability with respect to outcomes, but it also has important implications for the nature of admissions policies and for what constitutes student success in college—hence, for the nature of diversity of the student population.

12

ASSESSMENT OF HIGHER EDUCATION QUALITY: PROMISE AND POLITICS

Peter T. Ewell
National Center for Higher Education
Management Systems — NCHEMS

Many of the people whom I admire most in this business are represented in this volume, and I feel especially humble among them. And as always when I visit ETS, my humility is reinforced by the fact that I am a kind of ambassador from an elusive and somewhat seat-of-the-pants arena. Higher education assessment has always been a field composed of amateurs in the best sense of the word. As you know, most practitioners have been faculty themselves working in isolation, but occasionally guided by the examples of others which they gratefully snatch up wherever they can find them. And the kinds of assessment approaches that they have sought most eagerly are precisely those that are under discussion here, and that are so reflective of Warren Willingham's work—authentic, creative, and action-oriented.

Approaches that embody these qualities comprise the main tradition of the best in higher education assessment over the last three decades, and are embodied in the work of many of those in this book—Patricia Cross, Morris Keeton, Arthur Chickering, Alexander Astin, and Sister Joel Read. This creative tradition is fueled by the twin convictions that a) taken from the proper value perspective, assessment constitutes a powerful tool for collective improvement that is highly consistent with core academic values and b) infusion of the logic of assessment directly into classroom and curricular settings is perhaps the most powerful means we have at our disposal to transform the logic of pedagogy itself—from one-way instruction to collaboration and partnership.

I have been privileged to have been a part of this improvement-oriented, institution-centered agenda for some time now, and it is where my heart really lies. But it is not what I am going to talk about here. Instead, my principal topic is politics— and in particular, how these politics both fuel and frustrate what we do. Since the assessment of quality first emerged as a major *policy* topic in higher education about a decade ago, it has had a dual existence. One strand of development represents an internal reform movement within the academy, growing largely out of a rediscovery of undergraduate education in the 1980s. This was always a tradition that had curricular and pedagogical reform as its centerpiece and there was nothing about it that was new even then. What was important was the fact that it emerged at that time as a *national* conversation, stimulated by such widely-cited reports as *Involvement in Learning* and *Integrity in the College Curriculum*. But a second, intertwined strand of development was public, as elected officials and higher education agencies saw in assessment a powerful tool to help achieve greater accountability for higher education and to drive the kinds of structural changes needed to improve its responsiveness to public purposes. This strand too had its documents, the most prominent of which was a report issued by the National Governors' Association in 1986 under the telling title *Time for Results*.

The relatively brief policy history of assessment in higher education has always been a product of this strange dialectic—sometimes reinforcing, sometimes contradictory. And over the past 10 years, it has resulted in some curious outcomes. First, far more colleges and universities are actually doing assessment because somebody *told* them to than because they really believe in it. Most, for better or worse, remain content to construct what they do in terms of what others demand, principally state governments and accrediting bodies. Very few, moreover, are as yet engaging in assessment in the spirit of academic inquiry—directed toward collective improvement—that constituted the original heart of the movement. Ironically, however, it is precisely that spirit which public officials throughout the 1980s wanted higher education to adopt, with relatively non-directive policies to match. This potential positive alignment of internal and external forces represented by this irony, though, did not survive the decade. Since about 1990, the ground has begun to shift beneath the entire economic and technological "dance floor" for these two unlikely partners, providing new constraints and opportunities. And most ironic of all, it is these *structural* shifts, not good intentions or intrusive government policies, that are finally moving us of necessity toward a more systemic adoption of the kinds of assessments that we need.

It is this strange progression of circumstances that I would like to briefly address. First, I want to review the recent history of quality assessment as a policy tool in higher education and, in particular, the way deepening government frustration with the academy's apparent unwillingness to change has altered its character. Second, I intend to examine some deeper forces in the operating environment for higher education that are rapidly rendering assessment a necessary condition for doing higher education's business. Finally, I want to use both of these to draw some conclusions about the kinds of assessments we will need to meet this future and, unfortunately, whether we will really be allowed to build them properly.

THE CHANGING ROLE OF QUALITY ASSESSMENT

Let me begin with the first item promised—quality assessment's relationship to public accountability for higher education and, more particularly, how this has changed in recent years. This story begins essentially in the early 1980s at the state level, with a strong resurgence of interest in the potential public purposes of higher education. In part, this was a creature of public officials—most notably a set of governors that prominently included one from New Jersey, Thomas Kean. But in part, it was also a product of a rhetoric of investment on the part of higher education's own leadership, who increasingly argued throughout the 1980s that further allocations to higher education would pay off in greater workforce productivity and economic competitiveness.

The result of both was a cluster of state policies founded on what a number of us at the time labelled the "New Accountability." Fundamentally, this "new look" in the role of state government reflected a shift of perspective from higher education as a kind of public utility whose principal benefits were reaped by individual citizens, to a view of the state's colleges and university as a collective asset and an investment for the future. This in turn led to a conception of accountability based not just on the traditional twin anchors of access and efficiency—which made sense for the "public utility" model—but founded equally on the kinds of specific returns to society as a whole that might be expected. This shift, of course, corresponded to the academy's own internal curricular reform efforts in the 1980s, and occurred just as many states were making parallel efforts to reform and restructure K-12 education. But it is important to stress that higher education's accountability problem was never the same as K-12's. While the latter's was a true crisis of performance that demanded a highly directive change policy, ours was always more of a "crisis of confidence" based on lack of understanding of higher education generally, suspicion that it was not well managed, and a vague but growing conviction that it had lost sight of its original public charge.

The policy response to this condition was in retrospect curious and surprisingly enlightened. Most states chose to require institutions to develop their *own* local assessment processes consistent with their unique missions and student clienteles. At the same time, set-aside funds were made available to institutions in the form of grant-like incentive pools to encourage instructional innovation consistent with the results of what was found through assessment. A prominent example of this intended combination occurred in New Jersey in the form of the College Outcomes Evaluation Program (COEP) and the Governor's Challenge Grant Program which supported a range of curricular innovations in both public and private institutions throughout the 1980s. Mirrored at the federal level by the Fund for the Improvement of Postsecondary Education (FIPSE), which supported the development of many campus assessment programs, this basic approach had been adopted by some two-thirds of the states by 1990.

Enlightened as it was, this policy approach to assessment was always potentially flawed in at least two ways. First, as a strategy for achieving lasting change, a government mandate had a very different look to faculty than as part of their own conversation. (I recall one faculty member at a state college in New Jersey characterizing the state's position, and his own reaction, succinctly: "this [assessment program] is so wonderful that we're going to *make* you do it!") Secondly, this strategy depended heavily upon the presence of favorable fiscal conditions to support the conduct of assessment itself and, more importantly, to fund the following results-based improvements. In short, the times made it possible to afford significant numbers of investigations and improvements on the margin, without really affecting the main activities of most colleges and universities.

By the early 1990s, it was clear that these flaws were fatal. Severe budgetary difficulties in most states abruptly terminated investment in further innovation, including assessment approaches that did not demonstrably add value. At the same time, many public officials lost patience with the slow pace of change, and the occasional outright resistance of some (usually prominent) institutions to the assessment/innovation agenda. These twin conditions yielded a policy pattern surrounding assessment far more directive than that of the 1980s but, at the same time, one that remains highly uncertain. One of its aspects is a passion for performance indicators and directed budgeting at the state level. As of this writing, some eighteen states have developed statistical performance-indicator systems, usually in response to the perceived inability of decentralized institution-centered assessment systems to carry effectively the burden of increased accountability. Another aspect of this pattern is a highly visible federal agenda which emerged quite unexpectedly with the 1992 reauthorization of the Higher Education Act. This initiative--which created new and potentially intrusive oversight regulations and bodies, including the State Postsecondary Review Entities (SPREs)—caused great concern in higher education circles and provoked a highly visible initiative to restructure institutional accreditation on a national basis. The November 1994 elections have blunted the urgency of this agenda, but federal interest in higher education's performance has far from disappeared. Indeed, recent events suggest that it is likely to be tied more than ever to emerging federal workforce initiatives as part of a more comprehensive Department of Labor initiative.

This is the immediate policy environment within which discussions of collegiate quality are now occurring, and it provides a good example of the kinds of rapid changes in political character and salience that will likely continue to dominate our short-term future. But while these latest maneuvers constitute one term of the constellation of forces that we must react to, I believe that some longer term trends in higher education's operating environment will more decisively shape assessment's utility as both an internal and external policy instrument. These deeper trends form the basis of a more meaningful reaction on our part, and their consideration constitutes the second part of my argument.

CURRENT OPERATING CONDITIONS

In particular, I would like to cite two broad changes in recent operating conditions that lie beneath the surface of political events. The first is the increasingly public nature of the higher education enterprise and, in particular, what should constitute its outcomes. Here, the original premise of the "new accountability"—return on investment—has firmly taken root in the public's mind. At the individual level, it is visible in growing consumer consciousness and rising citizen unease about affordability. Indeed, recent poll results suggest that college costs remain the single dominant issue surrounding higher education for the majority of Americans. At the corporate and policy level, this theme is visible in an increasing unwillingness to let colleges and universities alone set the substantive agenda about what is to be taught and how. Grounding this unwillingness is more visible recognition on the part of employers that they constitute higher education's single most important customer and should exert a shaping influence as a result. And both developments now seriously challenge the academy's traditional conviction that disciplinary mastery should be the principal test of collegiate success.

In this regard, I'd like to cite particularly the results of some work that the National Center for Higher Education Management Systems (NCHEMS) completed in 1995 in conjunction with the Education Commission of the States (ECS). This project involved convening several dozen focus groups of corporate and political leaders in seven cities across the country, and posing to them the question of what the results of 4 years of college ought to be. While they took disciplinary and professional skills for granted in these conversations, what they said also provided an interesting twist on the list of essential attributes usually associated with general education in most college catalogues—which itself is not dissimilar to Cardinal Newman's list of outcomes so ably presented by Arthur Chickering in Chapter 2. Put in their terms, essential outcomes included:

- **higher-order applied problem-solving skills.** These differed in their minds from traditional "critical thinking" abilities in their strongly practical nature. At the same time, they included a large measure of creativity—in the words of one informant, not only solving problems but "being able to find the right problem to solve."

- **enthusiasm for learning on a continuous basis.** Again, this at first glance looks like "lifelong learning" as an end in itself; beneath it, though, were visible concerns about the need for workers to continually update rapidly changing skills and the consequent crucial nature of the meta-skills needed to learn at all levels of the workforce.

- **communication and collaboration skills.** Also high on the academy's list, the policy version of this attribute differed in particularly emphasizing oral communications. More importantly, it stressed the application of communications skills in real situations—most prominently, being an effective member of a team.

- **sense of responsibility for actions taken.** Though largely non-cognitive, this theme was extremely important for all external constituents. Prominent here were both an individual dimension—responsibility for the consequences of one's own actions—and a collective dimension—support of and contribution to one's own community or organization.

- **ability to bridge cultural and linguistic barriers.** While in some ways resembling the academy's own concern with cultural diversity, the emphasis here was again far more applied. At its center was the ability to work effectively with people drawn from different backgrounds and value systems, far more than simply personal tolerance for ethnic and national differences.

- **sense of "professionalism."** Again noncognitive, this attribute was perhaps the only one missing from the academy's traditional array. It embodied a cluster of motivations and the acceptance of standards surrounding professional practice and, more particularly, knowledge and support of the larger organizations of which individuals may be members. Also included here was a cluster of appropriate interpersonal behaviors—what one respondent aptly labelled "pure civility."

Though in many ways familiar, it is important to note two ways in which this list of essential attributes differs from its more academic version. First, *non-cognitive* traits are accorded equal weight with more cerebral outcomes. Indeed, for many respondents, the distinction disappeared entirely. Second, all are manifested in *action* not contemplation. The external test of quality is what students can do with what they learned, when confronted with complex real-life situations. The implications for policy of these observations are many, but one in particular stands out: for better or worse, our "customers" are increasingly pressing us to define more precisely the common meaning of the baccalaureate, they have some strong views about the subject, and they will want a place at the definitional table.

A second major condition shaping current practice is the growing need for higher education to restructure what it does in the face of escalating fiscal pressures. These pressures are, of course, partly a product of politics but constitute some very real and enduring conditions nonetheless. Despite some recent bright spots, most states are still experiencing sluggish economies and an eroded tax base as a consequence. More importantly, current structural conditions of state budgeting render higher education expenditures the "budget balancer"—the largest piece of discretionary spending under the control of state lawmakers after the mandatory deductions represented by such items as court-ordered school spending and federal health care program matching requirements. Finally, both taxpayer unrest and the lack of public perception that further investments in higher education are really needed continue to strongly constrain public support. In short, we are now in the curious position of having lost the ability to gain fiscal support from public bodies on the basis of "residual deference" without being in the public's mind "broken enough"—like K-12 or criminal justice systems—to warrant emergency investment.

All of these factors—plus the inability to raise tuition further—have placed enormous fiscal pressures on colleges and universities. Ironically, and as in corporate America more generally, this real fiscal pressure is in my view producing far more positive innovation than either voluntary reform or political mandate. In support of this, I'd like to note three trends in particular that point toward some profound changes in the ways in which collegiate instruction is beginning to be accounted for and delivered. First are the internal efforts of a number of institutsons to restructure their own curricula. Most notable in Virginia, where each public institution has been required to prepare and execute a restructuring plan to avoid further funding cuts, such efforts generally involve a mix of old and new initiatives. Some involve simple cost-cutting—reducing the number of credits needed to graduate, increasing faculty workloads and the number of large-enrollment sections, and the like. More significantly, though, many are concentrating on achieving greater curricular *coherence*, recognizing that "learning productivity" is increased by courses that fit together as part of a more rational curricular plan. More radically still, some are exploring self-paced and competency-based alternatives to traditional course delivery that may allow students to complete their programs in less time and with less expenditure of instructional resources. Many of these notions, of course, are not new and have been advanced repeatedly on their own merits since the mid 1960s. But they are only now being taken seriously by college and university leaders, not on the grounds of effectiveness, but because of their potential to reduce costs. All will require a greater use of assessment—both to determine individual competence for the assignment of credit and to guide the development of more effective curricular structures by examining their results.

A second notable trend is an increasing pattern of multiple-institution attendance patterns. In part, this has been encouraged by public policies that emphasize achieving greater economies by teaching lower-division courses at 2-year institutions. But more typically, it is the product of individual consumer choices on the part of a far more mobile population. Indeed, in many urban areas, the traditional "forward transfer" pattern of 2-year to 4-year attendance has been replaced by what enrollment planners call the "swirl"—a constant movement on the part of students among institutions of all types seeking the credits that they need at a price that they can afford. Such enrollment patterns are placing increasing strains on traditional articulation and transfer policies based solely on individual course content. Instead, states and institutions alike are beginning to discuss the alternative of basing such policies on assessed competencies at point of transfer. And this alternative is further stimulated by emerging attempts to restructure collegiate admissions standards on a competency basis in states like Oregon and Florida. Both policy initiatives, of course, will require valid assessment procedures to make them work at all.

A final trend is the now inescapable potential of instructional technology—which is seen by policymakers in virtually every state as exactly the magic bullet needed to slay the "cost-of-instruction" dragon. Although major questions continue to arise about its ability to actually deliver on reducing costs, the widespread adoption of new technology is probable in pursuit of this promise. And its impact on both the nature of instruction itself and on the kinds of assessment that will be needed will be profound. First, the use of new technologies raises the opportunity for a vastly changed "directionality" of instruction—converting it from a sequential path of delivery to one much more multifaceted; as a result, students may have mastered quite different parts of a given domain, or may come to current skill levels by traveling quite different routes. At the same time, the use of technology explodes most administrative categories for "accounting" instructional delivery—raising significant questions about how to count costs or allocate credit. Finally, the growing use of technology as an instructional alternative begs to be evaluated —are the outcomes of technology-based instructional modes really comparable to those of more traditional forms and are there significant unanticipated consequences of their widespread use? All three issues suggest that assessment will have a ready market as experiments with technology continue.

Together, these environmental trends yield two major implications for assessment's role and potential. First, all three areas suggest a growing pressure on "seat time" as the basis for higher education's credentialing and institutional reward system. All point in some way toward the eventual displacement of the Carnegie unit by "competency" as the unit for future curriculum-building, though no one at this point knows either which competencies should be so accounted or how to recognize them. While these problems—largely political—remain as formidable as ever, consensus on the *principle* of competency as the unit of solution continues to grow. Obviously, should this occur, assessment will become central to institutional operations. At the same time as innovations proliferate, a market for "quality control" will likely emerge. Current conversations about innovation have been driven far more by economics than by pedagogy, and it will be imperative that we have appropriate tools for both policymakers and institutional leaders to examine the "benefit" side of the cost/benefit relationship actually associated with this range of experiments.

THE ASSESSMENT AGENDA

These imperatives, of course, lead directly to our "bottom line:" What kinds of assessments will be needed in this new policy climate? On reflection, let me hazard three main characteristics. The first is apparently straightforward, and is already a part of our common parlance—the need for substantial "authenticity" in the instruments and approaches that we design and deploy. Now this is of course an extremely familiar admonition in educational measurement circles, and it has been with us for some time now as an educator's criterion. But it has historically been difficult to reconcile with the "quick fix" political responses that often occur in its name. Yet I advance the proposition that there will be a market for authentic assessment for some substantial public policy reasons that are strongly associated with the expected objectives of collegiate study. There is increasing agreement among our customers that "quality" is demonstrated not in the knowing but in the doing. Instruments that don't actually look at the doing, though cheap, will therefore badly miss the mark. We need instead, instruments that exhibit at least 3 important characteristics: a) approaches that are rooted in the context of actual practice; b) instruments and techniques that emphasize the deployment of the identified skills over a broad range of specific contexts, with the ability to work "messy" problems in alien circumstances prized above all; and c) that take adequately into account appropriate dispositional and motivational issues in addition to (indeed, in many ways fused with) pure cognition. All three characteristics, of course, are perhaps best illustrated by the work of Warren Willingham which we celebrate in this volume.

As we all know, it will be a singular challenge to reliably examine the kind of "intellectual broken-field running" that constitutes such abilities, but in the long term, I believe, that is where the demand is going to be. As the economist reminds us, however, the long term may be uncomfortably far away. As a result, I'd like to suggest two additional characteristics that I believe our instruments and approaches must possess in order to meet the more immediate political future, both in many ways suggested by recent experience, in New Jersey.

First, such approaches will need to be unusually *robust*, with this design criterion equivalent in importance to the traditional standards of reliability and validity. Experience in this business teaches us that we need to imagine each of our carefully-crafted instruments and data-collection rubrics "half implemented"—with half the funding, in half the time, and with half the levels of technical support originally planned. Application of this criterion may well lead us to make far different sets of choices about what will work under real policy conditions, regardless of the elegance of other measurement alternatives.

Second, the assessment approaches we ultimately deploy for higher education cannot be advanced to the policy community *unaccompanied*. Instead, they must be clearly linked with a larger change agenda and a clear strategy for *using* what is found to guide improvement. Considerable experience teaches us that we must be very clear about the nature of the particular problem we are trying to address through measurement, lest the measurement itself become the end of policy. I've noted some particular "policy hooks" for action earlier in this talk in the form of evaluating the effects of new technologies or in addressing the consequences of multiple-institution attendance. Others may emerge from the need to guide and rationalize local and state-system level attempts to restructure instructional delivery.

But it is clear to me from the fate of such efforts as the publicly-mandated General Intellectual Skills (GIS) assessment in New Jersey, and the consistent failure to fund a national effort to assess critical-thinking and problem-solving abilities as called for in the National Education Goals, that there is very little constituency for a number—especially, as seems likely, when the number in question will be very expensive. At the same time, to be useful internally, assessment results must be visibly "connectable" by institutional leaders to the real problems of teaching and learning that they face. The time is long past when "value-added" assessments in themselves can be afforded; increasingly, assessment approaches which themselves *add value* to instructional delivery will be in demand instead.

To conclude, let me restate my original premise. I believe that both current politics and a new operating environment for higher education are forcing an action agenda for colleges and universities that will increasingly have assessment at its center — whether we or they like it or not. The need for "quality assurance" for the academy's many publics is real and permanent, despite surface fluctuations. And internal restructuring is becoming imperative in our enterprise, just as it has become in every other major social institution in this country. To meet this challenge as assessment practitioners, I believe, will require a curious sort of recursiveness. To develop appropriate methods, we will need the same qualities in ourselves as those that we seek to measure. Among them prominently are three: the ability to shift contexts rapidly in the face of new conditions; with an eye to the main chance, a disposition to partner effectively with many strange bedfellows who may for better or worse be shaping the market for information; and, above all, thoroughness and integrity in what we do. In short, to meet the future, we will be required to fully model the message—in just such a way as Warren Willingham has done these many years in all his work.

13

ASSESSMENT, STUDENT DEVELOPMENT, AND PUBLIC POLICY

Alexander W. Astin
University of California, Los Angeles

A basic premise in my consideration of college impact and public policy is that the fundamental purposes of assessment activities in higher education should be to promote educational equity and to facilitate the student's educational development. As Sister Joel Read maintained in Chapter 6, assessment should promote success and access. Another way of saying this is that *assessment of students, more than anything else, should advance the educational mission of our colleges and universities.* McKeachie said essentially the same thing in Chapter 5 when he remarked that "educational assessment should be educational." I will also argue that many of our *traditional* assessment practices are not well-suited to higher education's basic educational purpose, and that some of these practices would appear even to undermine those purposes. I would first like to take a critical look at traditional assessment practices -- especially those that involve the use of standardized tests -- and then suggest some ways in which we might be able to reform these practices.

THE PURSUIT OF "EXCELLENCE"

Before getting to any specifics, I would briefly like to share the value perspective from which I am approaching this problem. Like all educators, I support the notion of "excellence" in higher education. For quite a while now I have been arguing that there are two traditional conceptions of excellence -- the *resource* and *reputational* approaches -- that govern much of what we do. The *resources* conception is based on the idea that excellence depends primarily on having lots of resources: the more we have, the more excellent our institution. Those resources that are supposed to make us excellent include *money, high quality faculty*, and *high quality students*.

The *reputational* view of excellence is based on the idea that the most excellent institutions are the ones that enjoy the best academic reputations. We academics have always had an interest in the pecking order of institutions, and these interests have been reinforced in recent years by the annual rankings published in magazines like *Money* and *U.S. News and World Report*. Reputation and resources are, of course, mutually reinforcing, since having a lot of resources enhances your reputation and having a good reputation helps you acquire resources.

In recent years I have been very critical of these traditional conceptions of excellence (Astin, 1985), primarily because they do not directly address the institution's basic purpose: the education of students. To focus our institutional energies more directly on this fundamental mission, I have proposed the adoption of an alternative approach called the *talent development* conception of excellence. Under the talent development view, excellence is determined by our ability to develop the talents of our students and faculty to the fullest extent possible. The basic premise underlying the talent development concept is that true excellence lies in the institution's ability to affect its students favorably, to enhance their intellectual and scholarly development, to make a positive difference in their lives. The most excellent institutions are, in this view, those that have the greatest impact--"add the most value," as economists would say--to the students' knowledge and personal development. In short, my argument will be predicated on the assumption that assessment, more than anything else, should enhance our talent development mission.

"EXCELLENCE" AND ASSESSMENT

Let's now turn to look at some of our traditional assessment practices. I'll begin with what's probably the most difficult and politically loaded policy issue: college admissions. When it comes to the question of equity, we need to keep in mind three basic facts about admissions testing. First, Blacks, Hispanics, American Indians, and poor students are substantially underrepresented in American higher education, especially in the more select or elite institutions.

Second, most selective institutions rely heavily on test scores to select their students. And third, African-Americans, Hispanics, American Indians, and poor students tend to receive lower test scores than other groups. Clearly, the continuing reliance on test scores by college and university admission offices will make it very difficult for these or any other educationally disadvantaged group to attain equal or proportionate access to the best higher education opportunities.

But the widespread use of norm-based testing has serious equity implications beyond the competitive disadvantage that it creates for certain groups. Since the lower schools tend to imitate higher education in their assessment technology, there is a heavy reliance on standardized tests all the way down to the primary schools. Given the normative nature of these tests, students who perform below "the norm" are receiving important negative messages about their performance and capabilities. At best, they are being told that they are not working hard enough; at worst, they are being told that they lack the capacity to succeed in academic work. A young person who regularly receives such messages year after year is not likely to come to view academic work in a positive way, and is certainly not likely to aspire to higher education. Why continue the punishment? In other words, it seems reasonable to assume that the use of norm-referenced tests causes many students to develop negative attitudes about education long before they reach an age where they might consider applying to college.

And research shows that, even among students who manage to finish school and apply to college, standardized test results have a major impact on *where* they choose to send applications (Astin, Christian, & Henson, 1980). As Fred Hargadon emphasized in Chapter 11, a great deal of college and university "selectivity" is, in fact, *self*-selection. Very few students with mediocre test scores apply to highly selective institutions. While some high-scoring students do apply to nonselective institutions, most of them apply instead to the more selective institutions. As a matter of fact, the self-sorting by student applicants is so extreme that most of our highly selective institutions could admit applicants at random and still end up with an entering class that scores very well in terms of test scores.

In short, the colleges' and universities' continuing reliance on norm-referenced tests in the admissions process poses a serious obstacle to the attainment of greater educational equity for disadvantaged groups, not only because of the handicap that it poses in the admissions process, but also because of the profound effects that it has on students' decision-making at the precollegiate level.

WHY DO WE TEST?

One of the principal driving forces behind the use of test scores in the admissions process is our continuing adherence to the resources and reputational views of excellence: High-scoring students are seen as a valuable "resource" (and, by implication, lower-scoring students as a liability) and having a select (high-scoring) student body enhances an institution's reputation because it is regarded as a sign of "excellence." That students, parents, teachers, and counselors are well aware of this reputational pecking order is reflected in the considerable self-selection just discussed.

Why do we persist in these practices? After thinking, researching, and writing about these issues for nearly three decades, it has become clear to me that the usual arguments that we use to justify selective admissions simply do not hold up under careful scrutiny. At the same time, the issue of "equity versus excellence" really turns out to be primarily a matter of *how we define excellence*. If we accept the reputational and resource approaches to excellence, we automatically create a conflict with the goal of equity since there are only so many "resources" of high-scoring students to go around. From the perspective of an individual institution, admitting more underprepared students forces it to admit fewer of the best-prepared students, thereby diluting its "quality" ("quality" in this context being defined as the mean test scores of the students who enroll). Conversely, if we decide to become more "excellent" by raising our admission standards, we must necessarily deprive admissions to more poor people and underrepresented minorities. Clearly, *under the resources and reputational definitions of excellence, there is an inherent conflict between excellence and equity.*

This zero-sum game also serves to foster a great deal of wasteful competition among institutions. If my institution succeeds in becoming more "excellent" by recruiting away some of your National Merit scholars, then your excellence is proportionally reduced. And the financial resources invested in this recruitment competition--something in the neighborhood of 2000-3000 dollars per student--are completely lost from the system with no gain in overall "excellence."

A talent development approach to excellence creates a very different scenario. From this perspective, our excellence depends less on whom we admit and more on what we do for the students once they are admitted. In other words, our excellence is measured in terms of how effectively we develop the educational talents of our students, rather than by the *initial level* of developed talent they exhibit when they enter. While it is possible to create a competitive pecking order of institutions using the talent development approach (e.g., which institutions' students show the greatest change, learning, and development?), there is nothing *inherently* competitive or normative about talent development. Nor is the total amount of "excellence" in the system finite. That is, if my institution manages to be highly successful in developing the talents of our students, this in no way constrains or limits what any other institution can do.

My advocacy of the talent development perspective toward excellence is by no means intended to suggest that there are not powerful forces supporting the resource and reputational approaches. College administrators are heavily rewarded for acquiring resources and enhancing their institutions' reputations. Regardless of where institutions stand in the pecking order, most of them want to move up, so administrators put a very high premium on enhancement of reputation and resources. At the same time, virtually every constituency of the institution -- students, faculty, administrators, trustees, alumni, members of the local community -- support the institution's drive for greater resources and reputation. Being associated with a prestigious institution makes each of us feel more important; it gratifies our egos. Clearly, for those who are interested in embracing a talent development conception of excellence and achieving a greater degree of equity for underrepresented groups, it is an uphill struggle. And the current attacks on affirmative action are not making it any easier.

To me the most potent conceptual tool for expanding educational opportunities and achieving a greater degree of educational equity is the talent development approach. Pat Cross put it well in Chapter 3 when she said that the purpose of assessment should be to *educate*, not just to select. This is especially true in the case of our public institutions, since they are presumably committed to "serving the public." Clearly, the most appropriate public service that can be performed by such institutions is education. Since the explicit charter of the public institution is thus to serve society by educating its citizens, no public institution can argue that it exists primarily to enhance its own resources and reputation or, to put it in the vernacular, merely to become as rich and as famous as it can.

What is particularly interesting about these issues is that contemporary spokespersons for higher education frequently use the "human capital" viewpoint as an argument for greater public support and funding. America's "competitiveness," they argue, depends upon educating all of our citizens to the greatest extent possible, not only to maximize the number of high-achieving scientists, inventors, and leaders, but also to minimize the number of lower-performing people who often represent a drain on the society's resources. The "human capital" argument, in other words, applies across the entire spectrum of ability and achievement. Such a view meshes very nicely, it seems to me, with the talent development approach.

ASSESSMENT AND "ACADEMIC STANDARDS"

When I make these arguments to my faculty colleagues, they will sometimes deny that they are driven by a quest for resources and reputation and will argue instead that the fundamental reason for selective admissions is to establish and maintain "academic standards." Without further elaboration, such arguments amount to an endorsement of motherhood, God, the flag, and apple pie: Who can object to "maintaining standards"? But what, exactly, are "academic standards"? I see at least two different meanings that can be extracted from this phrase, and each deserves a fair hearing. The first and most common meaning is that academic standards refer to the level of performance the student must demonstrate in order to be awarded particular grades or to earn a degree. When "standards" is used in this sense, the faculty are saying that they resist lowering admissions standards to accommodate more underprepared students because they are concerned that final (exit) performance standards will also be lowered. If we look at this argument more closely, it amounts to saying that admissions standards determine graduation standards.

The problem with this argument is that performance standards can be maintained independently of admissions standards. The lack of a necessary relationship between admissions standards and exit performance standards can perhaps best be understood with an analogy from the field of medicine. In much the same way that education seeks to develop the student's intellectual talent to the highest possible level by the time of graduation, the exit "performance standard" for all forms of medical treatment is a sound and healthy patient. If a patient is admitted to a hospital for, say, a hernia repair, the exit "standard" is basically no different than it would be for a patient who has to undergo a more difficult and complex procedure such as the removal of a tumor from the lung. In both cases, the goal is the same: a sound and healthy patient. It *is* understood, however, that more resources will need to be invested in the patient with the tumor: longer and more complex surgery, more intensive post-surgical care, a longer stay in the hospital, and possibly post-operative treatment with radiation or chemotherapy. (Edmund Gordon reminds us in Chapter 16 that equity in treatment doesn't necessarily mean equal treatment, especially if people differ from each other at the point of entry.) At the same time, it is recognized that the *probability* of "success" (reaching exit standards of sound health) is higher for the hernia patient, since the surgical risks are less and the prognosis better (e.g., much less chance of malignancy).

In short, if a hospital admits a patient who is more seriously ill than the typical patient at that hospital, it does not automatically set lower "performance standards" for that patient. On the contrary, the hospital's goal is for all patients eventually to get over their illnesses and be in good health when they leave the hospital. It *is* true that an extremely ill patient often requires a greater investment of resources to reach the hoped-for performance standards for discharge, and it *is* true that the probability of reaching those standards is often less than would be the case for an average patient, but the hospital does not automatically alter its performance standards simply because the patient has a poor prognosis at entry.

This medical analogy underscores one important reality about expanding educational opportunities. If an institution or a system of institutions wants to maintain exit performance standards and to enroll a greater proportion of underprepared students (students who, at college entry, have substantially lower standardized test scores than the average student), one or more of the following changes must occur: The underprepared students must be given more time to reach performance standards; a greater share of institutional resources must be deployed to deal effectively with the underprepared students' educational needs; or, the institution's dropout and failure rates must increase. In short, lowering admissions standards does not necessarily require any alteration in performance standards at the exit point.

In higher education our thinking about performance "standards" tends to be much more simplistic. Rather than attempting to achieve common performance standards by differential treatment, we try to "maintain standards" through selective admissions. This is basically no different in principle from trying to achieve "performance standards" in a medical setting by refusing to admit the sickest patients. Indeed, in American higher education we have developed a set of elite institutions that are so selective in their admissions that high performance standards at exit are almost guaranteed, even if the institution contributes little to the educational process. Ironically, these same institutions have the best facilities and the most resources of all institutions (Astin, 1985). To replicate such institutions in the medical field would be almost absurd: We would have an elite group of hospitals or clinics that would have the finest and most advanced equipment and facilities and the best-qualified and highest-paid staff but which would admit only people with common colds. All other prospective patients would be refused admission in order to maintain the highest possible performance standards at exit!

The second meaning of the "maintaining academic standards" argument expresses a concern for the talent development process itself. This argument goes as follows: If larger numbers of underprepared students are admitted to an institution, that institution's academic program will become less demanding and will therefore lose some of its potency in developing student talent. In other words, in attempting to gear its program to greater numbers of underprepared students, the institution will slight its better-prepared students, giving them a watered-down education that will lead to less talent development among the better-prepared students. It should be emphasized that this argument revolves around a problem that all institutions face, regardless of their admissions policies: How to deal effectively with students who come to college differing significantly in their levels of academic preparation. Even the most selective institutions face this difficulty, given their differential admissions policies for international students, alumni children, athletes, students with other special talents, and students from Wyoming! The considerable success that some selective universities have with their athletes demonstrates clearly that, given a sufficient incentive, any selective institution can succeed in developing the talents of less-well-prepared students. Moreover, there are some very promising pedagogical techniques for accommodating a diversity of students --such as cooperative learning--that have not yet been used on any substantial scale in most colleges and universities.

THE "PREDICTION" ARGUMENT

Another reason commonly given for relying on test scores in making admissions decisions is that the tests "predict grades in college." But let's look at the *validity* of the argument itself. Even if we accept college grades as a valid performance measure (and many educators are now questioning this practice), the "prediction argument" does not really hold up under scrutiny. Basically, this argument asserts that students with high test scores should be favored in the admissions process because they are likely to "perform well" later on in college. All this really means is that a high-scoring applicant is more likely than one with lower test scores to get good grades in college. This is simply another way of saying that pre-college performance correlates with college performance. And indeed it does. But colleges, unlike employers, are not in the "personnel selection" business when it comes to admissions. They are, rather, in the business of *educating* their students. Does the prediction argument really have anything to say about how much or how well the different students will actually *learn?* Does it say anything about how much talent *development* different students will eventually show? Unfortunately, it does not.

Consider the following scenario. Let's say that we were to admit all applicants regardless of their test scores. But instead of educating them, we put them in a deep freeze or in a state of suspended animation for 4 years and then revive them and give them a set of "final exams" in order to compute their college GPAs. Obviously, those who had the highest test scores at the point of entry will "perform better" on these final exams than those with lower test scores, even though *no learning or talent development took place!* The point is a subtle but very important one: Just because past performance correlates with or "predicts" future performance does not mean that high performers in high school will learn more or develop their talents more in college than low performers will. In other words, traditional selective admissions does not necessarily further the talent development mission of a college or university.

Supporters of selective admissions might respond that my argument is flawed because a student's college GPA is indeed a valid indicator of how much a student has learned in college. On a purely anecdotal level, most of us who have taught in college have had personal experiences that refute such an argument. For example, we have all had students who were so bright and so well prepared at the beginning of a course that they could do well on the final examination without exerting much effort and without really learning very much. On the other hand, most of us know of students who showed great improvements (learned a lot) but whose final exam performance was mediocre because they came to us so ill-prepared. But the evidence against the argument that "grades reflect learning" is not merely anecdotal. John Harris (1970), for example, has shown that students who get mediocre grades in a course can be learning as much (as measured by score *improvements* in standardized tests given before and after the course) as students with the highest grades.

The evidence usually cited in defense of the prediction argument is the moderate correlation of college grades with high school grades and admissions test scores. To see why "prediction" does not necessarily reflect "learning," one needs only to understand what a correlation really shows. Let's say that there is an admissions test that yields scores on a ten-point scale and that we have 3 high school seniors with scores of 4, 5, and 6, respectively. Suppose we admit them and they all gain two points during their 4 years of college so that, by the time they reach their senior year, they score 6, 7, 8, respectively. The "prediction" of college performance from high school performance would yield a perfect correlation of +1.0, even though all three students learned the same amount in college! How can we justify an admissions policy that would have excluded the two applicants with initial scores of 4 and 5? Is their two-point gain less "valuable" or less "important" than the two-point gain of the highest-scoring applicant? Let's suppose, on the other hand, that the students learned absolutely nothing in college, so that their scores remained the same over the 4 years. The correlation would still be +1.0, even though the students learned absolutely nothing! Indeed, even if the students got dumber during college, with each score declining two points to 2, 3, and 4, respectively, the correlation would *still* be +1.0! In other words, the only requirement for high school performance to correlate with college performance is that the students' positions *relative to each other* show some consistency over time. Nothing in the correlation tells us how much talent development has occurred, or even whether there has been any talent development at all!

EDUCATIONAL OPPORTUNITY AND THE DEVELOPMENT OF "HUMAN CAPITAL"

I want to emphasize that the principal obstacle to expanding educational opportunities is posed not by the tests themselves, but the way they are *used* to promote the reputational and resources conceptions of excellence. Both Cross (Chapter 3) and Gordon (Chapter 16) remind us that assessment should be linked to the learning process. While some critics have tried to argue that the talent development approach compromises and threatens "academic standards," when we look at the educational system as a whole, *there is no better way to promote "academic standards" than to maximize talent development.* To see why this is so, imagine that we have an entering freshman class to educate and that they come to us at the point of admissions with varying levels of developed talent. To simplify the argument, let's say that each applicant's level of developed talent can be ordered on a scale from 1 to 10. Level 1 would represent borderline literacy and level 10 would represent the intellectual talent level required for attaining a PhD degree. Let's assume further that the "minimum standards" required for the bachelor's degree is 6. If we were working, say, in a large state university, a typically diverse group of ten college freshmen might enter our college with the levels of developed talent ranging from 2 to 5. (The "5's," of course, are already close to the minimal level required for graduation.) Our first job as an educational institution, then, is to help as many of these ten students as possible to reach level 6. In essence, a talent development approach seeks to *add* as much as possible to each student's entering level of performance. Now if we are indeed successful in "maximizing talent development" among all ten students, we accomplish at least three important goals:

> First, we maximize the number of students who reach minimal performance standards (level 6).
> Second, we maximize the "margin of safety" by which students exceed this minimal level (that is, the number of 7s, 8s, 9s, and 10s).
> And third, we minimize the number of students with borderline skills (that is, levels 2 and 3).

This last accomplishment (# 3) is especially important, since we will seldom be successful in bringing all entering students up to performance standards. So even if some of our students fail to reach level 6 and drop out of college without a degree, we have still made some contribution to their intellectual functioning and have thus added to their chances of eventually becoming productive members of society. In other words, a talent development approach is the surest way not only to "maintain academic standards" but also to maximize the amount of "human capital" available to the society.

What I am really suggesting here is that the role of testing changes dramatically under a talent development perspective. Rather than being used to merely enhance institutional resources and to promote institutional reputations, tests are used to place students in appropriate courses of study and to determine how much talent development is actually occurring by repeated assessments over time. These longitudinal assessment activities would serve two functions: to document the amount and type of talent development that is occurring, and to provide, in combination with environmental information about the student's experiences in college, a basis for learning more about which particular kinds of educational policies and practices are likely to facilitate talent development for different kinds of students. If testing in higher education were revised in this fashion, it seems likely that proponents of expanding access and opportunity in higher education would come to see testing as an ally rather than as a threat.

TESTS AS OUTCOMES

Let's turn now to consider a very different use of standardized tests in academe: as outcome assessments to measure how much students have actually learned, that is, to assess how much talent development has occurred. I want to explore two policy questions: How well do norm-referenced standardized tests capture what is actually occurring in student development? And is it wise to base educational policy on the results of such outcome assessments?

An opportunity to explore such questions is provided by a large scale longitudinal study that we recently completed using data from the Cooperative Institutional Research Program (CIRP). This study involved more than 24,000 students at 217 baccalaureate-granting institutions. In addition to extensive longitudinal data on each student from our freshman survey and follow-up questionnaires administered 4-1/2 years later, we had retention data from the college registrars, college admissions test scores from the College Board and ACT, and graduate admission test results from the GRE, NTE, MCAT, and LSAT. We also obtained extensive environmental data by surveying 20,000 faculty members at these same institutions.

We used a total of 82 different student outcome measures, and some 21 of these could be classified as "cognitive" outcomes. These 21 cognitive measures can be further divided into three groups: standardized test scores (GRE, LSAT, etc.; 9 measures), behavioral measures (college GPA, retention and admission to graduate/professional school; 3 measures) and self-rated *growth* measures in several cognitive areas (such as general knowledge, critical thinking, writing ability, etc.; 9 measures).

The first thing that struck us about the findings was the high degree of correlation among all of the standardized test scores, especially between those administered 4 1/2 years apart. In fact, the SAT and ACT appear to be excellent pretests not only for the GRE, but also for most of the other professional school admissions tests. For example, the SAT/ACT Math and Verbal tests both correlate .85 with their GRE counterparts, and the SAT/ACT composite correlates .88 with the GRE composite! These would be impressive uncorrected test-retest correlations even if we were using exactly the same test! Besides their obvious ability to predict GRE scores, SAT/ACT scores account for more than half of the variance in all of the other graduate admissions tests.

After controlling for the effects of college admissions tests and other entering freshman characteristics, we were able to identify a number of environmental variables (college characteristics and experiences) that affected the students' performance on each of the 21 cognitive outcome measures (for more details of the methodology see Astin, 1991, 1993).

Perhaps the most important finding to emerge from all these analyses is that the college experiences that were found to affect standardized test scores are very different from the experiences that affect the 12 other cognitive outcomes. In a few instances the same environmental variables showed *opposite* effects on these two sets of outcomes. For example, the extent to which the faculty emphasizes research shows positive effects on several standardized test scores and negative effects on student retention.

A number of other potentially important college experiences that showed no relationship to the test score outcomes turned out to have significant positive effects on most of the 12 other cognitive outcomes. For example, the amount of interaction between students and faculty showed significant positive effects on all the behavioral outcome measures and on five of the nine self-reported growth measures. Similarly, the frequency with which the student interacted with other students positively affected two of the behavioral outcomes and five of the self-reported growth measures. And, while the amount of time that students spent studying and doing homework also showed no effect on test scores, this "time on task" measure showed significant positive effects on all three behavioral outcomes and seven of the nine self-reported growth measures.

The implications of these findings for educational policy are clear: If we were to base educational policy solely on the standardized test results, potent environmental variables such as student-faculty interaction, student-student interaction, and time on task would all be rejected as ineffectual strategies for enhancing cognitive development.

Given our heavy reliance on standardized tests at all levels of education in this country, it is important to realize that educational reform efforts that are designed primarily to improve students' ability to perform well on standardized tests may not contribute much to any other cognitive outcomes and may, in some cases, detract from them. The conflicting results associated with the Research Orientation of the faculty is just one of several examples of this problem (see Astin, 1993).

The point here is not necessarily to denigrate the use of standardized multiple-choice tests for assessing educational outcomes--such tests can be of value in assessing certain kinds of student talents--but rather to point out that they measure rather narrowly defined skills and do *not* appear to be good overall indicators of student development. In Chapter 8, Hunter Breland used the term "fidelity" in discussing writing tests. In the jargon of information theory, standardized multiple-choice tests have very high "fidelity" but very low "bandwidth." As a matter of fact, if we were also to consider the results with the 61 *affective* outcomes that were utilized in the larger study (Astin, 1993), the contrasts with standardized test results would be even more pronounced.

ALTERNATIVES TO STANDARDIZED TESTS

Many of the contributors to this volume--especially Gordon, Chickering, Keeton, McKeachie, and Sister Joel Read--tell us that we need to broaden our notions about what kinds of talents we should value and want to develop. In Chapter 10, Snow put it well when he said we should be "promoting a diversity of talents."

Educators who have been wedded to traditional standardized tests over the years forget that there are many alternative ways of assessing cognitive performance and development. Beyond the alternative measures used in the study I've just described, we can rely on creative *products* and *performances*. Creative products include such things as original writing, research papers, inventions, scripts, films, videos, works of art, and musical compositions. Creative performances include equally diverse activities such as public speaking, leadership, dance, musical recitals, and theater productions.

The temptations to continue relying on standardized tests are many: Such tests are already widely used, are familiar to both faculty and students, and are relatively inexpensive to administer and score. These conveniences make it very tempting to employ such tests in large-scale educational reform efforts and in large-scale studies of education such as the Coleman Report, High School and Beyond, the National Assessment of Educational Progress, and the National Educational Goals study designed at the federal level. Notice also that most of the evaluation that we do at the K-12 level is done through standardized tests. Practically every school district in the country administers norm-referenced standardized tests annually, and the presumption is that the tests are measuring those developmental qualities that are most relevant to the purposes of the schools. At a minimum, the results of this study suggest that we need to broaden our conception of how to measure cognitive development and to begin considering alternative methods.

AFFECTIVE OUTCOMES

The results that we obtained from the 61 noncognitive or affective outcomes used in the longitudinal study just described (Astin, 1993) convince me that we need to pay much more attention to the so-called "affective" side of student development.

Most of us are inclined to shy away from assessing affective outcomes because we think they are too "value-laden." We feel much more comfortable limiting our assessments to cognitive outcomes. College, after all, is supposed to develop the student's intellect, so how can we go wrong if we focus on cognitive variables? But if you read through a few college catalogs, you begin to realize that colleges claim to be concerned about a number of "affective" things such as good judgment, self-knowledge, citizenship, social responsibility, character, and the like. Indeed, most descriptions of the "liberally educated" person sound at least as "affective" as they do "cognitive."

What I am really suggesting here is that the stated missions of most colleges and universities give us plenty of license to begin assessing affective outcomes. To me one of the most important of these affective qualities is citizenship. Given the state of contemporary politics in the U.S., citizenship and social responsibility may be among the most important educational outcomes that we should try to assess.

In Chapter 12, Peter Ewell gave us a wonderful summary of the *political* context in which higher education is operating these days. And as Linn reminded us in Chapter 7, some politicians see higher education as an *obstacle* to change. But there is another aspect of our political scene that concerns me even more. Earlier this year one of the representatives from our own national congress observed that "*The United States is fast becoming a nondemocratic country*. We have the lowest voter turnout of any major industrialized country on earth...The simple fact is that the majority of Americans...no longer believe that the government is relevant to their lives."[1]

Democracy and citizenship provide excellent examples of the importance of affective qualities in higher education. Most of us probably think of democracy primarily as an *external* process, where people do things like discussing issues

---

[1]Rep. Bernard Sanders, writing in the *Los Angeles Times*, January 16, 1994.

and politics, campaigning for candidates, or voting. While these activities are indeed important elements of a healthy democracy, none of these "external" behaviors is likely to occur in the absence of appropriate "internal" conditions, such as an understanding of how democratic government is supposed to function, an appreciation of the individual's responsibilities under such a form of government, and a willingness, if not a determination, to be an active participant. What I am really saying here is that democratic *behavior* is most likely to occur when the person has acquired certain knowledge, understanding, beliefs, and values. These "internal" qualities are precisely the kinds of qualities that educational institutions are in an ideal position to foster, and there is no reason why we cannot begin to incorporate measures of such qualities in our outcomes assessments.

The miserable state of contemporary American politics suggests to me that we in the higher education community have not done a very good job of developing these qualities in our students (or in ourselves, for that matter). While many of my faculty colleagues may argue that the success or failure of our system of representative democracy is not higher education's responsibility or concern, they forget that promoting "good citizenship" is one of the most commonly stated values in the mission statements of most colleges and universities. We are, in other words, publicly on record as committing ourselves and our institutions to the value of promoting good citizenship. The challenge for those of us in the assessment field is to figure out how to measure qualities of good citizenship. Let's take a closer look at just what some of these qualities might be.

What about behavioral measures? Most of us would probably agree that political behavior in the United States today leaves much to be desired, even by the simple measure of citizen involvement. But we make a serious mistake when we assume that "democracy" amounts to allowing each of us to go into a voting booth every now and then to make our choices in secret, or that the practice of "good citizenship" consists merely of taking advantage of this opportunity whenever it is offered. It is true that, even by this simplistic standard, most of us are not very good citizens, but even if all of us voted all of the time, this would in no way ensure that we had a democracy that functioned the way it is supposed to function. Good citizens also read about political issues and events, discuss political issues with others, and actively support the political causes that they care about.

What sorts of "cognitive" measures should we consider? Comprehending our democracy involves a lot more than knowing what's in the constitution and being able to describe the three branches of government. The poor condition of our democracy today is a product of complex forces that have little to do with what we learn in high school civics courses. It has much more to do with such things as the economy, corporate business, lobbyists, the manner in which political campaigns are funded, and especially the role of the mass media. Knowledge of how these factors affect our democratic system would seem to be at least as important to the future of our country as knowledge of math or science.

If higher education really wants to get serious about its commitment to producing responsible citizens, it should be much more focused on helping students understand how our system of government actually works. Take the most basic of all ingredients in any functioning democratic system: *Information*. Even the most elementary understanding of how a democratic political system is supposed to operate recognizes the central role of information: A democracy works only to the extent that the voter is well informed. If citizens really understood and appreciated the importance of information in our system of government, they would take a much greater interest in learning more about the mass media that produce most of this information. The majority of Americans, for example, get their political news from prime-time TV newscasts. That this particular medium is *not* doing an acceptable job of keeping us informed is revealed in a frightening finding from a survey conducted during the 1992 presidential campaign: This study showed that a person's actual knowledge about the three major presidential candidates was *inversely* related to the extent to which that person relied on prime time TV as the major source of news.

What I am really suggesting here is that our educational system should help students not only to understand the key role that information plays in an effectively functioning democracy, but also to become better critics and analysts of contemporary mass media and of the information they produce. Most faculty put a high premium on the development of "critical thinking" skills in students, but we still have a long way to go before we can say that we are producing student/citizens who have sufficient critical understanding *and* the motivation to demand better information. I'm reminded here of a wonderful little book called *Teaching as a Subversive Activity*. (Postman and Weingartner, 1969), which argues that in an "information society" where so much of our "information" comes through the commercial mass media, an important function of education should be to help young people become expert "crap detectors." Given the nature of contemporary political campaigning, the need to develop better "crap detecting" capabilities in our students has never been greater.

There has been a lot of discussion in this volume about two issues that need to be joined: (1) diversification of our assessment in terms of which talents we value, and (2) the *linking* of assessment to the teaching/learning process. Can these two ideas be connected to the notion of developing more responsible citizens? H Let me propose one possible strategy for bringing about such a complex merger through a campus activity that has been getting a lot of attention lately: volunteer service or service learning. Why not use service learning as a means of rejuvenating some of our general education courses in the fields of humanities and social sciences? It's taken for granted in most natural science fields that abstract scientific laws and principles cannot be fully understood and comprehended without a *laboratory* experience. Why not look at service learning in the same way, as the *laboratory* component of humanities and social science courses? The Higher Education Research Institute at UCLA is currently engaged in an intensive longitudinal study of the long-term effects of service-learning experiences during the undergraduate years. The preliminary results are very exciting: Not only does performing volunteer work enhance undergraduate retention, but there are a number of post-college outcomes that are also positively affected, including *affective* outcomes such as commitment to helping others, environmental activism, and commitment to promoting racial understanding. Post-college *behavioral* outcomes that are positively affected include preparation for graduate school, actual entry to graduate school, continuing participation in volunteer work after college, job preparation, and--believe it or not--donating money to your alma mater!

THE ROLE OF VALUES:
SOME GRATUITOUS ADVICE FOR THE TESTING COMPANIES

While my discussion so far has focused on some of the limitations of standardized multiple-choice tests, I'd like to emphasize that the major limitations of these instruments are not so much with the tests themselves but rather in the way in which we have traditionally *used* them. And at the heart of all such decisions about test utilization is the question of *values.* Values lie at the heart not only of our decisions about which outcomes to measure, but also our choice of methods for assessing these outcomes. And when it comes to admissions testing, values once again enter into our decision, for example, to use standardized tests to promote our reputation and resources rather than our talent development mission.

Values even underlie the way that we score standardized tests. Many of the contributors to this volume--Cross, Chickering, and Keeton among others--have suggested that we need to move away from normative scoring. To use standard scores or percentiles is consistent with the values of resource acquisition and reputational enhancement, since normative scores make it easy to identify the "best" and "worst" students. Normative scoring, however, makes it difficult to use the results of standardized tests to promote talent development. The conversion of raw scores into normative scores basically wipes out fundamental educational information such as what percent of questions the students answered correctly, which ones were answered correctly, and so on. Normative scores also make it difficult to measure *improvement* or *change* in performance, the fundamental ingredient in a talent development or value-added approach to assessment. Clearly the time has come for us to consider converting all of our standardized tests into performance-based or criterion-referenced approaches.

In addition to criterion-referenced or performance-based scoring methods, there is also a powerful old idea that has received little attention in modern testing practices: the expectancy table. An admissions test score, perhaps in combination with other entering student data, can be expressed in several very useful ways: such as the probability of graduating in 4 or 5 years, the probability of gaining admission to graduate or professional school, and so on. With the longitudinal data in the large-scale study just described, we have found it useful to express SAT or ACT scores in terms of an expected performance on the GRE or even on the MCAT, the LSAT, or the NTE. By comparing such expected scores with the students' actual scores when they apply for graduate or professional school, the institution gains important data for curriculum evaluation and self-study.

Perhaps what is needed is a transition period during which the traditional normed scores are combined with expectancy scores or other kinds of criterion-referenced or performance scores, following which the normed scores could be phased out. The success of the American College Testing program proves, I think, that students and admissions people can get used to a different system of scoring college admissions tests.

In addition to a new scoring system, there is no reason why the testing organizations cannot also provide feedback to schools and teachers showing students' performance on individual test items. Knowing which items are easiest and hardest for their students and knowing the distribution of responses across various distracters on each test item would be invaluable for curriculum evaluation and planning, not only in the high schools but also in the college the student enters. Also, with modern data processing capabilities, such information from Advanced Placement tests and the College Board Achievement tests could be provided at relatively little cost.

A common objection to the provision of data on individual test questions is the need to protect test security. This objection has always puzzled me, given the *theory* underlying the construction of most standardized tests. According to test construction theory, the items for such tests are selected from a hypothetical "domain" of all possible test questions that could be asked about the subject in question. If providing individual item feedback violates the security of a particular set of items, then we can simply write a new set of items. If the domain is finite, then once all possible test items have been written and made public, the testing company can simply sample at random from this domain when it constructs each new test. It might be argued that having all items made public would simply encourage students to memorize the answers to as many of the items as possible. But if the student knows the answers to all possible questions that could be asked about a particular body of knowledge, then that student knows, by definition, that body of knowledge.

Another substantial service that testing companies could provide on behalf of talent development would be to conduct more equating studies of the various tests that they distribute. I harbor no illusions that academics are suddenly going to abandon normatively scored standardized tests in the near future. Indeed,

SATs, ACTs, GREs, and the like are probably going to be with us for a long time to come. But as long as these tests are scored normatively, and as long as there is no way to compare a score on one to a score on another, it becomes virtually impossible to assess learning or talent development by combining the results from comparable tests given at different times. Given the very high correlations between the SAT and the GRE, allow me to make still another gratuitous suggestion to our host organization: ETS could provide a major service to undergraduate institutions by conducting equating studies of these two tests. Similar equating studies could probably also be done using the College Board's Achievement tests and the Advanced Placement tests as "pretests" and the appropriate subject matter test of the Graduate Record Examination as "posttests." If the longitudinal correlations of these various instruments are anything like what we found with the SAT and the GRE, such equating studies could certainly be justifiable from a psychometric point of view.

Such equating would not only provide colleges with a simple way to assess how much *growth* or talent development students were demonstrating during the undergraduate years, but it would also have the more subtle effect of encouraging students, professors, and college administrators to begin thinking about test scores less as screening and selection devices and more as ways of measuring student learning and *development.* Certainly this would contribute immensely to helping shift our educational thinking away from resources and reputation and more in the direction of talent development.

In closing, I would like once again to make one last pitch for a much greater emphasis on affective outcomes. I am well aware of the many technical problems associated with defining and assessing such outcomes, but the literature on student development in higher education would certainly argue for the importance of assessing such outcomes. There is plenty of justification in the catalogs and mission statements of most colleges and universities for including such qualities as citizenship, interpersonal competence, leadership, honesty, empathy, and social responsibility in any battery of outcome measures. While our society can be justifiably proud of its many achievements in the cognitive realm--atomic energy, genetic engineering, modern agriculture, modern medicine, and electronic marvels of every conceivable type—it is important to realize that most of the problems of modern society are *affective* and *emotional*: racial tension, corruption in business and government, escalating materialism and individualism, crime, drug abuse, widespread poverty and homelessness, and noninvolvement in the political process. Higher education can play a major role in refocussing our attention on these affective processes by acknowledging their importance in its assessment practices. In short, it is time to begin shifting some of our educational interest and energy in the direction of our affective side—to begin concerning ourselves with the development of beliefs and human values that will serve to heal our societal divisions and to help to create a community that is less competitive and materialistic and more generous and cooperative.

REFERENCES

Astin, A. W. (1985). *Achieving educational excellence: A critical assessment of priorities and practices in higher education.* San Francisco: Jossey-Bass.

Astin, A. W. (1991). *Assessment for excellence: The philosophy and practice of assessment and evaluation in higher education.* New York: Macmillan/Oryx.

Astin, A. W. (1993). *What matters in college? Four critical years revisited.* San Francisco: Jossey-Bass.

Astin, A. W., Christian, C. E., & Henson, J. W. (1980) *The impact of student financial aid programs on student choice.* Los Angeles: Higher Education Research Institute.

Harris, J. (1970). *Gain scores on the CLEP General Examination and an overview of research.* Paper presented at the Annual Meeting of the American Educational Research Association, Minneapolis, Minn.

Postman, L., & Weingartner, C. (1969). *Teaching as a subversive activity.* New York: Delacorte Press.

PART V

ISSUES OF EQUITY AND FAIRNESS IN HIGHER EDUCATION ASSESSMENT

Equity and fairness are social values that apply whenever decisions are made or actions taken that affect individuals or groups. If these decisions or actions are based on test scores or assessment information in general, then equity and fairness become central measurement concerns that fall squarely in the area of validity. Indeed, validity is also a social value, and we should not let its technical underpinnings in psychometric theory obscure the fact that validity's power and legitimacy as a judgmental standard derive from its basis in societal values.

In recent years, the concept of validity has been extended to encompass the *adequacy* and *appropriateness* of *interpretations* and *actions* based on test scores or other assessment devices. The term "adequacy" refers to the evidential basis of test validity and "appropriateness" to the consequential basis. Equity and fairness are key issues with respect to the consequential basis of validity because they can ultimately be evaluated only by taking the intended and unintended consequences of test interpretation and use into account.

Moreover, equity and fairness are principles of social justice, a broader social value also closely linked to the consequential basis of validity. In the context of educational assessment, the major issues of equity are equal access and treatment as well as equal opportunity to learn. The major concern of fairness is to achieve a proper balance of the needs, rights, and demands of different individuals and groups in test interpretation and use. The relevant validity principle in establishing fairness is *comparability* of scoring, interpretation, and use across diverse individuals, groups, and settings. These issues of equity and fairness, as they bear on higher education assessment, are the topics of Part V.

In Chapter 14, Randy Bennett notes that congressional legislation along with federal regulations aimed at assuring test fairness for disabled examinees puts the testing community in a state of conflict. This conflict stems from the dual legislative requirements of accurate and valid assessment of the capabilities of disabled individuals simultaneously with the prohibition of inquiry about disabled status. Unable to guarantee the comparability of scores across standard administrations and those modified for disabled examinees, the testing profession resorted, at least temporarily, to flagging the latter scores, thereby violating the prior-inquiry prohibition.

Bennett then reviews the consequent flurry of intensive research activities aimed at understanding and accommodating the sources of noncomparability in both score meaning and task demands under standard and modified conditions. The results indicate that scores under nonstandard conditions are generally comparable to scores from standard tests except for modifications that allow extra time. Bennett then argues that the advent of computer-based testing affords numerous possibilities for improving comparability because of the multiplicity of options available for stimulus presentation and response mode as well as the computer's capability for individualizing timing requirements to minimize the role of speed in performance when it is not a relevant aspect of the construct being assessed. In Bennett's view, computer-based testing promises generalized accommodations to improve comparability of task requirements and score meaning for all examinees, disabled and nondisabled alike.

In Chapter 15, Richard Durán explores educational interventions and accompanying assessments aimed at improving our understanding of Latino and other linguistic minority students' cognitive and linguistic preparation for college. He argues that asking students whether English is their best language is not nearly as informative or predictive as students' self-appraisals of their specific English-language ability for academic purposes. Because non-English language learners expend more effort in recognizing the structural features of English than do native English speakers, their verbal problem-solving performance is depressed and they adopt a variety of information-processing strategies to compensate for difficulties in comprehension. As a consequence, probing of their wrong answers often reveals careful reasoning by students based on assumptions about the meaning of material not fully understood.

However, the problem is not just a matter of insufficient knowledge of English structure and rhetorical organization, Durán emphasizes. The difficulties faced by linguistic minority students also stem from their lack of socialization into academic culture, from an inadequate understanding of the purpose of academic tasks and an inability to adopt the social role appropriate for classroom interaction. This problem is exacerbated by exposing Latino students to cognitively and linguistically undemanding remedial activities that serve mainly to develop ungeneralized skills tailored to the remedial tasks as well as self-identities as remedial learners. What is needed are programs, probably beginning as early as the 4th grade, in which linguistic minority students can be socialized to engage in higher-order thinking while carrying out academic tasks and to develop communicative competence in realistic and demanding academic contexts.

In Chapter 16, Edmund Gordon argues that the problems of human diversity are not primarily problems of assessment but problems of education, that the problems of equity and fairness in educational assessment are secondary to the failure to achieve equity through educational practices. He argues further that diversity both in status and in functional characteristics leads to a categorizing of people within the social hierarchy in ways that influence their access to resources and opportunities as well as to rewards.   However, he maintains that the most crucial aspect of these invidious categories is not their basis in cultural experiences and practices but, rather, their contribution to the ways in which one identifies the self.   Thus cultural identity may be more important than culture per se in determining an individual's outlook, attitudes, and behavior.

Gordon also distinguishes diversity in status and function from the pluralism embodied in the social demand for multiple competencies enabling individuals to adapt to diverse contexts and circumstances.   He then explores some of the ways in which a concern for population diversity and pluralistic outcomes can impact teaching, learning, and assessment.   Specifically, he offers seven concrete suggestions for making both assessment and education more responsive to human diversity, not the least of which is a call for greater individualization to improve learning and the validity of local interpretations as opposed to rigorous standardization to sustain the comparability of interpretations and decisions across individuals and groups.   This is an example of the tradeoffs entailed in Gordon's proposed strategies, tradeoffs that contribute mightily to the complexities of test fairness, as highlighted from a systemic perspective in the following final chapter in Part V.

In Chapter 17, Warren Willingham, as is only fitting in a volume in his honor, provides a capstone treatment of the issues of test fairness.   Willingham maintains that test fairness, for both the public and the profession, has always been viewed in terms of comparable validity for individuals and groups.   Hence, the concept of fairness is just as complex as the concept of validity, and the two are difficult to disentangle in either theory or practice.   Indeed, in recent years the concept of validity has been elaborated to make explicit the concern for value implications and social consequences that has always been an integral, if often latent, aspect of validity judgments.

After examining multiple tradeoffs and other technical as well as social complexities intrinsic to attempts to establish fairness for individuals or for groups under different assessment conditions and for different assessment purposes, Willingham proposes a four-stage framework for evaluating fairness issues at each step in the assessment process from initial test design to ultimate test use.   Within each of the four stages of design, development, administration and scoring, and interpretation and use, he enumerates specific steps implicating fairness issues and underscores interconnections that need to be attended to.   The intent is to do everything practical to increase test fairness as comparable validity across all aspects of the assessment process from the initial choice of constructs and test design to the consequences of test use.

14

COMPUTER-BASED TESTING FOR EXAMINEES WITH DISABILITIES: ON THE ROAD TO GENERALIZED ACCOMMODATION

Randy Elliot Bennett
Educational Testing Service

This chapter examines how the advent of computer-based testing (CBT) might improve postsecondary admissions assessment for examinees with disabilities. We begin by reviewing the context and current status of testing examinees with disabilities, using "comparability" as a fundamental standard. Next, we assess the implications of computer-based testing for improvements in this comparability. We conclude by introducing the concept of "generalized accommodation" as one avenue for potentially resolving the comparability issues raised by modified tests.

FAIRNESS IN TESTING

In 1973, Congress passed the Rehabilitation Act, Public Law 93-112. Section 504 of that act called for nondiscrimination on the basis of handicap in all programs receiving federal funds.[1] The implementing regulations, which included educational admissions and recruitment, contained several test-related stipulations (Non-discrimination on Basis of Handicap, 1977). First, the regulations essentially required that tests accurately reflect the capabilities of disabled applicants and not their impairments (except where those impairments overlapped with the skills the tests were intended to measure). Second, in the event of adverse impact, tests were

---

[1]   In its entirety, Section 504 states, "No otherwise qualified handicapped individual in the United States as defined in Section 7(6), shall, solely by reason of handicap, be excluded from the participation in, be denied the benefits of, or be subjected to discrimination under any program or activity receiving federal financial assistance."

to be validated with samples of disabled examinees as predictors of success for the programs in question. Finally, the regulations prohibited inquiry about an applicant's disability status.

Section 504 introduced an immediate conflict, for it assumed that tests could be modified (e.g., translated to Braille) and still produce scores comparable to those from standard administrations. Absent data, testing programs could not guarantee comparability and so included the designation, "NON STD," on score reports (Sherman & Robinson, 1983), thereby violating Section 504's preadmission inquiry prohibition. Recognizing the conflict, the U.S. Office of Civil Rights (OCR) took two actions. It endorsed interim guidelines permitting "flagging" on a temporary basis (Redden, Levering, DiQuinzio, & the Task Force on a Model Admissions Policy, 1978), and it called for a blue-ribbon panel to study the issue.

In response to OCR's request, the National Academy of Sciences appointed a Panel on Testing of Handicapped People in 1979 to reconcile the law's requirements with available testing technology and practice. The Panel's report, released in 1983, concluded that the then-current psychometric theory and practice did not allow full compliance (Sherman & Robinson, 1983). Nevertheless, the panel asserted that the technical problems could be solved and recommended that testing agencies be compelled to complete the necessary studies within 4 years.

Answering the panel's recommendation, Educational Testing Service (ETS) began a program of research supported in collaboration with its two major admissions test sponsors, the College Board and the Graduate Record Examinations Board. The primary concern of this effort was test fairness, which Warren Willingham (1986, 1988a) argued was best indicated by "comparability." Willingham saw comparability as having two components. *Score* comparability was a psychometric construction implying like *meaning and interpretation* of test performance (but not necessarily equivalent score levels) across population groups. Willingham (1986, 1988a) posited that score comparability could be examined empirically through studies of reliability, factor structure, item functioning, predicted performance, and admissions decisions. That is, scores would be comparable if, across population groups, they had similar measurement precision, assessed the same underlying constructs, were free of item classes that operated differentially, had similar predictive relations with important external criteria, and encouraged the same inferences by decision makers.

The second component, *task* comparability, implies equivalence in the cognitive demands placed on the individual by the admissions testing task (Willingham, 1988a). The analysis of task comparability requires consideration of the appropriateness of test content, accommodations, and timing. So, the test should be free of material that is inaccessible by virtue of its presentation or that calls upon experience atypical for one of the groups (unless that experience or accessibility is central to the purpose of the measure). Additionally, the availability of ancillary services (e.g., test preparation materials), physical arrangements at the center, and the importance of speed in responding should be as close as possible for both groups.

While studies based on these comparability notions were being conducted, the 1985 edition of the *Standards for Educational and Psychological Testing* (American Educational Research Association, American Psychological Association, National Council on Measurement in Education, 1985) was released. This document lent professional legitimacy to the flagging dilemma by concluding that "until test scores can be demonstrated to be comparable in some widely accepted sense, there is little hope of happily resolving...the issue of reporting scores with or without special identification " (p. 78). Additionally, the *Standards* required test publishers to issue "cautionary statements in manuals and elsewhere" regarding the interpretation of such scores, but stopped short of explicitly sanctioning flagging (Standard 14.2, p. 79).

Three years after the *Standards'* release, the results of the ETS studies were published as *Testing Handicapped People* (Willingham, Ragosta, Bennett, Braun, Rock, & Powers, 1988b), one of the most comprehensive investigations of selection tests for examinees with disabilities ever carried out. Conducted with the then-current version of the Scholastic Assessment Test (SAT) and the paper-and-pencil Graduate Record Examinations (GRE), this work found that scores from nonstandard tests were generally comparable to those from standard ones (Willingham, 1988b), although some noncomparability in test scores was associated with the provision of extra time.[2]   Although this source of noncomparability appeared to affect both admissions tests, the evidence was clearer for the SAT, which had a much larger database.

Several lines of evidence pointed to timing. Examinees with disabilities who took extended-time tests were more likely than nondisabled examinees taking the standard administrations to (1) finish, (2) find items near the end differentially easy, and (3) have their subsequent college grades overpredicted. This last finding was particularly true for students with learning disabilities, by far the largest group using modified examinations. Among these students, overprediction rose as the amount of extra time increased. Also, no overprediction was found when those same students' grades were projected from their high school records, suggesting that the noncomparability was localized to the test.[3]

Willingham (1988b) pointed out that this source of noncomparability was, in

---

[2]   Other instances of noncomparability were detected but not as easily linked to the test. For example, the subsequent performance of deaf students who attended a special college program was substantially underpredicted by modified versions of the SAT (even to some degree when scores were combined with high school grades). This result could be because English, akin to a second language for many such students, is not the primary mode of communication in special college programs. Alternatively, it could be associated with differences in grading practice between the segregated program and the mainstream one on which the prediction equation was based.

[3]   Further indication of noncomparability for this group comes from research on the ACT Assessment, the Law School Admission Test, and a subsequent study of the SAT, each of which also found learning disabled students' college grades to be overpredicted (Farmer & Laing, 1987; Ragosta, Braun, & Kaplan, 1991; Wightman, 1993; Ziomek & Andrews, 1996).

theory, correctable by adjusting time limits for modified tests such that examinees with disabilities finished in similar proportions to nondisabled examinees taking the standard examination. This suggestion was consistent with the *Standards*, which recommended that time limits be empirically based rather than simply set as a multiple of the standard allocation (AERA, APA, NCME, 1985, p. 79). For this suggestion to be workable would require a system composed of timing guidelines for each of several disability-by-test-condition categories, a mechanism for departing from those guidelines to satisfy individual circumstances, and a method for assuring that only those with legitimate need received this modification.

With the passage of the Americans with Disabilities Act of 1990 (PL-101336), testing provisions similar to the 504 regulations were universally extended (Nondiscrimination on the Basis of Disability by Public Accommodations and In Commercial Facilities, 1991).[4] This extension prompted the American Psychological Association's Division of Evaluation, Measurement and Statistics to question publicly whether the comparability goal could be achieved (Division 5 APA, 1993). Their statement, which covered educational as well as employment tests, raised two primary concerns. The first was that modified tests may measure different attributes for examinees with and without disabilities (i.e., the accommodation may change the cognitive demands of the task as, for example, occurs when differential time limits cause speed of responding to be more important for one group than another). Second, even if the same attributes are measured, there is no standard method for equating the scores, a point on which the ETS research strongly agreed (e.g., Powers & Willingham, 1988). As for flagging, the statement recognized the complexity of the issues involved but conceded that it might be justified under some circumstances, particularly in the presence of strong evidence for over or underprediction (Division 5 APA, 1993, p. 13).

Where do testing programs stand on the flagging issue? Those who direct programs would probably agree that flagging should be permitted to continue, for they must view comparability also from the perspective of the integrity of the admissions testing process and fairness to examinees generally (Willingham, 1988b). Program directors perceive the potential for increased abuse if flagging is restricted (Willingham, 1989). Especially troublesome is the case of learning disabilities, for which diagnosis often cannot be made with reasonable certainty (Shepard, 1989) and for which abuse has been reported (e.g., see Dribben, 1996; The Learning Disability Scam, 1996; Machan, 1996; Rubin, 1996). In the testing programs' view, the flag can deter dishonest students from employing this

---

[4] Unlike 504, the ADA regulations contain no specific language on preadmission inquiry or on validation for the educational program in question (Nondiscrimination on the Basis of Disability by Public Accommodations and In Commercial Facilities, 1990). However, ADA does not absolve those covered under Section 504 from the latter's mandates. Testing programs, which often do not receive federal funds, are impacted by 504 indirectly as their user institutions almost invariably do accept government support.

diagnostic uncertainty to increase their scores through extra time. Although attempts have been made to design a workable system using empirically based time limits and stricter eligibility criteria (e.g., Ragosta & Wendler, 1992; Wright & Wendler, 1994), the current legal consensus is that timing decisions are best made on a case–by–case basis. Hence, most programs continue to identify scores from modified administrations under the original interim waiver of the 504 preadmission inquiry regulation (Redden, Levering, DiQuinzio, & the Task Force on a Model Admissions Policy, 1978).[5]

COMPARABILITY AND COMPUTER–BASED TESTING

As the above context suggests, score and task comparability have not yet been achieved for modified versions of paper-and-pencil admissions tests. What is the situation for computer-based tests? Because it is empirically based, score comparability takes time to assess. Computer-based testing is a relatively recent phenomenon and few examinees with disabilities have participated, so no score comparability studies have been published.[6]

From the perspective of *task* comparability, CBT offers substantial promise. One reason is that computers have become life-style accommodations for many people with disabilities. Those who have difficulty using a pencil can often use a word processor instead; those who cannot read text can have it directed to a speech synthesizer, Braille printer, or Braille display; and those who can't get around physically can get around virtually--working, playing, learning, or communicating through electronic networks. To help disabled users in these pursuits, an industry has evolved that produces dozens of alternative devices for getting information into and out of personal computers.

Because computers play a central role in the lives of many people with disabilities, these machines may offer a natural way to test--more so than paper-and-pencil methods. As a result, ETS' CBT programs now permit eligible examinees to use such alternative input devices as a trackball, a head-mounted mouse emulator, or an enlarged keyboard that duplicates the functions of both the mouse and the standard console. Examinees may magnify portions of the screen, change the foreground and background colors to get appropriate contrast, and have

---

[5] The flagging story is not over. A recent development is the extension of extra time by some professional licensing programs to examinees with limited English proficiency (Kirsch, personal communication, January 19, 1995). Putting aside the soundness of such an extension, it is interesting to speculate on the consequences were admissions testing programs to follow suit. One outcome would be an increase in the proportion of noncomparable scores--probably not a desirable result. A second would be to make the flag less useful as an identifier of disability status which, from the 504 perspective, is perhaps more positive.

[6] From July 1993 to December 1994, the computer-based GRE General Test was taken by some 71,000 examinees, of which just over 300 were special administrations (Gioella, personal communication, January 17, 1995). From April 1994 to December 1994, 200 out of 155,000 candidates took special administrations of the National Council Licensure Examinations for nurses.

computer equipment placed on a special surface that can be adjusted to any of a variety of positions.

These accommodations are only initial steps toward a more complete CBT infrastructure that provides full access to those with disabilities (ETS Conference, 1992). Such an infrastructure might, for example, include multi-modal tests that make information available through various representational systems (D. Forer, personal communication, August 18, 1993). Test directions and help functions would be redundantly encoded as text, audio, video, and Braille, with the choice of representation(s) left to the examinee. The digital audio would allow for spoken directions, whereas the video could present instructions in sign-language or speech-readable form (e.g., Loeding & Crittenden, 1994). Among other things, these standardized presentations should reduce the noncomparability associated with the uneven quality of human readers and sign-language interpreters (Ragosta & Kaplan, 1988).

Although CBT programs have taken important steps to become accessible, there are trends that could negatively affect task comparability. One such trend is toward graphical user interfaces, in which actions are represented by icons and initiated using a mouse. These interfaces are enormously popular, as evidenced by the success of Microsoft Windows. Intended to make computers easier to use, graphical interfaces are especially valuable in the presence of response complexity.

Response complexity is, of course, one common characteristic of performance assessment, toward which CBT is moving from its predominantly multiple-choice roots. The pressure for this movement is great, as the education community calls for tests more in keeping with a constructivist approach to instruction (e.g., Wiggins, 1993). In the CBT environment, some examples might involve typing a word, sentence, or essay; moving objects on the display to create a simulated electrical circuit; or selecting symbols from an on-screen array to build a mathematical expression. Some rudimentary performance tasks have already been introduced and development of more elaborate ones is well underway (e.g., Bennett, Steffen, Singley, Morley, & Jacquemin, 1997; Bejar & Braun, 1994).

Although response complexity may be necessary to assess some valued types of problem solving, it can also threaten task comparability, especially for examinees with physical impairments. In particular, the need to enter lengthy character strings or precisely manipulate screen objects may introduce irrelevant difficulty. Simplifying the interactions by using graphical interfaces is not a fully effective solution as it may, in turn, impede blind candidates (Coombs, 1995). As CBT developers, our challenge will be to design interactions from the test's inception that are equally easy for all (e.g., by using icons that identify themselves multi-modally through text messages and speech). In addition, we'll need to make effective tutorial instruction widely available for whatever particular machine-human interactions such performance tasks require.

CBT has not only changed the mechanics of how the examinee interacts with the test but it has the potential to change the timing constraints, again with important implications for comparability. Because paper-and-pencil tests were administered to large groups in single sittings, timing had to satisfy opposing constraints. These constraints were (1) allowing most examinees to finish and (2) not detaining too long those who completed early. (Permitting the latter group to move on to the next separately timed section while the former was still working on the previous one would be administratively unworkable.) Most programs choose to err in the direction of not detaining early completers, so the typical timing for admissions tests introduces some speededness (Willingham, 1988b, pp. 177-178). For the SAT in particular, the ETS studies suggested that the modified paper-and-pencil test was more of a power measure for examinees with disabilities precisely because of the amount of extra time involved (see, e.g., Bennett, Rock, Kaplan, & Jirele, 1988, pp. 89-90).

Rather than being given in groups, computer-based tests are administered individually. As a result, time limits can, in principle, be set to eliminate the role of speed in performance. Two factors currently work against this outcome. Some programs, such as the GRE, retain a degree of speededness to preserve links with paper-and-pencil versions (e.g., Schaeffer, Steffen, Golub-Smith, Mills, & Durso, 1994, p. 18). As programs eliminate these paper-and-pencil counterparts, such linking will become unnecessary. A more stubborn problem, however, may be affordability: Programs pay for the use of commercially owned CBT centers on an examinee-time basis. How much more liberal time limits for all examinees can become without threatening the economic viability of CBT is not clear. Even so, the general sentiment appears to be toward reducing speed as a performance factor and, coincidentally, to achieving greater task comparability.

TOWARD GENERALIZED ACCOMMODATION

Many changes are occurring in our society to accommodate people with disabilities. As a result of Section 504, and the more recent Americans with Disabilities Act, curb cuts are appearing in cities and small towns, audio cues help identify the floors in elevators, buses kneel closer to the sidewalk, and ramps have become almost seamlessly embedded in new buildings. These modifications have made the "tasks" of daily living more comparable by making physical access easier.

It is noteworthy that the modifications are not simply add-ons restricted to those with disabilities but are instead integral components. Consequently, the way *nondisabled* people interact with the environment has changed too, even if only subtly. Nondisabled individuals use the curb cuts, the ramps, and the kneeling buses--often thankfully, when laden with packages, children, or simply fatigue. (And the elevator audio cues appear effective also, alerting those lost in thought just in time to make the proper exit.)

These environmental modifications were made in keeping with the "full inclusion" principle, the notion that regardless of severity, individuals with disabilities should be guaranteed access to the activities, benefits, and services that all other members of our society are granted. As in Brown vs. Board of Education, full inclusion does *not* suggest "separate-but-equal" treatment. Rather, it connotes the general adaptation of existing structures to make them usable by all. That the principle can succeed is illustrated by the fact that general modifications have made such tasks of daily living as getting onto and off of buses and into and out of elevators more comparable for those with and without disabilities. Who pays for these modifications? We all do. But, arguably, we all benefit by having a fairer society, as well as adaptations most of us can use.[7]

Algozzine (1993) maintains that the full inclusion principle should be applied to testing by avoiding any practices that create separation among groups. For Algozzine, all students should be expected to take all tests and any modifications allowed for one student should be permitted for all.

At first glance, Algozzine's assertion may seem impractical, if not hopelessly naive. However, upon deeper reflection it becomes more meaningful, for in the future it may be possible to relax CBT time limits generally, thereby moving closer to task (and score) comparability. Thus, it may be appropriate to ask how we might fully include all examinees in testing programs by changing assessment practices that, now inviolate, could with the proper innovation prove generally modifiable. For the framers of the next generation of computer-based admissions tests, this should be a timely question.

CONCLUSION

We have contended that CBT offers an important opportunity to make admissions testing fairer for examinees with disabilities, particularly by improving task comparability. Generalized accommodation is one conceivable avenue to such improvement. At the same time, work on score comparability should continue, including the exploration of methods for adjusting test results statistically (see Division 5 APA, 1993, p. 9, and Geisinger, 1994, for some possibilities).

As Willingham (1986) noted, score and task comparability go hand in hand; among other things, empirical evidence on scores informs judgment about how to structure the admissions testing task and that judgment in turn guides new data collection. Thanks to Willingham, a substantial amount of empirical work and logical analysis has been done for paper-and-pencil tests, making possible nascent thinking about the comparability of CBTs. Whether timing persists as the primary source of noncomparability, and whether other unwanted variation is rising to replace it, are pertinent empirical questions. In the interest of fairness, the

---

[7] The full inclusion principle is by no means universally accepted. For arguments against its application to the education of students with disabilities, see Fuchs and Fuchs (1994/1995) and Shanker (1994/1995). For the proponents' view, see Wang Reynolds, and Walberg (1994/1995).

investigative process should continue with an eye toward the significant prospects for betterment that CBT brings.

ACKNOWLEDGMENTS

Appreciation is expressed to Bill Ward, Doug Forer, Catherine Nelson, and Pat Taylor for their helpful comments on a previous draft of this manuscript, and to Brent Bridgeman and Craig Mills for their suggestions.

REFERENCES

Algozzine, B. (1993). Including students with disabilities in systemic efforts to measure outcomes: Why ask why? In National Center on Educational Outcomes (Ed.), *Views on inclusion and testing accommodations for students with disabilities* (pp. 5-10). Minneapolis, MN: National Center on Educational Outcomes.

American Educational Research Association, American Psychological Association, National Council on Measurement in Education. (1985). *Standards for Educational and Psychological Testing.* Washington, DC: American Psychological Association.

Bejar, I., & Braun, H. I. (1994). On the synergy between assessment and instruction: Early lessons from computer-based simulations. *Machine Mediated Learning, 4,* 5-15.

Bennett, R. E., Rock, D. A., Kaplan, B. A., & Jirele, T. (1988). Psychometric characteristics. In W. W. Willingham, M. Ragosta, R. E. Bennett, H. I. Braun, D. A. Rock, & D. E. Powers, *Testing Handicapped People* (pp. 83-97). Boston, MA: Allyn & Bacon.

Bennett, R. E., Steffen, M., Singley, M. K., Morley, M., & Jacquemin, D. (1997). Evaluating an automatically scorable, open-ended response type for measuring mathematical reasoning in computer-adaptive tests. *Journal of Educational Measurement, 34,* 162-176.

Coombs, N. (1995). Closing the windows on opportunity. *Educom Review, 30*(2), 28-29.

Division 5, American Psychological Association. (1993). Psychometric and assessment issues raised by the American with Disabilities Act (ADA). *The Score, 15(4),* 1-2, 7-15.

Dribben, M. (1996, October 10). Getting an edge on the SATs, etc. *The Philadelphia Inquirer*, p. B1.

ETS conference examines the technology of computer-based testing for people with disabilities. (1992, Fall). *ETS Developments*, 6-7.

Farmer, M., & Laing, J. (1987). Characteristics of students with learning disabilities who take the ACT Assessment under special conditions. *Journal of Postsecondary Education and Disability, 5,* 27-32.

Fuchs, D., & Fuchs, L. S. (1994/1995). Sometimes separate is better. *Educational Leadership, 52*(4), 22-26.

Geisinger, K. F. (1994). Psychometric issues in testing students with disabilities. *Applied Measurement in Education, 7,* 121-140.

The learning disability scam. (1996, March 18). *New York Magazine, 29,* 11-12.

Loeding, B. L., & Crittenden, J. B. (1994). The development of SHIPS: an interactive videodisc assessment for youth who use sign language. *Exceptional Children, 61,* 148-158.

Machan, D. (1996, August 12). An agreeable affliction. *Forbes.* Available online: http://www.forbes.com/forbes/081296/5804148a.htm

Nondiscrimination on the basis of handicap, 42 Fed. Reg. 22676 (1977).

Nondiscrimination on the basis of disability by public accommodations and in commerical facilities, 28 C.F.R. Part 36 (1991).

Powers, D. E., & Willingham, W. W. (1988). The feasibility of rescaling. In W. W. Willingham, M. Ragosta, R. E. Bennett, H. I. Braun, D. A. Rock, & D. E. Powers (Eds.), *Testing handicapped people* (pp. 133-142). Boston, MA: Allyn & Bacon.

Ragosta, M., Braun, H., & Kaplan, B. (1991). *Performance and persistence: A validity study of the SAT for students with disabilities* (CBR-91-3). New York: College Entrance Examination Board.

Ragosta, M., & Kaplan, B. A. (1988). Views of disabled students. In W. W. Willingham, M. Ragosta, R. E. Bennett, H. I. Braun, D. A. Rock, & D. E. Powers (Eds.), *Testing handicapped people* (pp. 59-70). Boston, MA: Allyn & Bacon.

Ragosta, M., & Wendler, C. (1992). *Eligibility issues and comparable time limits for disabled and nondisabled SAT examinees* (CBR-92-5). New York: College Entrance Examination Board.

Redden, M., Levering, C., Diquinzio, D., & the Task Force on a Model Admissions Policy. (1978). *Recruitment, admissions, and handicapped students: A guide for compliance with Section 504 of the Rehabilitation Act of 1973.* Washington, DC: American Association of Collegiate Registrars and Admissions Officers and the American Council on Education.

Rubin, B. M. (1996, April 14). Learning disability the new 'advantage.' *The Chicago Tribune,* p. 10.

Schaeffer, G. A., Steffen, M., Golub-Smith, M. L., Mills, C. N., & Durso, R. (1994). *The introduction and comparability of the computer adaptive GRE General Test* (GRE Board Professional Report 88-08a). Princeton, NJ: Educational Testing Service.

Shanker, A. (1994/1995). Full inclusion is neither free nor appropriate. *Educational Leadership, 52*(4), 18-21.

Shepard, L. A. (1989). Identification of mild handicaps. In R. L. Linn (Ed.), *Educational measurement* (3rd ed., pp. 545-572). New York: American Council on Education/Macmillan.

Sherman, S. W., & Robinson, N. M. (1983). *Ability testing of handicapped people: Dilemma for government, science, and the public.* Washington, DC: National Academy Press.

Wang, M. C., Reynolds, M. C., & Walberg, H. J. (1994/1995). Serving students at the margins. *Educational Leadership, 52*(4), 12-17.

Wiggins, G. (1993). Assessment: Authenticity, context, and validity. *Phi Delta Kappan, 75*(3), 200-214.

Wightman, L. F. (1993). *Test takers with disabilities: A summary of data from special administrations of the LSAT.* Newtown, PA: Law School Admissions Services.

Willingham, W. W. (1986). Testing handicapped people--The validity issue. In H. Wainer & H. I. Braun (Eds.), *Test validity* (pp. 89-103). Hillsdale, NJ: Lawrence Erlbaum.

Willingham, W. W. (1988a). Introduction. In W. W. Willingham, M. Ragosta, R. E. Bennett, H. I. Braun, D. A. Rock, & D. E. Powers (Eds.), *Testing handicapped people* (pp. 1-15). Boston, MA: Allyn & Bacon.

Willingham, W. W. (1988b). Discussion and conclusions. In W. W. Willingham, M. Ragosta, R. E. Bennett, H. I. Braun, D. A. Rock, & D. E. Powers (Eds.), *Testing handicapped people* (pp. 143-185). Boston, MA: Allyn & Bacon.

Willingham, W. W. (1989). Standard testing conditions and standard score meaning for handicapped examinees. *Applied Measurement in Education, 2*, 97-103.

Willingham, W. W., Ragosta, M., Bennett, R. E., Braun, H., Rock, D. A., & Powers, D. E. (Eds.). (1988). *Testing handicapped people.* Boston, MA: Allyn & Bacon.

Wright, N., & Wendler, C. (1994, April). *Establishing time limits for the new SAT for students with disabilities.* Paper presented at the annual meeting of the National Council on Measurement in Education, New Orleans.

Ziomek, R. L., & Andrews, K. M. (1996). *Predicting the college grade point averages of special-tested students from their ACT Assessment scores and high school grades* (ACT RR-96-7). Iowa City, IA: ACT.

15

DIRECTIONS IN THE ASSESSMENT OF LINGUISTIC MINORITIES

Richard P. Durán

University of California, Santa Barbara

My professional association with Warren Willingham began when I undertook a study sponsored by the College Board regarding the population validity of college admissions tests for use with Hispanic populations. This led to a monograph entitled, *Hispanics' Education and Background: Predictors of College Achievement* (Durán, 1983). Most significantly, this 1983 monograph included a synthesis of research on Hispanics' schooling achievement and educational attainment and their relation to socioeconomic and sociolinguistic background factors. This direction proved productive, for it was responsive to College Board's careful and timely review of college preparation issues among Latinos. The direction coincided as well with the view of many minority education researchers calling for such a review in the context of interpreting college admissions test scores. The direction was also responsive to Latinos outside ETS who claimed that ETS and the College Board were recalcitrant to undertake such a review that might question the validity of the SAT for Latinos.

The main findings were that one measure of predictive efficiency, namely, the squared validity coefficient between admissions test scores and grades, indicated about 9 percent less predictive accuracy for Latino as opposed to non-Latino students at the same institutions. I did not systematically review evidence of lack of predictive accuracy based on differences in the standard error of measurement for prediction--an alternative method for addressing this issue. However, Maria Pennock-Roman later undertook research of this sort, but using different data, and found no major differences in error of prediction for Latino and non-Latino students in the samples of students she investigated (Pennock-Roman, 1990).

The College Board study I undertook was a means to a further end. It allowed me to expand the issue of validity of the SAT so as to consider a broader set of educational issues that needed airing regarding obstacles that Latinos faced in progressing through the educational system--issues that Latino and minority education researchers believed needed the attention of testing firms and institutional test developers. This was in keeping with developing views that test validation should take into account the social and educational consequences of test use (Messick, 1989, 1995). I believe that the main outcome of my research was to point to the importance of exploring educational interventions aiding Latino and other linguistic minority high school students and to ways to create accompanying assessments improving the quality and depth of our understanding of students' cognitive and linguistic preparation for college.

IMPROVING ASSESSMENT OF NON-ENGLISH BACKGROUND STUDENTS

In 1985 in collaboration with Mary Enright and Donald Rock (Durán, Enright, &, Rock, 1985), I published a research study sponsored by the College Board surveying connections between the language background of Latino SAT test takers and their College Board test scores. At the time, the College Board Student Descriptive Questionnaire contained one question on language background: SDQ # 38, "Is English your best language? (yes or no)". One research issue addressed was whether students' self-appraisal of their English language ability for academic purposes was more related to SAT test scores than answers to question 38. The English ability questions on the survey probed students' self-appraisal of speaking, writing, reading, and listening skills in academic contexts.

The results showed that responses to SDQ 38 correlated under .20 with SAT Verbal test scores, while the median correlation of responses to academic English ability questions with SAT Verbal scores was .36. Responses to one of the English ability self-rating questions (How well do I understand vocabulary terms I read?) correlated .45 with SAT Verbal test scores—a rather high correlation of a magnitude similar to the high relationship encountered between SAT test scores and college grades.

This survey study also found that the correlations of Test of Standard Written English (TSWE) scores with responses to SDQ question 38 were lower than correlations between TSWE scores and self appraisals of academic English ability—the median correlation was .34 for the latter. Responses to one academic English ability question regarding use of appropriate grammar in writing correlated .43 with TSWE scores, again of a similar magnitude as relationships encountered between SAT test scores and grades.

The results cited offer some useful insights and directions for further investigation. If we want to understand how English ability affects readiness for college, we need to probe more deeply into the ways that particular English skills are tied to the demands of academic work.

The National Assessment of Educational Progress (NAEP) has also provided useful information on the readiness of ethnic minority subgroups to perform at advanced proficiency levels in reading or mathematical problem solving based on knowledge of English for academic purposes. Data (e.g., from the 1987-88 NAEP) indicated that Hispanic high school students have more difficulty in reading comprehension and reasoning than non-Hispanic White students. Over 46 percent of non-Hispanic White students scored at the "Adept" level of reading achievement on the NAEP reading achievement test as compared to just over 24 percent of Hispanic students (U.S. Department of Education, 1991). The "Adept" level was defined as being "able to find, understand, summarize, and explain relatively complicated literary and informational material." Latino high school students, as would be expected given this lag, also lagged behind non-Hispanic White students in scoring at an "Advanced" level on the NAEP reading assessment. A little over one percent of Hispanic students scored at this level as compared to nearly six percent of non-Hispanic White students. The "Advanced" level was defined as being "able to understand the links between ideas even when those links are not explicitly stated and to make appropriate generalizations even when the texts lack clear introductions or explanations." More recent NAEP data from 1992 and 1994 corroborate these findings (U.S. Department of education, 1995). Taken at face value these data suggest that Latino high school students as a group are sorely underprepared both to comprehend English and to reason in English as would be required in college.

Research on NAEP 8th-Grade Mathematics Items

The National Center for Research on Evaluation, Standards, & Student Testing has sponsored informative research on the relationship between English language demands of NAEP 8th-grade mathematics test items and the performance of English and non-English background students on test items. In this work, Jamel Abedi (1994) and linguist colleagues at UCLA analyzed NAEP mathematics test items recording the incidence of:

- low-frequency vocabulary use of the passive voice,
- use of lengthy nominal phrases,
- use of conditional clauses,
- use of relative clauses,
- complex phrasing of questions, and
- abstract as opposed to concrete wording.

The research then examined performance of students on mathematics items and found that non-English background students performed somewhat more poorly than English background students on NAEP mathematics test items heavily utilizing the foregoing features of English. A follow up study found that elimination of these features led to improved performance on items by both non-English and English background students, with greater effects for non-English background students. The research program merits replication given that the findings reached only marginal statistical significance. Nonetheless, the results suggest that lack of familiarity with particular kinds of English structures is related to lower academic test performance.

ALTERNATIVE PARADIGMS FOR CONSTRUCT VALIDITY RESEARCH

The research just described suggests two main lines of inquiry informing improved assessment design in the service of improving academic preparation of non-English background students. One direction is related to application of information processing cognitive research to the design of diagnostic and dynamic assessments. The second direction is tied to qualitative study of the acquisition of critical communicative skills in naturalistic teaching and learning contexts.

Cognitive Information Processing Research

Not surprisingly, research with non-English language learners suggests that they expend more effort in recognizing the structural features of English than native English speakers and that this extra effort may depress or alter the English verbal problem-solving performance of non-native English speakers when they have limited knowledge of the subject matter at hand. Research has begun to identify and probe specific linguistic difficulties encountered by students and has also uncovered evidence of adaptive information-processing strategies used by students to compensate for difficulties in comprehending reading-comprehension test items and academic texts.

For example, Durán, O'Connor, and Smith (1988), drawing on the work of Fillmore (1983) and Kay (1987), analyzed protocols from seventh-grade Latino language minority students as they worked sample reading–comprehension test items drawn from popular standardized reading tests. Students read English test–item passages in a line-by-line manner, and they were asked to reason aloud about what they understood and what might come next in a passage. They were also asked to explain how they picked multiple–choice answers to questions based on a test–item passage. Qualitative analysis of students' protocols and responses to the examiner's question-probes showed that students' multiple–choice responses to questions were not often consistent with accounts of how students reasoned as they read. In particular, students' incorrect answers were often strategic. Wrong answers often revealed careful reasoning by students about how to answer questions given what was understood from a text and assumptions about the meaning of material not fully understood. Students' on-line reading and reasoning performance was found to be affected by their ability to:

1)   envision the meaning of a text as a whole;
2)   resolve the meaning of individual words and phrases;
3)   recognize and reason from the genre of a passage;
4)   call up relevant cognitive schemata appropriate for understanding a passage; and
5)   recognize grammatical and rhetorical features organizing a passage given a genre.

As another instance, Collins and Smith (1982), in a synthesis of reading–comprehension research and metacognition, identify specific cognitive strategies used by readers encountering comprehension difficulties, strategies that resonate with the findings of the foregoing research. These strategies apply to readers regardless of language background and include:

- ignoring an uncomprehended word, sentence, or relationship and continuing to read on;
- suspending judgment about what a word or sentence or a relationship means;
- forming a tentative hypothesis about a meaning;
- rereading the current sentence or sentences;
- skipping-back and rereading text from a previous context; and,
- getting help from an expert source.

The interaction of specific strategies of this sort with text and learner characteristics has been investigated with ESL (English as a second language) students and non-ESL students at the college level. Goldman and Durán (1988) presented oceanography text passages and passage questions to students taking courses in this subject-matter area. They presented passages on a computer screen in sentence segments and tracked students selection of portions of a text passage to re-read. As students made their decision about whether and what to review from a text, they spoke aloud about how they were trying to answer a text question at hand. Analysis of native English and ESL students' protocols and responses to questions and patterns of text search revealed that all students just beginning study of the subject matter (oceanography) read the passage very differently from students with more experience in the subject matter. Beginning students matched the terms occurring in questions with the same terms in a passage when first initiating work on answering a question. In contrast, students who had studied more of the subject matter were more likely to rely on memory as they began answering questions. Regardless of expertise in the subject matter, ESL students tended to expend more effort on understanding a target passage. These students were more likely to reread a passage and to search through it for specific information that might be relevant to answering a question.

A series of studies by Goldman (1988) investigated native English background and ESL program students' ability to recall a sequence of ideas introduced in text passages from a psychology text as it unfolded on a computer video screen. Passages were taken from real psychology texts and were modified so as to systematically manipulate the occurrence and non-occurrence of sequential connector terms (e.g. "first," "second", "next", etc.) marking enumeration of ideas in a passage. The results of the research showed that *both* native English users and ESL students used a mixture of three global reading strategies: a) read a text all the way through and quit; b) read a text all the way through and then go back and reread portions; and c) stop and reread as you go through a text.

ESL students, however, spent more time in strategies involving rereading of a text. The results also showed that all students, regardless of language background, recalled passage information somewhat better when it was foregrounded by a sequence marker; however, occurrence or non- occurrence of sequence markers had little effect on the recall of ESL students who were classified as having the least proficiency in English.

Another series of studies by Goldman and Murray (1989, 1992) investigated native English and ESL students' ability to complete cloze items in psychology text passages that required selecting an appropriate logical connector term. The terms signaled additive (e.g. "in addition"), adversative (e.g., "however"), causal (e.g., "because"), and sequential (e.g., "next") relations among adjoining clauses. Protocols were collected from students regarding how they made decisions to fill-in cloze items. These protocols were analyzed subsequently in order to gain information about the reasoning of students as they chose an appropriate connector term from a list representing each possible connector type. The results showed that native English students were more likely to make a correct connector choice than ESL students and that native English students also showed significantly higher confidence ratings about judgments than ESL students for correct responses involving adversative and sequential connectors. ESL students appeared to be aware of the isolated meaning of alternative connectors outside of their occurrence in a text, but they showed difficulty in identifying the logical relationship required to adjoin clauses in a text passages using those same connectors. Other research on the verbal reasoning of high school students suggests that these students show a similar pattern of correct and incorrect judgments when solving conditional reasoning problems, but that non-English background students do not perform as well as English background students (Durán, Revlin, & Havill, 1995).

Qualitative Study of the Acquisition of Critical Communicative Skills in Naturalistic Teaching and Learning Contexts

While psycholinguistic studies of text comprehension and reasoning strategies of English language learners have proven informative, they typically involve tasks and materials that simulate rather than sample authentic academic reading assignments. Because of this their findings *may or may not* generalize to authentic academic activity. A number of educators and investigators have found value in addressing issues pertinent to the assessment of language minority students through including qualitative study of communication practices in academic classrooms (see e.g., Moss, 1996, for a discussion of the need for such a reapproachment).

In his book, *Lives on the Boundary*, Rose (1989) discusses the language problems of entering freshman at UCLA who come from language minority and inner-city backgrounds. He suggests that many of the academic difficulties of these students are tied to students' lack of socialization to academic culture. The reading difficulties of students are not just a matter of insufficient knowledge of English structure and rhetorical organization. More deeply, these difficulties are tied to understanding the purpose of academic tasks and to the ability of students to realize the social role appropriate to interaction in the classroom as well as to the ability to establish a relationship with the voice of text authors. These issues were investigated by Kris Gutierrez (1995) in her Ph.D. research. She reported that Latino college students enrolled in remedial English courses were given language arts remedial assignments utilizing prepackaged worksheets and workbooks emphasizing learning of word decoding and grammatical rules. Interviews revealed that, prior to college, these students had not had much experience in high school with academic assignments requiring extensive discussion and reasoning from texts and extensive essay writing. Gutierrez concluded that remedial students were ill prepared for college work because they had not been socialized in earlier schooling to engage in higher-order thinking while carrying out academic assignments. Research on the development of language skills among bilinguals and second language learners supports the notion that language acquisition can occur effectively when learners are required to participate in meaning-making activities requiring rich interaction with more fluent speakers who model appropriate language use (Krashen 1981; Wong-Fillmore, 1979).

Taken as a whole these findings highlight the intimate connection between the students' appropriation of social identities in the classroom and their communicative competence. The findings suggest that exposing Latino students to cognitively and linguistically undemanding activities does not equip them to acquire communicative competence needed for advanced academic learning. Gutierrez's results suggest that Latino students exposed to remedial tasks, such as isolated word decoding practice, acquire forms of communicative competence tailored specifically for such remedial tasks, along with self-identities as "remedial learners."

DEVELOPMENT OF COMMUNICATIVE COMPETENCE IN THE 4TH GRADE AMONG STUDENTS ACQUIRING ENGLISH

More detailed study of educational survey data such as NAEP indicates that reading comprehension achievement begins to show declines among minority students relative to European-origin students as early as the 4th grade. While the concern of this volume is with college performance and access to college, evidence is emerging from qualitative studies of language use in classrooms that the process of preparing for advanced academic work begins quite early on in the elementary grades for language minority and other students. In an on-going research project we are currently conducting, the goal is to investigate how students acquire academic competence in English and Spanish within a language arts cooperative learning curriculum known as CIRC (Cooperative Integrated Reading and Composition). The target children are 3rd to 5th graders in bilingual education programs. The children in question are just transitioning from Spanish language to English language instruction.

The project is focusing on ways that language and cognitive competence are socially constructed through face-to-face interaction among student peers as well as interaction with a teacher. One of the aims is to develop quantitative and qualitative methods of individualized and group assessment that improve our understanding of how students acquire important *genres* of thinking and language use. Our initial focus has been on how 4th grade students acquire ability to answer questions based on a story they have read. While the 4th-grade might seem far removed from college, we believe that students at this grade level are expected to acquire critical academic language-use skills that are essential to students' long term academic growth along the path towards college preparation. Children's learning how to answer questions based on a text is one of these early demands being studied in detail.

Preliminary findings show that dramatic transformations occur in students' ability to answer questions in a group and individually over the course of the school year. The evidence is both quantitative and qualitative. Quantitative data from pre and post individual measures of question answering capacity show statistically significant improvement in students' performance (Szymanski and Durán, in preparation). Evidence from qualitative research suggests that a teacher's modeling and direct instruction of appropriate question answering is picked up by students as they interact in cooperative groups. For example, students pick up that typical questions start with a linguistic marker such as "what", "who", "when", "why", "where" and "how" that need to be interpreted in light of meaning conveyed by a story text. Students also pickup that answers should be complete sentences and that the start of a written answer should or can be preceded by an "echoing" of the "given" information of a question. Discourse analysis of the teacher's direct instruction to students on how to answer questions and students' cooperative learning interactions reveals that students appropriate the cognitive framing for how to answer questions from the teacher in their own talk in cooperative groups.

Research such as this may lead us to new vistas on how to assess the development of important academic communication skills required for advanced academic functioning among language minority and other students. In pursuit of this goal, we need to consider a developmental approach to the design of innovative assessments that begins to probe how socialization into classroom academic functioning creates a foundation for the development of skills leading to college preparation. Research currently underway suggests that this foundation has its origins in the early elementary grades.

REFERENCES

Abedi, J. (1994). *Language background as a variable in NAEP mathematics performance.* Los Angeles: Center for the Study of Evaluation, UCLA.

Breland, H. (1979). *Population validity and college entrance measures.* New York: The College Board.

Collins, A., & Smith, E. (1982). Teaching in process of reading comprehension. In D. K. Detterman & R. J. Sternberg (Eds.), *How and how much can intelligence be increased* (pp. 173-186). Norwood, NJ: Ablex.

Durán, R. P. (1983). *Hispanics' education and background. Predictors of college achievement.* New York: College Entrance Examination Board.

Durán, R. P., Enright, M. K., & Rock, D. A. (1985). *Language factors and Hispanic freshman's Student Profile.* College Board Report No. 85-3. New York: College Entrance Examination Board.

Durán, R. P., O'Connor, C., & Smith, M. (1988). *Methods for assessing reading comprehension skills of language minority students.* Technical Report, Center for Language Education and Research, University of California, Los Angeles.

Durán, R. P., Revlin, R. & Havill, D. (1995). *Verbal comprehension and reasoning skills of Latino high school students.* Research Report 13. Santa Cruz, CA: National Center for Research on Cultural Diversity and Second Language Learning, University of California, Santa Cruz.

Goldman, S. R. (1988). *The role of sequence markers on reading and learning strategies.* Paper presented at the annual meeting of the American Educational Research Association, New Orleans.

Goldman, S. R. & Durán, R. P. (1988). Answering questions from Oceanography texts: Learner, task and text characteristics. *Discourse Processes, 11,* 373-412.

Goldman, S. R. & Murray, J. (1989). *Knowledge of connectors as cohesion devices in text: A comparative study of native English and ESL speakers* (Report to the Office of Naval Research). Santa Barbara, CA: University of California, Santa Barbara.

Goldman, S. R. & Murray, J. D. (1992). Knowledge of connectors as cohesion devices in text: A comparative study of native-English and English-as-a-second language speakers. *Journal of Educational Psychology, 84*(4), 504-519.

Gutierrez, K. (1995). Unpackaging academic discourse. *Discourse Processes, 19,* 21-37.

Fillmore, C. J. (1983). *Ideal readers and real readers.* (Cognitive Science Report No. 5). Berkeley, CA: University of California, Cognitive Science Program.

Kay, P. (1987). Three properties of the ideal reader. In R. Freedle & R. P. Durán (Eds.), *Cognitive and linguistic analyses of test performance* (pp. 208-244). Norwood, NJ: Ablex.

Krashen, S. D. (1981). *Second language acquisition and second language learning.* New York: Pergamon Press.

Messick, S. (1989). Validity. In R. L. Linn, (Ed.), *Educational measurement* (3rd ed.) (pp. 13-103). New York: Macmillan, 1989

Messick, S. (1995). Validity of psychological assessment: Validation of inferences from persons' responses and performances as scientific inquiry into score meaning. *American Psychologist, 50,* 741-749.

Moss, P. (1996). Enlarging the dialogue in educational measurement: Voices from interpretive research traditions. *Educational Researcher, 25,* 20-28.

Pennock-Roman, M. (1990). *Test validity and language background.* New York: The College Board.

Rose, M. (1989). *Lives on the boundary.* New York: Penguin Books.

Szymanski, M. & Durán, R. P. (in preparation). Literate action among bilingual children.

U.S. Department of Education, National Center for Education Statistics (1995). *NAEP 1994 reading: A first look.* Washington, D.C.

U.S. Department of Education, National Center for Education Statistics (1991). *The condition of education, 1991, Volume 1, elementary and secondary education.* Washington, D.C.

Wong-Fillmore, L. (1979). Individual differences in second language acquisition. In C. Fillmore, D. Kempler and H. Wang (Eds.), *Individual differences in language behavior.* New York: Academic Press.

16

HUMAN DIVERSITY AND EQUITABLE ASSESSMENT

Edmund W. Gordon
Yale University and The College Board

The topic of human diversity and its implications for assessment is extremely complex. In this chapter, I will address just four of the major issues arising in this contentious domain. The first issue concerns the relationship between assessment and pedagogy itself. The second issue has to do with the implications of assessment that grow out of an assertion that the problems of diversity are probably not primarily problems for assessment but problems for education. Third, I will discuss the complexities of diversity as distinct from pluralism, both of which have implications for education and assessment. Finally, I explore some notions of how educational assessment can be made more sensitive and more appropriate for persons from diverse cultural backgrounds.

PROBLEMS OF ASSESSMENT OR OF PEDAGOGY

With respect to the first issue, I argue that the most fundamental problem concerning human diversity and equity in educational assessment has to do with the effectiveness, sufficiency, and adequacy of teaching and learning. When teaching and learning are sufficient, when they are truly effective, most of the problems posed for equitable assessment as a function of diverse human characteristics become manageable. The problems are not eliminated but they at least become manageable when the educational work on the front end is appropriate. Unfortunately, it often is not. It is when teaching and learning are insufficiently effective for the universe of students served that problems arise in the pursuit of equity for diverse human populations. It can be argued that the problems of equity in educational assessment are largely secondary to the failure to achieve equity through educational treatments. However, the fact that equitable educational assessment is only secondarily a problem of assessment does not mean that those of us in the assessment enterprise have no responsibility for doing something constructive.

It is not by accident that existing approaches to standardized assessment of educational achievement are insufficiently sensitive to the diversity of the student population served as well as to pluralism and the social demands placed upon students—shortly, I will clarify what I mean by pluralism. Prevailing standards by which academic competence is judged are calibrated in large measure against either what most people at a specific level of development are considered able to do or what we agree is necessary in order for students to engage effectively in the demands of the next level of work. The fact that some persons have greater difficulty than others and seem unable to achieve these standards is usually thought to be a problem in the individual or reflective of group differences in abilities. It is not often thought to be a problem of the appropriateness of the assessment instruments or of educational practices.

In our efforts to be responsive to diverse learning characteristics and plural social standards, prevailing wisdom suggests that there may be limits to what can be done to design and develop sensitive assessment technology and procedures. We may be able to make the assessment processes more instructive; we may make them more supportive of diverse learning experiences; we may find more varied contexts and vehicles through which students can demonstrate their competencies; the items can be made more process sensitive and could give less emphasis to narrowly defined products. But in the final analysis, any assessment procedure is most likely to reveal the effectiveness of the teaching and learning to which students have been exposed. Thus the facts of diversity and pluralism may have more serious implications for teaching and learning than for equitable educational assessment technology and practice.

Previously, I asserted that this does not mean that those of us in the assessment community are off the hook. What I think it does mean is that both the teaching and learning end and the assessment end need to give greater attention to better understanding of the complexities of human diversity.

COMPLEXITIES OF DIVERSITY AND PLURALISM

When I speak of diversity of human characteristics, I am generally referring to the different positions people hold in this society, differences in status as well as differences in function. In both education and assessment if we do not distinguish between status characteristics and functional characteristics, we are likely not to make much progress.

Status defines one's position in the social hierarchy and that status, that position, often determines one's access to the resources of the society, to the economic and political power structures. Status influences access to opportunity and access to rewards. It influences how other people treat you, what other people may expect of you, and often what one expects from one's self. Traditionally, differential status has been assigned on the basis of social class or caste, of ethnicity or race, of gender, even of language and national origin. There is a host of so-called social dividers by which we define status.

In contrast, diversity in functional characteristics refers to the *hows* of behavior, to the ways in which behavior is manifested, the ways in which people act. These functional characteristics may be locally associated with certain status groups, but the manner of behavior is not associated with status. We include as functional characteristics such traits as cognitive styles, interests, and identity. With each of these functional characteristics—remembering now that they define the how of behavior, the way people behave—we think more and more that they reflect the way persons engage learning experiences and the way people engage the environments to which they are exposed.

In the past year or so, I have been thinking that this may be too narrow a view of either functional or status characteristics. It may be that the most crucial aspect of the categories into which one falls is its contribution to the way one feels about oneself. Cultural identity may be more important than culture itself. In the modern world there is so much overlap in the manifestations of culture that if we were to focus only on cultural practices, only on the external facts of culture, we would have a hard time explaining how it is that Ed Gordon, who is exposed to so much of what is the mainstream culture of the United States, still acts like an African American, functions like an African American, and most important thinks of himself as an African American. What is important here is Ed Gordon's identification of self with that symbolic culture we call African American. Even when one deconstructs the culture itself, it has elements of many other cultures. Now this point may be made for all of the functional characteristics, that the differences between groups with respect to these functional characteristics are less important than the differences within groups. What may be most important is the contribution that the point of reference—the culture or the group—makes to the way the person identifies the self.

In order to clarify some of their implications for assessment and education, diversity of status and function needs to be distinguished from pluralism. In many of our writings we tend to use pluralism and diversity interchangeably as if they were synonymous. However, pluralism refers to the social demand of demonstrating multiple concurrent competencies in situationally relevant contexts. We recognize pluralistic demands most readily with respect to different cultures and languages. Those of us who are bilingual or multilingual have clear advantages over those of us who are monolingual. Similarly, those of us who can make ourselves at home in more than a single culture have advantages over those who can function in only one culture. I take great pride in being able to go back to North Carolina and be at home with my colleagues there or to come to Princeton or to City College and be at home with my colleagues there. If the context of the settings in which I am called upon to express my competencies qualitatively affects their expression, then this is tantamount to the development of pluralistic competencies. The requirement that all of us are being called upon to develop pluralistic competencies in a diverse world and a diverse society presents problems for us in what to teach and what to assess.

Let us turn next to the questions of equity and equality, which I contend often get confused. Much of our legal approach to democracy has been based upon ensuring that people are treated equally. However, when we come to human services, particularly education and health, equal treatment may actually be dysfunctional for some folks. What one needs is equitable treatment, that is, treatment that is appropriate to the characteristic and sufficient to the need. When we begin to talk about the issues of diversity and of pluralism in the context of equity, I am simply contending that equity in these terms requires considerably more attention, first, so we can better understand it and, second, so that this understanding can inform what we do about inequity.

Because the issues concerning diversity and pluralism are far more complex than is often reflected in public debates, it may be useful to identify some of the possible ways in which a concern for population diversity and pluralistic outcomes impacts upon teaching, learning, and assessment. It is becoming more and more obvious that these sources of variance influence student motivation to engage in academic learning and to master its content. Recent research shows that some African American students are unwilling to engage in appropriate academic activity because they view those activities as identified with another group (Fordham & Ogbu, 1986). Furthermore, it is dysfunctional in their primary social interactions to exhibit behaviors that set them apart from their group rather than place them within the group. In my own work with Thomas and Allen where we are trying to help young citizens improve their cognitive skills and strategies, we found that many of these students actually have relevant strategies (Gordon, Allen, & Armour-Thomas, 1988). The students used them appropriately in a different context but were unwilling to use them in the academic context. Hence, the primary problem is not one of cognitive deficiency but the absence of a disposition to use particular kinds of cognitive skills in particular kinds of situations.

My oldest son, who is an anthropologist, talks about the possibility that much of the behavior we see in young Black males that we call dysfunctional or antisocial is actually resistant behavior. If the society is going to do something productive with these young people, we have to find ways to turn their resistant behavior into socially productive activities rather than try to control or contain the resistant behavior itself.

As a consequence, the ways in which I identify myself, the ways in which I perceive my status and my functional relationships with society, influence the way in which I engage in the learning opportunities of that society. Parenthetically, they probably also influence the ways in which I engage in assessment experiences. Not only do cultural identities influence the ways in which things are acquired but also the ways in which things are played out in day-to-day behavior as well as in assessment functions.

TOWARD MORE EQUITABLE ASSESSMENT

Many years ago, actually it was in the 1950s, I had the good fortune to work with a German woman who had come to this country just about the time of the rise of Hitler. Her name was Elsa. Elsa was a gentile but she did not want to be part of a society gearing itself up to treat Jews and Gypsies and other so-called undesirable folk the way Germany was treating them at that particular moment. And if I can digress formally at my age, I take advantage of this opportunity to express my politics. It is troubling to me that we see beyond the horizon in this country some of the same mean spirit that one saw in Germany in 1929, 1930, and 1931, namely, efforts to divide people in terms of their group characteristics, some as desirable versus others as undesirable and, more seriously, some as superior versus others as inferior. Worse still, there is a strong tendency to view these group differences as God-given and genetically determined. These beliefs led to the destruction of German society, and many of us have been troubled by Herrnstein and Murray's (1994) treatment of these issues for similar reasons. But, many of us are almost as troubled by the concerted rush to reject these ideas because in the process of doing so we also gave undue prominence to that point of view.

Unfortunately, the nation seems to be ready for this kind of minority-group baiting because we seem to be increasingly fearful of the sufficiency of our material resources to serve all of us adequately, so some of us are to be set apart. Elsa saw this happening in Germany, but she was not politically assertive enough to fight it there. However, she did say that she would not stay in Germany and be a part of it. But Elsa's great contribution was not political but rather her scientific work in trying to assess educational potential in neurologically impaired children. She went to great lengths to construct alternative procedures for doing so. But the piece of her message that I want to stress as we move into a discussion of what can be done to make assessment more responsive to diverse human characteristics is her argument that any serious changes one might wish to make in assessment procedures need to be preceded by a change in our perception of the purpose of assessment.

Elsa saw the traditional purposes of assessment as being focussed primarily, almost exclusively, on classification and prediction. She argued that what we really need in assessment is better description and understanding as a basis for prescribing and intervening. It seems clear that Elsa's message is more appropriate for lower levels of education than for higher education and more appropriate for youngsters with serious disabilities than for those in the normal range. However, there are messages in her work that can be applied to higher education and to a wide range of diverse individuals because, in her view, the assessment experience should result in the examinees having more and better understanding of how they function and of how they can use the assessment information for subsequent learning and development.

What can be done to improve assessment? It must be 20 or 25 years ago now that Sam Messick and I put together a little proposal (that was never funded) to unbundle standardized test data in an effort to identify task demands and associated cognitive processes contributing to the total score. We wanted to isolate clusters of items with common task requirements so that subscores could be constructed at the process level. We hoped to better understand the construct-relevant sources of task difficulty in relation to the ways in which examinees engage or fail to engage relevant cognitive processes, so that we could provide richer score interpretations for informing instruction. Although our study died aborning, recent work by Snow and his colleagues has pursued similar aims in a much more sophisticated fashion, using rich data sets and detailed multivariate analyses (Hamilton, Nussbaum, Kupermintz, Kerkhoven, & Snow, 1995; Kupermintz, Ennis, Hamilton, Talbert, & Snow,1995).

In the past few years we have seen the emergence of what has been called portfolio assessment, which aims to collect a wide array of qualitative and quantitative information about students in an effort to improve understanding of the person being assessed. Portfolios afford an opportunity for students to present themselves in a variety of ways, even in ways that offer the best picture of the self. Another vehicle is to embed assessment in the curriculum itself or to embed teaching and learning experiences within assessment procedures. However, some of us worry that the assessment tail could wag the instructional dog. We become cautious when assessment is used for instructional as well as for evaluative purposes.

To dispel some of these concerns and to provide some concrete suggestions as to how to make assessment more responsive to human diversity, I next present seven assessment/educational interventions.   These seven suggestions are not offered as firm recommendations but rather are in the spirit of needed research and development.   The first suggestion is to radically increase the teaching, learning, and assessment experiences, to increase the diversity of the kinds of learning and assessment tasks available as well as diversity in the contexts and demands of learning and assessment.   This particular suggestion stems from considerations outlined in earlier sections of this chapter that what we have to build into the assessment experience is a much wider opportunity for choice in ways in which students can demonstrate what they know and do not know.

Incidentally, I recognize that there are problems in systematizing evaluative judgments based on individualized choice of tasks, whether by students or by teachers.   This issue of systematization or standardization takes me back to one of Elsa's abiding concerns.   Elsa went into retirement and ultimately to her death complaining that she was never able to standardize her assessment procedures.   Some of us thought that if her procedures had been standardized, this would have defeated her purpose.   It may very well be, as we think about our other research and development suggestions, that if we give too much attention to how we standardize scores now, to how we calibrate them systematically to make comparable judgments across persons and circumstances, it may be counterproductive to the purposes behind assessment responsive to human diversity.

The first of these suggestions was for far greater diversity in the opportunities to learn and to express one's learning in test situations.   The second has to do with increased flexibility in the timing of assessments, which was examined by Bennett in Chapter 14.

The third suggestion has to do with recognizing and enhancing the multiplicity of perspectives to which students are exposed in their learning as well as the perspectives from which they are encouraged to express themselves in their assessments.   What we see is influenced by the frame of reference or perspective we bring to the stimulus field.   When I am exposed to a phenomenon or come to any experience, I see through eyes that have been shaped by a particular background and by particular experiences.   If what is being looked for by the person who is assessing or what is being offered by the person who is teaching does not take my perspective into account, my responses and constructions may be misinterpreted.   Insensitivity to student perspectives presents problems for us because it is not just that multiple perspectives represent alternative viewpoints, some of them right and some of them wrong.   The question of how one selects from a variety of perspectives and makes judgments is one of the research issues that needs to be pursued.   I am convinced that at both the instructional level and the assessment level if one is insensitive to student perspectives the interpretation of assessment data will be off-target, distorted, or otherwise invalid. Furthermore, a way of seeing is also a way of not seeing in our assessment and teaching. We have to be much more sensitive to differences in perspective and recognize that these differences are influenced by the cultural backgrounds from which people come.

The fourth suggestion is a proposal to sample from noncanonical as well as canonical voices, knowledge, and techniques. The key question is what is appropriate to the canon in the context of cultural diversity? As we hear new voices in different cultures, their automatic inclusion in the canon is almost as bad as their exclusion. If one is confronted with bad literature from Asian culture or African culture, say, it does not do justice to students from those cultures by accommodating them with the inclusion of bad literature in teaching or assessment. Rather, it is patronizing them. One of the practical problems here is not being sufficiently familiar with these new and diverse voices in literature in general so as to select appropriately a representative teaching or assessment package. Selections from noncanonical sources need to be made with the same care and attention that we give to the more familiar canonical selections.

The fifth suggestion has to do with allowing student self-selected choice as opposed to teacher- or examiner-determined options for demonstrating what is known. The introduction of widespread student choice into assessment presents problems because there is some evidence that students, the people being tested, are not often the best judges of what they ought to be tested on or of the best way of presenting themselves. Hence, we need to do more research not only on the effects of self-selected choice in learning and assessment, but also on how to help students make better decisions about what they need as well as what they want and about how to put their best foot forward. If we go back to my work with Armour-Thomas and Allen (Gordon, Allen, & Armour-Thomas, 1988) on cognitive modifiability, what we began to recognize was that when the target students were able to identify what we were talking about in a context familiar to them, when they were able to use their own experience base, they understood the concepts. But when we presented material in the academic language and academic context, they did not. This finding implies that we should provide choices in learning and assessment that are compatible with the students' own experiences.

As a sixth point, we need to provide opportunities for both individual and cooperative learning as well as cooperative performance opportunities. In Lauren Resnick's (1987) article on learning in and out of school, she reminds us of how in school settings and formal assessment settings, we do not want people to cooperate with each other. Yet on entering the world of work, if you cannot cooperate with others you are lost.

The final suggestion is for student design of tests to cover learner- or examinee-generated knowledge. If you are trying to learn what I know about chemistry, biology, English, or the social sciences, why not give me the opportunity to define the domain of knowledge I think I am an expert in? Some years ago out at the Rand Corporation they were experimenting with approaches to computer-based instruction. One of the lines of investigation being pursued was self-designed tests whereby an examinee constructed his or her own assessment from a pool of items and assessment situations. Letting students define the boundaries of their knowledge and understanding in a subject area may be the best way of assessing their knowledge structures.

Having laid out this program of research-and-development to make assessment more responsive to human diversity, I must remind us of the point at which we began: Unless persons have had adequate educational and social opportunities to learn and develop, whatever we do in assessment is not going to help very much.

REFERENCES

Fordham, S., & Ogbu, J. U. (1986). Black students' school success: Coping with the "burden of 'acting white'." *Urban Reveiw, 18*, 176-206.

Gordon, E. W., Allen, B. A., & Armour-Thomas, E. (1988). *The development and enhancement of cognitive competence of educationally disadvantaged high school students.* A Report to the Exxon Foundation.

Hamilton, L. S., Nussbaum, E. M., Kupermintz, H., Kerkhoven, J. I. M., & Snow, R. E. (1995). Enhancing the validity and usefulness of large-scale educational assessments: II. NELS:88 science achievement. *American Educational Research Journal, 32*, 555-581.

Herrnstein, R., & Murray, C. (1994). *The Bell Curve: Intelligence and Class Structure in American Life.* New York: Free Press.

Kupermintz, H., Ennis, M. E., Hamilton, L. S., Talbert, J. E., & Snow, R. E. (1995). Enhancing the validity and usefulness of large-scale educational assessments: I. NELS:88 mathematics achievement. *American Educational Research Journal, 32*, 525-554.

Resnick, Lauren B. (1987). Learning in school and out. *Educational Researcher, 16*(9), 13-20.

17

A SYSTEMIC VIEW OF TEST FAIRNESS

Warren W. Willingham[1]
Educational Testing Service

My theme—as implied by the title—is that the measurement profession needs to broaden its thinking about the nature of test fairness. Test fairness has always been associated in the public's mind as well as in professional literature with variations in validity. The nature of and reasons for differential validity have been a strong personal interest throughout my career, so test fairness seems a fitting topic for my contribution to the fine set of chapters in this volume.

Why are measures more or less valid for different purposes, in different situations, for different individuals? I think back on my earlier work on a variety of projects: to evaluate the accessibility of higher education, to decide which qualities and achievements of applicants warrant admission to a demanding educational program, to assess the academic capabilities of disabled students, to develop principles of good practice in the assessment of experiential learning, to determine which students should be placed on academic probation, or to characterize a student's success after 4 years of college. Each of those lines of work involved judgments of fairness. Few of the judgments were clearcut or entirely satisfactory.

A salient reason for the ambiguity and the unease, I am persuaded, is that fair measurement is a good deal more complex than the largely technical interpretations we tend to give it. Involvement with colleagues at ETS over the past sev-

---

[1]I am greatly indebted to Nancy Cole, who has given me the benefit of her experience and insight in many conversations that have shaped and broadened my understanding of test fairness. I am also grateful to Carol Dwyer, Robert Linn and Samuel Messick for their helpful comments on earlier drafts. These valued colleagues bear no responsibility, of course, for the views expressed here or for any lapses.

eral years in a study of gender differences and implications for fair assessment has intensified my interest in the theoretical underpinnings of test fairness. In the course of that work, it quickly became clear that a coherent discussion of practical test fairness issues that are often raised with regard to gender requires a rationale that can include but needs to go beyond traditional psychometric definitions. This chapter comes out of that work, though it is concerned with fairness issues as they apply to individuals and subgroups generally, rather than to gender specifically.

To limit the scope, I focus mainly on high-stakes educational tests, though much important analysis in recent years pertains to employee selection, and many of the important precedents have been established in the legal, regulatory, and judicial arenas (Bersoff, 1981; Camara & Brown, 1995; Novick, 1981; Sharf, 1988). Furthermore, my interest here lies more in drawing attention to several critical issues than in advancing solutions. Since the topic is nonetheless extraordinarily broad, I direct my comments to two limited objectives. One is to describe what I mean by a systemic view of test fairness. Another is to illustrate a systemic view by associating fairness issues with a framework of the assessment process that may be helpful in addressing such issues in practice. But first, a few comments on recent history of the topic.

TEST FAIRNESS, PAST AND PRESENT

There have always been two main arguments in favor of objective testing: One is the utilitarian belief that tests enhance the effective development and utilization of talent; another is the egalitarian belief that tests can help to insure equal opportunity for education and employment. Significant aspects of the utilitarian belief are subject to empirical evaluation (Schmidt, Ones, & Hunter, 1992; Manski & Wise, 1983); the egalitarian belief stems from a meritocratic value system that stresses individual rights (Glazer, 1970).

Hard as it may now be to imagine, measurement specialists more or less discovered group-based test fairness as a major issue only some 30 years ago. Certainly, prior to that time, there was discussion of the cultural fairness of a test or its appropriateness for some examinees, but it was the Civil Rights Movement in the 1960s that gave social identity and political dimension to the topic. That was the period when hard questions were first asked as to whether the egalitarian belief in testing was justified in the face of observed subgroup differences in test performance. The public and test specialists alike asked whether tests were inherently biased against some groups, particularly Black and Hispanic examinees.

I recall a meeting in about 1965, when several senior staff from the College Board and some senior researchers at ETS gathered to consider what studies might be helpful in determining whether tests were biased. That first discussion was singularly unhelpful. The group could suggest no way to research the problem because they saw no fully comparable basis for judging fairness. I will return to that seemingly naive but oddly prophetic judgment.

Ideas did emerge, and soon thereafter two of the most frequently cited ETS Research Reports were completed. They proved to be landmark studies because they focused attention on two workable methods for judging fairness (Cleary, 1968; Cleary & Hilton, 1968). These two studies gave impetus to research on differential regression and differential item functioning among subgroups—the two lines of inquiry that have done most to inform our thinking about test fairness or, as it was often called, test bias. Soon thereafter came a considerable outpouring of research on the topic.

In employee selection, test validity is strongly associated with criterion relationships because such selection typically focuses sharply on a particular utilitarian goal—predicting success on the job. Analysis of prediction results led to the generally accepted conclusion that ability tests did not differentially predict job success of Black and Hispanic applicants (Hartigan & Wigdor, 1989; Hunter, Schmidt & Hunter, 1979; Wigdor & Garner, 1982. See R. L. Linn, 1982, for a review of similar results in academic prediction). There were, however, substantial mean differences on these tests between minority and majority applicants. Regulations of the Equal Employment Opportunity Commission (EEOC, 1970) specified that use of an employment test having adverse impact on a protected group would constitute discrimination prohibited by Title VII of the Civil Rights Act (1964) unless two conditions were met: demonstration of validity and demonstration that alternate selection procedures with equal validity and less impact were unavailable.

This rigorous requirement for using a test that shows adverse impact on subgroup selection rates—as often proved to be the case—is frequently credited with a sharp decline in employment testing and a shift in enforcement attention to affirmative action goals (Sharf, 1988). As I will later argue, fairness issues in educational testing differ in fundamental ways from those in employment testing. Nonetheless, the enormous importance attached to criterion-related validity had a heavy impact on views of test fairness and how it is assured, often at the expense of construct validity and the possibility of a deeper understanding of the meaning of test scores and the effects of their use (Tenopyr, 1995).

Fair Selection Models

Meanwhile, measurement specialists were conceiving and debating a variety of selection models that advanced alternate views of fairness (Cole, 1973; Darlington, 1971; R. L. Linn, 1973; Thorndike, 1971). All of these models derive from the fact that any imperfect predictor will fail to select members of a low scoring group in proportion to their rate of criterion success, even if individuals at the same score level are equally likely to succeed, regardless of group membership—Cleary's (1968) definition of an unbiased predictor. This common situation is illustrated in Figure 1.

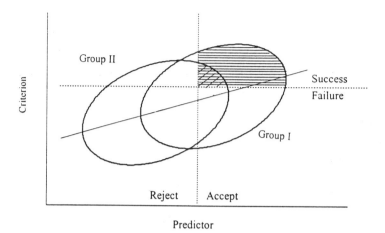

FIGURE 1. The conditional probability model for fair selection (based on Cole, 1973).

Since the two groups in Figure 1 have a common regression line, the predictor meets Cleary's definition of an unbiased test. But among the applicants who could be successful if admitted, most from Group I were selected (grey area), while a relatively small proportion of Group II were selected (cross-hatched area). Cole's conditional probability model for fair selection is based on this principle: Among the applicants who can achieve a satisfactory criterion score, the probability of being selected should be the same regardless of group membership. In order to meet such a definition of fair selection in this hypothetical situation involving a cut-score on one predictor, the score that qualifies for admission would need to be set at different levels for Group I and Group II so that the shaded areas represent the same proportion of potentially successful students in the two groups.

The effort to determine which model, among the variety of such models proposed, best represented fair selection was perhaps the policy debate of the decade among measurement specialists. The spring 1976 issue of the *Journal of Educational Measurement* included Petersen and Novick's (1976) detailed analysis and critique of a number of models with rejoinders. There was general agreement that Cleary's (1968) original regression model remained the standard technical basis for defining an unbiased selection test.

The authors of the various models also agreed that fair selection models are based on different values, are often inconsistent, and may affect different groups in contradictory or undesirable ways. They did not agree on a preferred model, mainly because different value judgments support different models (Shepard, 1982). They did agree that a choice could be made if different social utility were assigned to correct or incorrect selections within different subgroups.

Darlington (1971) had earlier expressed a similar view, namely., that group fairness in selection requires a subjective value judgment concerning the relative importance of maximizing predictive validity versus minimizing subgroup differences in selection rate.

Because of the lack of professional consensus, the fair selection models never made it to the 1985 revision of the *Standards for Educational and Psychological Testing* (American Educational Research Association, American Psychological Association, & National Council on Measurement in Education, 1985). Moreover, this debate apparently had little effect on selection practices in colleges and universities. One reason was technical complexity. The graphics, such as shown in Figure 1, were enough to cause many eyes to glaze over— to say nothing of the equations that fair selection models often entail. A more fundamental reason was the substantive oversimplification. There is no obvious way to apply a univariate model in a selective institution that is using multiple measures and procedures in order to meet a variety of admissions objectives (Willingham & Cole, 1997). Instead, selective institutions have practiced affirmative action without benefit of statistical rationale.

Employee selection is ordinarily not as complex and therefore suggests the possibility of reducing subgroup differences in selection rate while minimizing the effects on overall predictive validity. It was the prospect of such a tradeoff that led a National Research Council (NRC) Committee to recommend subgroup norming for the General Aptitude Test Battery (GATB). In simplest terms, the NRC committee recommended that the U.S. Employment Service express GATB scores as percentiles (or some modified version thereof) based on each examinee's particular subgroup when making job referrals (Hartigan & Wigdor, 1989)

The rationale followed Cole's (1973) argument as illustrated in Figure 1. The proposal ran into a storm of controversy, two views of which are described by Gottfredson (1994) and by Sackett and Wilk (1994). In response to these developments, Congress specifically prohibited any form of score adjustment on the basis of race, color, religion, sex, or national origin (Civil Rights Act of 1991). Three decades earlier researchers had been right for reasons they could not fully appreciate. It was possible to find psychometric criteria that are ostensibly comparable but not possible to find comparable value criteria for deciding whether the outcomes of test use are fair.

There were, of course, other major issues in recent years involving test fairness: whether ability tests can be used to place children in different school tracks (Larry P. vs. Riles, 1980); what constitutes adequate opportunity to acquire the knowledge and skills represented on a school-leaving examination (Debra P. vs. Turlington, 1979); whether differences in subgroup performance should be considered in selecting test items (Anrig, 1987); whether it is permissible to flag scores of tests administered to disabled examinees under nonstandard conditions (Rehabilitation Act of 1973); whether scored answer sheets and test forms must be routinely disclosed to examinees (New York State Testing Act, 1980). All of these issues involved either legislation or litigation. Together they illustrate the range and importance of test fairness issues. The foregoing 30-year perspective on fair selection is sufficient, however, to illustrate the principal observation I wish to make about the current status of test fairness in psychological and educational assessment.

The Current Issue

The measurement field is burdened with a persistent structural dichotomy because it employs technical tools in order to serve social ends. The dichotomy is often reflected in divergent professional and public views of test fairness and an understandable reluctance of professionals to take on fairness issues considered to lie in the public domain. We are where we are for good reason. Test fairness issues are extraordinarily complex and often lie beyond the reasonable purview of measurement specialists. Nor is the field of one mind and action. There have long been signs of adaptation to this dichotomy, as well as obstacles.

It is certainly true that fairness issues have been a major concern in the measurement literature for some time (Cole, 1981; Diamond & Tittle, 1985; Flaugher, 1978; Gipps & Murphy; 1994; Gottfredson & Sharf, 1988; Hartigan & Wigdor, 1989; Jensen, 1980; Messick, 1964, 1980; Shepard, 1982; Wigdor & Garner, 1982). Test fairness has been formally incorporated in mainstream measurement theory (Cole & Moss, 1989; Messick, 1989), and there have been effective appeals by leading scholars for greater rapprochement regarding technical and social issues (Cronbach, 1980; R. L. Linn, 1980; Shepard, 1993; Tenopyr, 1995; Wild & Dwyer, 1980).

Furthermore, there have been energetic and promising efforts to provide more specific professional guidelines on issues that may involve fair interpretation and use of test scores (AACD/AMECD, 1992; Eyde et al., 1993; Joint Committee on Testing Practices, 1988; NCME Ad Hoc Committee, 1995). The 1985 *Standards* added several sections specifically on test use (AERA, et al, 1985). Helpful as these developments are, there are counter currents and impediments.

First, there is the traditional division of responsibility between test developers and test users. As stated by the 1985 *Standards*, "Although the test developer and publisher should provide information on the strengths and weaknesses of the test, ultimate responsibility for appropriate test use lies with the user." (p. 41) This responsibility can prove difficult to carry out if test use is circumscribed by the design and delivery of test information.

A closely related problem is the common distinction in measurement literature between bias and fairness. Bias is advanced as a technical term used by professionals and is more likely to be associated with the test itself. Fairness is associated with the use of tests and is evaluated by more subjective means in a political context. For example, the 1985 *Standards* state that the accepted technical definition of bias (predictive or selective) is based upon two groups having a common regression line; that is, the Cleary model. The *Standards* go on to say,

> Unlike selection bias, however, fairness is not a technical psychometric term; it is subject to different definitions in different social and political circumstances. At present a consensus of technical experts supports only one approach to selection bias as technically appropriate. This approach is adopted in the *Standards* with the understanding that it does not resolve the larger issue of fairness. (AERA, et al, 1985, p. 13)

Beyond this introductory explanation, the *Standards* are largely silent on test fairness—how fairness differs from bias, what the fairness issues are, and in what way the measurement profession should aid in their resolution. As a result, selection issues that are of great concern to the public appear somewhat removed from professional standards. This is one reason that I have reservations about the current use of the terms bias and fairness. The bias-fairness distinction seems like a symptom of dysfunction, albeit a non-trivial symptom, on which I will comment in more detail. The distinction hints at a more fundamental issue: How should the measurement profession deal with social issues concerning the fairness of tests? There is an important need, I believe, for a more coherent structure that can better link technical issues and public concerns on the common ground of assessment practice; that is, a more systemic view of test fairness. To that end, subsequent sections of this chapter describe the assessment context in which test fairness issues arise, and propose a framework for relating test fairness issues more directly to the assessment process. First, we must distinguish several related ideas and define what is here meant by test fairness.

TERMS AND CONCEPTIONS

Since the main purpose of this discussion is to enlighten the meaning of "systemic view of test fairness," it is first necessary to define somewhat prematurely what is being discussed. If all goes well, the definition and its merits will be more apparent at the end. Test fairness has a critical connection to three other closely related ideas: equity, validity, and bias.

Equity is a social value strongly associated with equal opportunity and equal treatment in education and in the workplace (Klein, 1985; Wellesley College Center for Research on Women, 1992). It is often connected with issues concerning fairness in testing (Diamond & Tittle, 1985; Gipps & Murphy, 1994), though equity is much broader in conception and application. Equity is primarily concerned with social justice and, for that reason, is subject to rival interpretations.

In recent years there has been increasing national concern about the effectiveness of education generally and about equity issues associated with a clearly uneven distribution of quality education. In this context, the role of tests is hotly debated. It is clear that there are differences as well as substantial overlap in the test performance of various groups of examinees, and that group differences stemming from wide disparities in education and social condition—as well as personal experience and interests—do not necessarily reflect test unfairness.

The important distinction between equity and test fairness is the necessary involvement of tests—directly or indirectly. There are several reasons why the measurement profession should be actively engaged in equity issues. One is the fact that assessment practices have the potential for negative impact on equity in education and employment. As a corollary, assessment can also have a positive influence. Avoiding the former and enhancing the latter is much more likely if measurement issues are informed with sufficient understanding of equity issues.

Fairness and Validity

The word fairness suggests justice that comes from impartiality, lacking in prejudice or favoritism. This implies that a fair test is comparable from person to person and group to group. Comparable in what respect? The most reasonable answer is validity, since validity is the raison d'être of the entire assessment enterprise. The systemic view offered here derives from this principle: The basis of test fairness is comparable validity.

Individual Fairness. For individual examinees, defining test fairness as comparable validity means that fairness is proportional to, if not synonymous with, validity. The parallelism lies in the fact that judgments of both validity and fairness are based on the extent of errors in individual scores. For individuals, fairer assessment requires smaller errors of estimate or inference, which means more comparable accuracy and validity from person to person and greater validity overall. The relationship is clear in those facets of Messick's (1989) validity framework involving the evidential basis of test interpretation and test use. For example, strong evidence of construct validity would lie in the demonstration of a strong true-score relationship with another measure that is conceptually quite similar; i.e., from person to person scores on one measure are comparably valid (accurate and fair) estimates of scores on the other. Similarly, a measure gives fair prediction of criterion performance to the extent that errors of estimate are minimal, that is, equally accurate and valid.

As R. L. Linn (1994) emphasizes, validity is always a matter of degree. So it is with individual fairness. The more valid the test, the smaller the errors and the fairer the interpretations in actual use. The longer the inferential leap from what is actually on the test to a complex and distal criterion of possibly questionable validity itself, the more likely are those inferences to suffer in validity and fairness. For individuals, improved validity is the road to fairness. A more valid test or a test that adds to a multiple correlation adds to predictive validity and to fairness in like proportion.

Group Fairness. Basing the interpretation of group fairness on comparable validity does not depart from traditional definitions. For some time differential predictive validity, differential prediction, and Differential Item Functioning (DIF) have been commonly accepted technical definitions of bias (AERA et al. 1985; Cole & Moss, 1989; Linn, 1982; Shepard, 1982;). Each is based directly or implicitly on the assumption that a fair test is comparably valid across subgroups. Thus Cole and Moss (1989, p. 205) define the technical meaning of bias as ". . . differential validity of a particular interpretation of a test score for any definable, relevant subgroup of test takers."

Fairness in terms of differential validity is a useful principle with even greater generality: Test fairness is comparable validity across all aspects of the assessment process from the initial design to the consequences of use. For groups, the fairness objective is to make the test as comparable as possible within the framework of its purpose and an agreed basis for deciding what is comparable. With this organizing principle, the challenge is to identify and resolve the important fairness issues, that is, potential sources of noncomparability. Like individual fairness, group fairness is, from a measurement perspective, a relative term. A test that is equally valid in all respects to all groups is theoretically possible if all sources of bias or invalidity are randomly distributed among subgroups—a circumstance that is perhaps too implausible to hope for in practice.

The idea that a partly valid test is therefore partly fair for individual examinees may be accurate from a psychometric perspective, but it feels unacceptable and is, in fact, misleading. From a social perspective, fairness is an ethical conception concerned with the justice and impartiality inherent in actions. The justice and impartiality of actions can only be judged in relation to available alternatives. From this perspective, a test can be judged fair if it is as comparable as any test or basis for decision can reasonably be for a given purpose and a given situation.

The distinction here suggested between individual and group fairness is closely akin to within-group versus between-group variation. An interaction between subgroup performance and a test characteristic can raise a consequential fairness issue but have little negative effect on—or even increase—overall validity. For example, adding SAT-Verbal to SAT-Math leads to underprediction of the grades of language minority students but improves overall validity (see Ramist, Lewis and McCamley-Jenkins, 1994). The same principle applies conceptually, if not statistically, to any aspect of validity and fairness. Finally, clarifying what is meant here by test fairness requires a few more comments on the distinction between bias and fairness.

Test Bias Versus Test Fairness

In 1968 Cleary tied the term "test bias" to a statistical relationship between a test score and a criterion—a quite specific operational definition to be contrasted with the broader conception of test fairness. The idea took well. It was consistent with the distinction between the adequacy of a test and the ethics of its use (Messick, 1980). In addition, the definition was clear-cut and encouraged research. As Jensen (1980) commented, "The assessment of bias is a purely objective, empirical, statistical and quantitative matter entirely independent of subjective value judgments and ethical issues concerning fairness or unfairness of tests and the uses to which they are put." (p. 375)

Subsequent writers noted the consensus view that fairness refers to ethical questions or value judgments involving use of the test results. Some have referred more directly to bias as reflecting intrinsic characteristics of the test (Diamond & Tittle, 1985) or flaws in the test (Sackett & Wilk, 1994) as distinct from conditions of use. And as previously noted, the technical-social distinction between bias and fairness was codified in the 1985 *Standards*. The distinction poses several problems.

First, there has been little discipline in the use of the two terms. Shepard (1982, p.10) referred to the "muddle" that results from expecting bias and fairness to be used with consistent meaning from one author to another. For example, even well-informed scholars have used a range of terms in describing fair selection models, and this literature has been characterized as "bias in selection," even though selection obviously refers to test use, which strains objectivity in many ways (see *Journal of Educational Measurement*, Spring issue, 1976). Later, the *Standards* (AERA et al., 1985), as well as Cole and Moss (1989) in their major review, also use "selection bias" in apparent contradiction with the bias-fairness distinction.

The contradiction stems from the incorrect assumption built into the bias-fairness distinction, namely, that bias is objectively determined and independent of the value judgments associated with fair use of tests. Prediction or selection bias assumes a particular use, that is, a specific criterion, sample, and situation. As Ramist et al. (1994) have shown, differential prediction results in higher education can vary substantially, depending upon the choice of GPA criterion, sample of students within an institution, type of college, and what other predictor variables are included or omitted. Such choices depend heavily upon value considerations.

Furthermore, there is a dysfunctional side to the bias-fairness distinction. From a theoretical perspective, the distinction makes it too easy to distance evidence from consequences, features that Messick (1989) has successfully championed as facets, not compartments of validity. Fairness profits from an integrated view for the same reasons as does validity. From a practical perspective, the distinction has tended to distract the attention of measurement specialists from wider equity issues (Gipps & Murphy, 1994), and runs the risk of defining for the profession a safe technical domain of insufficient social relevance.

It is certainly possible to make distinctions between bias and fairness, though they can be more misleading than helpful. So it is not clear what the solution to the muddle might be. Because of these problems, Gipps and Murphy (1994) elected to use bias as little as possible in their book on fair testing. In his measurement text, Cronbach (1990) avoids both terms. My purpose here is not to sort all this out, but to comment on the conceptual problem and to explain my use of "fairness" here as an inclusive term, incorporating the issues normally ascribed to both bias and fairness.

This groundwork sets the stage for further illustration and needed context. The general interpretation of test fairness offered here is no more than a compass orientation. As Scriven (1980) has warned, brief and all-purpose definitions are usually not very helpful and also somewhat misleading. If a systemic view of test fairness is to add meaning to the topic, we need more of a roadmap, that is, some consideration of the assessment system and connections to the actual process of assessment.

ASSESSMENT IN CONTEXT

According to Churchman (1971), society handles important functions by building complex systems that can be viewed as manifolds of interlocking problems. The design of such systems poses conceptual as well as practical challenges. In order to understand the parts, how they work, as well as their strengths and weaknesses, it is useful to seek a more complete view of the system. The assessment process with all of its procedures, participants, and interlocking problems can be seen as such a system. We examine the assessment system from two perspectives: the nature of the "test fairness manifold" and the "social matrix" in which it operates.

The Test Fairness Manifold

Part of the difficulty in sorting out and acting on test fairness issues is that the domain is considerably more multidimensional than is implied by traditional interpretations. The manifold of fairness issues is complex partly because people see it in different ways (Flaugher, 1978), but the complexity is more fundamental than that observation implies. As the previous discussion of fairness and validity should make clear, fairness is complex because validity is complex. As Shepard (1993, p. 423) comments, Messick's (1989) treatise in R. L. Linn's *Educational Measurement* "...extends the boundaries of validity beyond test score meaning to include relevance and utility, value implications, and social consequences." The review by Cole and Moss (1989) in the same volume confirms that broadened domain by addressing a wide variety of test fairness issues.

Failure to take account of that complexity is a frequent problem in the professional rendering of test fairness issues. This happens in two ways: overlooking multiple components and overlooking interconnections. Too often, test fairness issues are viewed in isolation, which can make an issue appear unrealistic and difficult to communicate to another party who is, so to speak, focusing on a more interesting part of the elephant. There are three important aspects of assessment that contain such multiple, interconnected components: the situation, the participants, and the process. Examples of oversimplified test fairness issues are readily found in each.

The Situation. The particular situation in which a given test is used can vary in numerous ways—the purpose to which the test is put, the side effects of its use, additional variables that are used along with the test, the criterion that is used, the particular context of use, and the specific sample that is involved. It is by now well understood that particular score interpretations are validated (and are more or less fair), not the test itself (Cronbach, 1971). Indeed, as Cronbach (1980) later elaborated, "The whole selection system is to be justified, not the test alone." (p. 103)

Nonetheless, fair selection models and selection data are routinely discussed as univariate matters. The practice persists despite Linn and Werts (1971) having demonstrated a quarter-century ago the incorrect impressions that can result from leaving out an important variable, and the incorporation of that admonition in the *Standards* (AERA, et al., 1985). The misleading effects can be consequential (see Chapter 7, Willingham & Cole, 1997).

Another example lies in the tendency to accept and generalize educational prediction data uncritically. This despite the time-honored skepticism directed to "the criterion problem" (Fishman, 1958; R. L. Linn, 1976; Cronbach, 1980) and frequent questions as to: What justifies this criterion? What biases does it have (Wild & Dwyer, 1980)? While validity generalization has been argued with some success in employee selection (Schmidt et al., 1992), a substantial amount of institutional specificity in predictive validity has been demonstrated by Willingham and Lewis (1990)—variability that is apparently due to lack of criterion consistency and comparability (Ramist, Lewis, & McCamley, 1990). A subsequent study showed that differential prediction for women and men also varied substantially with different criteria, in different types of colleges, and different samples within those colleges (Ramist et al., 1994).

The Participants. There are two ways of viewing the multiple participants in assessment—by desegregating the pool of examinees or the various groups of professionals and institutions who have different connections with the process. Both views suggest important fairness issues for different reasons. The institutions and professionals who sponsor and use tests have one view as to what is fair; examinees have another. They will not necessarily always agree, though both have a legitimate claim.

A more obvious potential conflict lies in differential effects of assessment on examinees. Principles of good practice, rights of examinees, and similar codes help to protect individual examinees from professional ignorance and negligence, but the interests of individuals generally are not always weighed systematically when group interests are advanced. More surprising is how seldom in research literature a proposed modification in testing practice that might favor one group is formally evaluated for its possible effect on another. For example, good arguments for essay assessment, on which women tend to score well, do not ordinarily take into account possible negative effects of this assessment format on language minority groups.

The Process. The enlargement of construct validity to include the consequences of test use and the ethical basis for evaluating those consequences did much to bring test theory in line with public perception of important issues regarding test fairness (Messick, 1980, 1989). That does not mean that test practice keeps in pace with test theory, or that we have a clear picture of the fairness implications of specific aspects of assessment.

Indeed, potential mishaps lurk at a number of steps in the assessment process. The steps are frequently interconnected and thus harbor possibilities for misconstruing the origin of the problem. For example, underprediction of women's grades in freshman math courses may initially suggest a design flaw. More thorough analysis may suggest using different, or at least additional, criteria. In a following section we examine the assessment process in a bit more detail because it provides a useful framework for identifying test fairness issues and recognizing their interconnections. First, it is useful to consider briefly the context for reaching decisions about assessment.

The Social Matrix

How do test fairness issues get resolved? It is one thing to identify, evaluate, and debate specific aspects of a test as to its fairness. It is another thing to resolve those issues and decide, yes or no, whether the test use or interpretation passes muster, how the test should be modified, whether its development and use is justified. Tests do not tend to get developed without an expectation that they will be used, and developers normally have intended uses in mind that will justify the effort to produce the test. I refer to whether the effort will be seen as worthwhile, not whether it is a good business decision—though the two may often be related. There is a social matrix in which the resolution takes place, at least implicitly. Three criteria are prominent:

- How useful the test is in serving its intended function.
- How fair the test is for individuals and groups of examinees.
- How well the test meets practical constraints.

These criteria overlap in various ways. Each is usually more a qualitative order-of-merit than a yes-no characteristic. Normally, these three criteria are likely to be important in the order listed. On the other hand, each criterion is complex in its own right, and failing on a particular aspect of any one of the three can easily render a test untenable. Scoring high on one criterion does not make up for failing on another. The three can be elaborated briefly as follows.

Usefulness. We develop and employ tests because the intended function is worthwhile. The social justification of testing requires that intended function include both the immediate purpose and the systemic effects of using the test. The immediate purpose is to provide a good measure of the construct of choice (with content relevance, favorable discriminant-convergent evidence, and so on) in order to obtain information (e.g., competency statements, predictive relationships, etc.) that is useful in making educational decisions about students and programs. Two types of systemic effects can be distinguished. One is the long-term gain we expect to accrue through improvements in social effectiveness; another is the anticipatory consequences of testing, that is, the "washback" effects on students and schools which can be both positive and negative (Messick, 1996; Resnick & Resnick, 1992).

If serving the immediate purpose is perceived as motivating the whole testing enterprise, then that specific use of the scores may be seen as quite separate from the so-called "side effects." But in evaluating test validity it is wiser, for both theoretical and practical reasons, to view tests as an intrinsic part of the larger system in which they operate. For example, admissions tests serve not only the immediate needs of college administrators in considering applicants, but also the social need for a process of moving students from secondary to higher education that is perceived by the parties as efficient, fair, and effective for the educational system generally.

Fairness. Even if a test serves a useful purpose, it must meet an acceptable standard of fairness. Since fairness can be viewed as synonymous with validity for individuals, fairness comes into play as an additional criterion of acceptability when sources of inappropriate differential performance (i.e., invalidity) can be associated with identifiable groups of examinees. The differential performance may be associated with construct representativeness or with construct irrelevant difficulty or easiness. Examples might include using material on a history test that is not in the syllabus in some schools, or employing an item type that is susceptible to short-term coaching tricks, or using a test that seriously underrepresents a criterion component on which women excel, or designing a test so that it requires a calculator unfamiliar to many inner-city Black students.

Any such situation can be seen as a serious breach of fairness, even though the detrimental effect on overall validity may actually be minor. These group-based threats to test fairness result from interactions between characteristics of the assessment process and shared experiences of the particular group such as similar interests, habitual activities, social learning, formal schooling, etc. Examples will be apparent when we consider the assessment process. It doesn't have to be a legally protected group, though that will likely raise the visibility and seriousness of the issue. Speaking generally, examinee "background" poses formidable problems—conceptual, legal, and practical—in determining what constitutes fair assessment and how to insure it.

Practicality. There are a surprising number of practical constraints that tend to determine whether an otherwise useful and fair test will be sanctioned and actually used. In the main, these have to do with acceptability and feasibility. Both are poorly understood, especially by test critics and reformers whose interests and experience often do not provide direct familiarity with the development and operation of testing programs. Tests can prove unacceptable to examinees, users, and sponsors for a variety of reasons. Most common is the feeling that the test takes too much time, is too complicated, or costs too much. Invasion of privacy is another constraint that is not often appreciated. Many types of tests are not feasible because it is not technically possible to produce sufficient forms that are different but also parallel, or provide equated scores, or maintain test security, or get scorers to agree, or meet minimum generalizability requirements. Many of these problems involve fairness issues as well.

The social justification of a test sits on this three-legged stool of usefulness, fairness, and practicality. It is quite possible for an alternate test to be more useful than an existing test (e.g., more predictive) for individuals overall, but because of its nature, be less fair for some particular groups. It is, in fact, very common that a promising type of assessment fails for some reason related to its fairness or its practicality. Knowledge of auto mechanics, for example, might well provide better prediction of success for women and men in auto repair school than would a general ability test, but underestimate the likely success of women because, as a group, women have less prior knowledge of the workings of automobiles. In this case, resolution of the test's overall fairness depends on the tradeoff between individual and group fairness.

It is good to recall that the evaluation is always in relation to some alternative. In all societies individuals are evaluated in some manner. If not with this test or a better test, then real-life decisions will get made in other ways. The alternate procedures may be less burdensome or less subject to some flaw of immediate concern, but may well be less defensible on other grounds. No test or other means of evaluation can be perfect with respect to usefulness, fairness, and practicality. As R. L. Linn (1994) has said, "Validity is always a matter of degree rather than an all-or-none judgement." (p. 6) So it is with fairness and practicality. All three must be weighed because tests are not justified on the basis of one factor in isolation.

FAIRNESS AND THE ASSESSMENT PROCESS

There are two reasons why the assessment process plays a critical role in describing what I characterized earlier as the test fairness manifold. One reason is that the numerous steps in the assessment process provide a heuristic framework for identifying fairness issues. It is an intrinsically valid framework because the steps in the assessment process include all the decisions that can result in a less fair test, all the places where the process can go wrong. Indeed, in the Cole and Moss (1989) major review of test bias, several of their categories of issues were closely associated with phases of the assessment process.

The second reason is related to the first. Defining fairness issues in terms of actual decisions in the assessment process forces the discussion of those issues closer to the real situation and the practical alternatives that should be considered. As it turns out, different stages in the assessment process feature different types of fairness-related decisions that suggest different strategies for meeting threats to fairness. Furthermore, the strategies have a common organizing principle. First, consider the nature of the process.

Four Stages in Assessment

Figure 2 distinguishes four overlapping and interconnected stages in assessment: Design, Development, Administration, and Use. The four stages follow in sequence with feedback. The design determines how the test is developed, and then administered, and then put to use. What is learned at each succeeding step

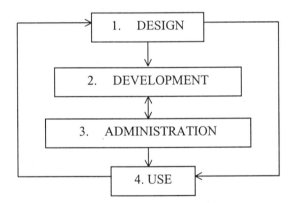

FIG. 2: Four stages in the Assessment Process.

serves to confirm or modify previous steps. Building a fair test is not, however, a simple linear process. Fairness issues interact in various ways and much depends upon the function served by the test and the context of its use. As the figure suggests, test design is closely linked with test use. Design is determined by intended use; use should be consistent with design. Similarly, development and administration are closely linked because test construction depends upon information from field trials.

Figure 3 illustrates a number of critical decisions that are made at these four stages in the assessment process. Decisions at the design stage determine the specifications (i.e., continuing characteristics) of a test; decisions in the course

1. Design
   a. Describe the test's purpose, examinee characteristics, intended interpretation and use, context of use with what other measures
   b. Choose constructs and evaluate their representativeness
   c. Specify the construct instantiation and item types
   d. Choose assessment mode and conditions
   e. Specify test timing, scoring paradigms, statistical characteristics
   f. Evaluate test quality, usefulness, fairness, consequences of use, and the adequacy of the rationale and evidence regarding validity

2. Development
   a. Choose items, topics, and exercises
   b. Review content for accuracy, balance, and irrelevant difficulty or easiness
   c. Review appropriateness and comparability of the test in relation to characteristics of examinees and opportunity to learn
   d. Review sensitivity of the test and its administration
   e. Analyze item characteristics and differential item functioning

3. Administration and Scoring
   a. Define and ensure standard conditions and timing
   b. Determine accommodations appropriate to individual disabilities
   c. Review irregularities (breaches of security, standard conditions, comfort)
   d. Define provisions for examinee choice
   e. Score, scale, and equate
   f. Evaluate reliability, comparability, group performance

4. Interpretation and Use
   a. Specify other measures relevant to interpretation and use
   b. Specify decision models and conditions of use
   c. Specify, collect, and evaluate criterion information
   d. Evaluate validity evidence regarding intended interpretation and use
   e. Evaluate other consequences and systemic effects (for individuals, groups, instruction, educational outcomes, and social outcomes)
   f. Evaluate comparability and impact for subgroups

FIG. 3: Critical decisions in assessment

of development and administration affect individual forms of the test. Each decision can, explicitly or implicitly, affect the fairness of the test. Thus unfairness can be introduced at any stage, regardless of the care that may have been previously exercised. Different instances of unfairness are likely to accumulate if the specific problem is not corrected or the test specifications are not modified. This particular listing in Figure 3 is limited to fairness issues in tests used for individual decisions in admissions, guidance, placement, instruction, graduation requirements, certification, or licensing but the principle applies to other tests as well.

Important decisions about a particular test feature often occur at multiple stages of the assessment process. For example, test content is determined initially by the choice of construct to measure (e.g., verbal reasoning), then by the manner in which the construct is instantiated in test specifications (e.g., by choice of item types such as paragraph comprehension and verbal analogies), and finally by the specific material chosen (e.g., reading passages on a particular subject). As we see in the following discussion, these consecutive decisions are interconnected, but they involve different fairness issues and call for different fairness control procedures.

Fairness Issues

Poor assessment practice can impair validity and fairness in many ways. The *Standards* (AERA, et al., 1985) and other professional guidelines previously cited describe many aspects of test use and misuse that can threaten fairness (AACD/AMECD, 1992; Eyde et al., 1993; Joint Committee on Testing Practices, 1988). Such guidelines frequently refer to specific lapses due to negligence, ignorance as to principles of good practice, technical missteps, ethical problems, and similar issues that can degrade assessment in the hands of particular practitioners or for individual examinees. The importance of such problems notwithstanding, the focus here is on more systematic threats to fairness for classes of examinees, that is, fairness issues that tend to be built into the assessment process as indicated in the following paragraphs.

Test Design. In designing a test, the overarching concern is always validity. Within that framework, fair test design should provide examinees comparable opportunity, insofar as possible, to demonstrate knowledge and skills they have acquired that are relevant to the purpose of the test. The intended use of a test and the systemic effects of its use are key considerations in its design because they determine what knowledge and skills (i.e., constructs) are relevant. Comparability should always be judged on the bases of all measures with which a test is used in making decisions about students because the test is often not intended to measure all relevant knowledge and skills. It is the decision or action, when a test is used as intended, that can be judged fair or unfair, not the design of the component measures in isolation. Opportunity to demonstrate proficiency may be affected either by underrepresentation of relevant constructs or by any aspect of test design that introduces construct-irrelevant difficulty and thereby tends to differentially hinder examinees' efforts to perform at their best.

Different features of test design may advantage or disadvantage different examinees to some degree despite all efforts to minimize such effects. Furthermore, the purpose of a test may narrowly determine the choice of useful constructs, and practical considerations may strongly influence the choice of assessment mode. The following aspects of test design illustrate possible threats to fairness:

- Failure to represent important knowledge and skills on which some examinees may perform quite well.

- Use of test formats and methods of delivery that have significant effects on the performance of some examinees.

- Specification of test characteristics (e.g., subject matter, item types, length, timing, scoring) that may disadvantage some examinees.

Test Development and Administration. Fair development and administration of tests should provide tasks, testing conditions, and scaled scores that are as comparable as possible for all examinees, taking any form of the test at any time and location. The goal is functional equivalence of the assessment task and scores from one examinee to another. This principle extends to comparability among subgroups of examinees and from one testing situation to another. From the standpoint of test fairness, it is useful to think of scores as comparable if they do not include any consequential source of difficulty that is unrelated to the skills and knowledge that the test is intended to measure. Accordingly, the fairness of a test with respect to its development and administration can be judged primarily on the basis of the adequacy of steps taken to insure comparability and evidence that examinees are not disadvantaged for reasons unrelated to the skills and knowledge being tested.

Meeting this objective tends to require an assessment that is as objective and standard as practical, even if the test is a holistic performance assessment. This principle may require accommodating examinee differences in order to insure that assessments are, in fact, functionally equivalent. Testing disabled examinees is a good example because, in this instance, accommodation is mandated by federal regulation. Taking steps to insure fairness through comparability of scores may sometimes be incompatible with the goal of insuring the opportunity of examinees to demonstrate individual proficiency. The following aspects of test development and administration illustrate possible threats to comparability:

- Test content that is not reasonably balanced with respect to its familiarity to different examinees.

- Questions posed in contexts that are much less familiar to some examinees than to others.

- Test forms of unequal scaled difficulty.

- Disadvantage to some examinees due to nonstandard conditions during testing.

- A test environment that is inhospitable or distracting to some examinees.

- Test features that result in some examinees being more test-ready than others.

- Tests that hamper demonstration of relevant skill.

Test Use. Fair test use should result in comparable treatment of examinees by avoiding adverse impact due to incorrect inferences or inappropriate actions based on scores. Treatment refers here to decisions (interpretations, inferences, or other actions) based at least in part on test scores. What constitutes comparable treatment requires close attention to the individual instance of test use and will depend upon the purpose of the test, the context of its application, and the consequences of its use. Comparable treatment requires appropriate consideration of all relevant information concerning the individual's background, characteristics, and competencies; use of the same decision process for all individuals and groups; and balanced attention to the interests of all individuals and groups. Fair test use also requires agreement on what constitutes comparable treatment because competing views of distributive justice place different value on different outcomes of assessment. The following aspects of test use illustrate possible threats to comparable treatment in test interpretation and use:

- Using less valid measures than are available.

- Underestimating performance.

- Placing undue weight on a single score.

- Basing decisions on a limited view of relevant proficiency.

- Using an inconsistent decision process.

- Using arbitrary standards.

Evaluating Fairness

The foregoing paragraphs suggest three criteria for evaluating the fairness of a test: comparable opportunity for examinees to demonstrate proficiency, comparable assessment exercises and scores, and comparable treatment of examinees in test interpretation and use. Comparability is the organizing principle, the paradigm that helps to recognize what aspects of a test and its use may threaten fairness, and what modifications may be appropriate. These aspects of comparability and the various points of application outlined above can be seen as facets of fairness, all potentially relevant and none substituting for the other. Thus test fairness, being a corollary of validity, is no less complex than validity. It is useful to think of evaluating the fairness of a test in three steps—more properly, phases of inquiry that involve different types of questions. The distinguishable steps involve identifying possible fairness issues, assessing their impact, and resolving the fairness status of a test.

Identifying issues. Like validity, test fairness involves an extensive complex of potential issues. One does not do justice to the topic or its importance by focusing either criticism or defense of a test on an isolated statistic or a favored argument. Nevertheless, given a particular test and its intended use, some threats to fairness are more plausible and potentially more consequential than others. It is never possible to check everything, so deciding what threats to examine is a nontrivial first step.

Examination of rival hypotheses is an accepted validation strategy (Cronbach, 1990; Messick; 1989). It applies here quite well because the appropriate fairness question is often whether groups differ in unexpected ways or for unexpected reasons. Messick's (1995a) six aspects of construct validity provide the most general framework for entertaining rival hypotheses. Other authors propose variations and examples (Kane, 1992; Shepard, 1993; Snow, 1993). Possible sources of or noncomparability associated with different decisions in the assessment process (Figure 3) is such a framework specifically focused on threats to test fairness.

Testing disabled examinees illustrates the problem of identifying which issues within that framework pose the most likely threat to fairness. In response to federal regulations that mandated comparable tests for disabled and nondisabled people, a series of studies were undertaken to evaluate eight aspects of comparability (Willingham, Ragosta, Bennett, Braun, Rock, & Powers, 1988). These studies gave little attention to construct choice, which was accepted as a given. They focused rather on aspects of testing disabled people that had raised the most serious questions: for example, cognitive comparability of the tests, the functional comparability of testing conditions, and whether "flagging" scores earned under nonstandard conditions had a biasing effect on the use of tests in selection.

Assessing Impact. To assess the impact or importance of a potential fairness issue requires quantifying it in some way. It is certainly true that there are many ways of quantifying the comparability of assessment for two groups of examinees, for example, comparability of factorial structure, reliability, or predictive relationships. By its nature, however, fairness in assessment evokes concerns about the intrinsic justice of invidious judgments and decisions about people and, by extension, groups of people. So it is parsimonious and germane to assume that in most cases the critical fairness concerns are related to differential outcomes of the process.

Two types of outcomes are important: test performance and test-related decisions. Test performance outcomes are the underlying concern in fairness issues that pertain to the first three stages of assessment—design through administration. In these three stages, fairness issues hang specifically on whether group differences in test performance would be different—normally, less discrepant—with valid alternatives to the existing test. The fairness impact question is how much difference would it make if different decisions were reached regarding choice of constructs, choice of format, conditions of administration, etc.

The baseline in answering such questions is the level of differential subgroup performance—the standardized effect size—on the existing test. For example, if a multiple-choice version of a test shows a -.25 effect size favoring males, and a free-response version of the test shows a +.10 effect size favoring females, then we have a differential effect size—a gender format effect—of .35. This metric is generally applicable to most important test fairness questions that pertain to the first three stages of assessment. A number of examples appear in Willingham and Cole's *Gender and Fair Assessment* (1997). The principle is the same in DIF analysis, though the metric is different since it compares item performance on groups assumed to be matched on the construct.

In the fourth stage of assessment, test interpretation and use, fairness questions concern decision outcomes. Normally, the metrics of interest focus directly on what counts, for instance, differential selection rates or the amount of error in estimating criterion performance. One approach to assessing impact is parallel to that described above, that is, how much difference would it make if selection decisions were based on a different set of measures, a different decision process, or if all the weight were put on one score?

A second approach to assessing fairness impact at this stage is to compare decision outcomes for two groups on the basis of an accepted standard. For example, given predictions of likely criterion success, the extent of errors for two groups can be interpreted directly for fairness purposes. Similarly, the proportion of an applicant group that is admitted can be compared directly with the proportion expected on the basis of admissions qualifications. This brings us to the question of deciding what standard to employ in making such assessments, handling disagreement on that point, and more generally, sorting out contradictory evidence as to whether a test is acceptably fair.

Resolving Fairness Status. The final step in evaluating test fairness is to resolve the status of the test and its use. It is one thing to recognize and assess individual fairness issues; it is another thing to decide whether a test must be modified, whether it is acceptably fair for a given purpose, and what constraints should be placed on its use. This is first a matter of assimilating such evidence as that just described. It is then necessarily a matter of weighing the consequences and the alternatives—that facet of construct validity that Messick (1989) has labeled the consequential basis of test use.

A number of considerations bear on the decision to use a test in a particular situation, or a modified test, or no test at all—a complex of factors I referred to earlier as the social matrix of test fairness. There may be specific unresolvable fairness questions about a test that serves, overall, a useful social function. Flagging of nonstandard scores of disabled examinees is a fairness issue that has been researched and debated for more than two decades with no resolution.

Testing procedures and outcomes that seem fair to one group may seem unfair to another. Desirable educational programs and jobs are scarce resources and their allocation engages difficult problems of distributive justice. Justice can be defined in quite different ways on the basis of different value systems (Deutsch, 1975; Rawls, 1971). Messick (1989) applied these ideas to the fair use of tests, pointing out that judgments as to what is fair depend upon which values one wishes to emphasize. For example, should test scores be used in ways that reward accomplishment, improve efficiency, insure equal opportunity, or some other clearly desirable but potentially contradictory social objectives?

Pursuing such value questions, Howe (1994) described three competing conceptions of what is required to obtain equality of educational opportunity. Each supports a different perspective on what constitutes just educational testing, and the choice of terms itself suggests a value orientation. Howe calls testing a paradigm case of an acceptable basis for selecting students in a "formal" conception of equal opportunity that simply requires an absence of barriers to access. A "compensatory" conception adds a requirement for programs that will mitigate disadvantage. A "democratic" conception of equal educational opportunity requires a shift from summative testing that serves institutions to formative testing that serves individual needs, as well as substantial changes in education itself (Howe, 1994, p. 30). Howe's formal and compensatory views of equal opportunity can be seen as the Cleary and the Cole selection models, respectively. The third view apparently sets aside the notion of comparable standards in selective admissions altogether. Clearly, at this level of debate, the resolution of test fairness is largely concerned with different views of distributive justice (Deutsch 1975, Messick, 1989).

CONCLUDING OBSERVATIONS

Recognizing the dynamics of the social matrix in which usefulness, fairness, and practicality determine how we test does not mean that the matrix always works well. Several issues deserve a final comment.

One important issue concerns the need for greater consciousness of fairness at test design rather than examining a test after the fact to see how fair it is. Most tests that have the potential for consequential effects on the life of the examinee are not spawned to a life of their own, to be used or not used depending upon whether the test is judged sufficiently valid in a given situation. Most tests are developed with an intended use in mind. Clearly, tests are likely to be fairer if the implications of design alternatives are carefully examined at the outset. Practically speaking, that is likely to prove quite difficult to do well for most tests. The reason is simple: Such a step presumes much more knowledge of subgroup strengths and weaknesses within the relevant domain and criteria than is normally available.

As Darlington (1971) urged a quarter-century ago, we need a better basis for resolving value issues in measurement. This is partly a conceptual problem, but also a very practical matter of narrowing the present gap between public and professional discourse—a prominent symptom being the acknowledged absence of any consequential discussion of test fairness in the *Standards*. To borrow from Cronbach (1980, p. 105), calling for value-free standards on fairness is a contradiction in terms, a nostalgic longing for a world that never was.

A closely related issue is, "Who is responsible for test fairness?" Is fair design the sole responsibility of test sponsor or test developer? Is fair use the sole responsibility of those who actually handle the scores? These parties cannot deliver on those responsibilities alone, especially since other parties often play a more direct role: school boards, legislatures, courts. Fairness will often ride more on political compromise than on technical precision. We need better ways to involve the measurement profession in the adjudication of what "comparable" can mean and is to mean.

A fundamental value dilemma has always plagued the public view of fair measurement: Does one insure fairness more by standardizing or by individualizing assessment? That is, "Assure me that we are all running the same race" versus "Why don't you test me on something I'm good at?" Individualizing may be critical when the primary purpose of the assessment is to aid student learning (Keeton & Associates, 1976). Standardization has been paramount in testing that is intended to support administrative decisions about individuals and programs where comparability of scores is critical. As Howe's (1994) discussion of equal educational opportunity makes clear, these are different functions, based on different values.

Providing examinees some choice on what they are tested is a forceful example of the standardize-individualize dilemma. Wainer and Thissen (1994) examined empirical evidence of the effect of examinee choice on a traditional psychometric interpretation of comparability. In effect, they argue as follows. If offering examinees a choice makes any difference in their performance, we do not have the technical wherewithal to make their scores comparable and therefore fair for administrative decision-making. If the choice makes no difference in performance, then the fairness advantage of having a choice is unclear.

Reconceptualizing what can be meant by comparable scores may be a way out of the individualize-standardize fairness dilemma if there is more than one functional and useful definition of comparable. Alternate meanings of comparable could presumably be based on educational standards achieved through alternate routes. The challenge is to find communicable ways of relaxing the promises of equivalence that are implied by "comparable" without losing the essential value that lies in an objective assessment of an understandable construct.

A number of writers in recent years have urged that other types of measures might prove fairer for groups with different backgrounds—in addition to or because of greater validity (Frederiksen, 1984; Gordon, in prep.; M. C. Linn, 1992; Resnick & Resnick, 1992; Sternberg, Wagner, Williams, & Horvath 1995; Wiggins, 1993). These hopes turn especially on performance measures that are context-rich and more closely represent the cognitive complexity of real-life situations than is often the case with many current tests. These prospects give all appearance of raising the stakes on fairness in assessment, that is, the promise of gain through more interesting and more relevant tests, the hazard of loss through diminished generalizability and comparability of scores. As Messick (1995b) cautions, alternative measures must meet the same level of rigor regarding standards for validity—and for fairness—that are common to all tests. For fair testing, those standards require a clear understanding of the constructs being assessed and the consequences of their use for all examinees.

REFERENCES

American Educational Research Association, American Psychological Association, & National Council on Measurement in Education. (1985). *Standards for educational and psychological testing.* Washington, DC: American Psychological Association.

Anrig, G. R. (1987, January). 'Golden rule': Second thoughts. *American Psychological Association Monitor, 18*(1), 3.

Association for Measurement and Evaluation in Counseling and Development. (1992). *Responsibilities of users of standardized tests.* Alexandria, VA: American Association for Counseling and Development.

Bersoff, D. N. (1981). Testing and the law. *American Psychologist, 36*, 1047-1056.

Camara, W. J., & Brown, D. C. (1995, Spring). Educational and employment testing: Changing concepts in measurement and policy. *Educational Measurement: Issues and Practice, 14*(1), 5-11.

Churchman, C. W. (1971). *The design of inquiring systems: Basic concepts of systems and organization.* New York: Basic Books.

Civil Rights Act of 1964. (1964). *Pub.L. No. 88-352*, 78 Stat. 243.

Civil Rights Act of 1991. (November 21, 1991). *Pub. L. No. 102-166*, 105 Stat. 1071.

Cleary, T. A. (1968). Test bias: Prediction of grades of Negro and White students in integrated colleges. *Journal of Educational Measurement, 5*(2), 115-124.

Cleary, T. A., & Hilton, T. L. (1968). An investigation of item bias. *Educational and Psychological Measurement, 28*, 61-75.

Cole, N. S. (1973). Bias in selection. *Journal of Educational Measurement, 10*(4), 237-255.

Cole, N. S. (1981). Bias in testing. *American Psychologist, 36*(10), 1067-1077.

Cole, N. S., & Moss, P. A. (1989). Bias in test use. In R. L. Linn (Ed.), *Educational measurement* (3rd ed., pp. 201-219). New York: American Council on Education, & Macmillan.

Cronbach, L. J. (1971). Test validation. In R. L. Thorndike (Ed.), *Educational measurement*, (2nd ed. pp. 443-508). Washington, DC: American Council on Education.

Cronbach, L. J. (1980). Validity on parole: How can we go straight? In W. B. Schrader (Ed.), *New directions for testing and measurement, 5. Measuring achievement over a decade. Proceedings of the 1979 ETS Invitational Conference* (99-108). San Francisco: Jossey-Bass.

Cronbach, L. J. (1990). *Essentials of psychological testing* (5th ed.). New York: Harper Collins Publishers.

Darlington, R. B. (1971). Another look at "cultural fairness." *Journal of Educational Measurement, 8*(2), 71-82.

Debra P. v. Turlington. (1979). 474 F. Supp.244 (M.D. Fla. 1979).

Deutsch, M. (1975). Equity, equality and need: What determines which value will be used as the basis of distributive justice? *Journal of Social Issues, 31*(3), 137-149.

Diamond, E. E., & Tittle, C. K. (1985). Sex equity in testing. In S. Klein (Ed.), *Handbook for Achieving Sex Equity Through Education* (pp. 167-188). Baltimore, MD: Johns Hopkins University.

Equal Employment Opportunity Commission. (1970). Guidelines on employee selection procedures. *Federal Register, 35*, 12333-12336.

Eyde, L. D., Robertson, G. J., Krug, S. E., Moreland, K. L., Robertson, A. G., Shewan, C. M., Harrison, P. L., Porch, B. E., Hammer, A. L., & Primoff, E. S. (1993). *Responsible test use: Case studies for assessing human behavior*. Washington, DC: American Psychological Association.

Fishman, J. A. (1958). Unsolved criterion problems in the selection of college students. *Harvard Educational Review, 28*(4), 340-349.

Flaugher, R. L. (1978). The many definitions of test bias. *American Psychologist, 33*(7), 671-679.

Frederiksen, N. (1984). The real test bias: Influences of testing on teaching and learning. *American Psychologist, 39*, 193-202.

Gipps, C., & Murphy, P. (1994). *A fair test? Assessment, achievement and equity*. Buckingham, England: Open University.

Glazer, N. (1970). Are academic standards obsolete? *Change*. (November-December), 38-44.

Gordon, E. W. (in press). Human diversity and equitable assessment. In S. Messick (Ed.), *Assessment in Higher Education: Issues of Access, Quality, Student Development and Public Policy* (pp. 203-212). Mahway, NJ: Lawrence Erlbaum Associates.

Gottfredson, L. S. (1994). The science and politics of race-norming. *American Psychologist, 49*, 955-963.

Gottfredson, L. S., & Sharf, J. C. (Eds.). (1988). Fairness in employment testing [Special issue]. *Journal of Vocational Behavior, 33*(3).

Hartigan, J. A., & Wigdor, A. K. (Eds.). (1989). *Fairness in employment testing: Validity generalization, minority issues, and the general aptitude test
battery*. Committee on the General Aptitude Test Battery, Commission on
Behavioral and Social Sciences and Education, National Research Council.
Washington, DC: National Academy Press.

Howe, K. R. (1994). Standards, assessment, and equality of educational opportunity. *Educational Researcher, 23,* 27-33.

Hunter, J. E., Schmidt, F. L., & Hunter, R. (1979). Differential validity of employment tests by race: A comprehensive review and analysis. *Psychological Bulletin, 86,* 721-735.

Jensen, A. R. (1980). *Bias in mental testing.* New York: Free Press.

Joint Committee on Testing Practices. (1988). *Code of fair testing practices in
education.* Washington, DC: Author.

Journal of Educational Measurement (1976). On bias in selection, *13*(1), [Spe-
cial issue].

Kane, M. T. (1992). An argument-based approach to validity. *Psychological
Bulletin, 112,* 527-535.

Keeton, M. T., & Associates. (1976). *Experiential learning: Rationale, characteristics, and assessment.* San Francisco: Jossey-Bass.

Klein, S. S. (Ed.). (1985). *Handbook for achieving sex equity through education.* Baltimore, MD: Johns Hopkins University.

Larry P. v. Riles (9th Cir., Jan. 17, 1980). 495 F. Supp. 926 (N.D. Cal. 1979)
appeal docketed, No. 80-4027.

Linn, M. C. (1992). Gender differences in educational achievement. In J.
Pfleiderer (Ed.), *Sex equity in educational opportunity, achievement, and
testing. Proceedings of the 1991 ETS Invitational Conference* (pp. 11-50).
Princeton, NJ: Educational Testing Service.

Linn, R. L. (1973). Fair test use in selection. *Review of Educational Research,
43,* 140-161.

Linn, R. L. (1976). In search of fair selection procedures. *Journal of Educational Measurement, 13*(1), 53-58.

Linn, R. L. (1980, September). *Admissions testing on trial.* Paper presented at
the annual meeting of the American Psychological Association, Montreal,
Quebec, Canada: also *American Psychologist,* 1982, *37,* 279-291.

Linn, R. L. (1982). Ability testing: Individual differences, prediction, and differential prediction. In A. Wigdor & W. Garner (Eds.), *Ability testing:
Uses, consequences, and controversies, Part II (Report of the National
Academy of Sciences Committee on Ability Testing* [pp. 335-388]). Washington, DC: National Academy Press.

Linn, R. L. (Ed.). (1989). *Educational measurement* (3rd ed.). New York:
American Council on Education, Macmillan.

Linn, R. L. (1994). Performance assessment: Policy promises and technical
measurement standards. *Educational Researcher, 23*(9), 4-14.

Linn, R. L., & Werts, C. E. (1971). Considerations for studies of test bias. *Journal of Educational Measurement, 8*(1), 1-4.

Manski, C. F., & Wise, D. A. (1983). *College choice in America.* Cambridge, MA: Harvard University Press.

Messick, S. (1964). Personality measurement and college performance. *Proceedings of the 1963 Invitational Conference on Testing Problems* (pp. 110-129). Princeton, NJ: Educational Testing Service. (Reprinted in A. Anastasi [Ed.]. [1966]. *Testing problems in perspective* [pp. 557-572]. Washington, DC: American Council on Education.)

Messick, S. (1980). Test validity and the ethics of assessment. *American Psychologist, 35,* 1012-1027.

Messick, S. (1989). Validity. In R. L. Linn (Ed.), *Educational measurement* (3rd ed., pp. 13-103). New York: American Council on Education & Macmillan.

Messick, S. (1995a). Validity of psychological assessment: Validation of inferences from persons' responses and performances as scientific inquiry into score meaning. *American Psychologist, 50*(9), 741-749.

Messick, S. (1995b). Standards of validity and the validity of standards in performance assessment. *Educational Measurement: Issues and Practices, 14*(4), 5-8.

Messick, S. (1996). Validity and washback in language testing. *Language Testing, 13*(3), 241-256.

NCME Ad Hoc Committee on the Development of a Code of Ethics. (1995). *Code of professional responsibilities in educational measurement.* Washington, DC: National Council on Measurement in Education.

New York State Testing Act (1980) Education Law, Section 340, *et seq.* Amended 1981, 1986.

Novick, M. R. (1981). Federal guidelines and professional standards. *American Psychologist, 36,* 1035-1046.

Petersen, N. S., & Novick, M. R. (1976). An evaluation of some models for culture-fair selection. *Journal of Educational Measurement, 13*(1), 3-29.

Ramist, L., Lewis, C., & McCamley, L. (1990). Implications of using freshman GPA as the criterion for the predictive validity of the SAT. In W. W. Willingham, C. Lewis, R. Morgan, & L. Ramist, *Predicting college grades: An analsysis of institutional trends over two decades* (pp. 253-288). Princeton, NJ: Educational Testing Service.

Ramist, L., Lewis, C., & McCamley-Jenkins, L. (1994). *Student group difference in predicting college grades: Sex, language, and ethnic group* (CB Report No. 93-1, ETS RR-94-27). New York: College Entrance Examination Board.

Rawls, J. (1971). *A theory of justice.* Cambridge, MA: Harvard University Press.

Rehabilitation Act of 1973. (September 26, 1973.) PL 93-112; 87 Stat. 355.

Resnick, L. B., & Resnick, D. P. (1992). Assessing the thinking curriculum: New tools for educational reform. In B. R. Gifford & M. C. O'Connor (Eds.), *Changing assessments: Alternative views of aptitude, achievement, and instruction* (pp. 37-75). Boston: Kluwer.

Sackett, P. R., & Wilk, S. L. (1994). Within-group norming and other forms of score adjustment in preemployment testing. *American Psychologist, 49,* 929-954.

Schmidt, F. L., Ones, D. S., & Hunter, J. E. (1992). Personnel selection. *Annual Review of Psychology, 43,* 627-670.

Scriven, M. (1980). Methods of inquiry in the philosophy of education. In R. M. Jaeger (Ed.), *Alternative methodologies in educational research.* Washington, DC: American Educational Research Cassette Series.

Sharf, J. C. (1988). Litigating personnel measurement policy. *Journal of Vocational Behavior, 33*(3), 235-271.

Shepard, L. A. (1982). Definitions of bias. In R. A. Berk (Ed.), *Handbook of methods for detecting test bias* (pp. 9-30). Baltimore, MD: Johns Hopkins University.

Shepard, L. A. (1993). Evaluating test validity. In L. Darling-Hammond (Ed.), *Review of research in education* (pp. 405-450). Washington, DC: American Educational Research Association.

Snow, R. E. (1993). Construct validity and constructed-response tests. In R. E. Bennett & W. C. Ward (Eds.), *Construction versus choice in cognitive measurement: Issues in constructed response, performance testing, and portfolio assessment* (pp. 45-60). Hillsdale, NJ: Lawrence Erlbaum Associates.

Sternberg, R. J., Wagner, R. K., Williams, W. M., & Horvath, J. A. (1995). Testing common sense. *American Psychologist, 50*(11), 912-927.

Tenopyr, M. L. (1995). *Measurement at the crossroads.* Paper read at meeting of American Psychological Association, NY, NY.

Thorndike, R. L. (1971). Concepts of culture-fairness. *Journal of Educational Measurement, 8*(2), 63-70.

Wainer, H., & Thissen, D. (1994). On examinee choice in educational testing. *Review of Educational Research, 64,* 159-195.

Wellesley College Center for Research on Women. (1992). *The AAUW report: How schools shortchange girls: A study of major findings on girls and education.* Washington, DC: American Association of University Women Educational Foundation and National Education Association.

Wigdor, A. K., & Garner, W. R. (Eds.). (1982). *Ability testing: Uses, consequences, and controversies.* Washington, DC: National Academy Press.

Wiggins, G. (1993, November). Assessment: Authenticity, context, and validity. *Phi Delta Kappan,* 200-214.

Wild, C. L., & Dwyer, C. A. (1980). Sex bias in selection. In L. J. van der Kamp, W. F. Langerak, & D. N. de Gruijter (Eds.), *Psychometrics for educational debates* (pp. 153-168). New York: Wiley.

Willingham, W. W., & Cole, N. S. (1997). *Gender and fair assessment.* Mahwah, NJ: Lawrence Erlbaum Associates.

Willingham, W. W., & Lewis, C. (1990). Institutional differences in prediction trends. In W. W. Willingham, C. Lewis, R. Morgan, & L. Ramist, *Predicting college grades: An analysis of institutional trends over two decades* (pp. 141-158). Princeton, NJ: Educational Testing Service.

Willingham, W. W., Ragosta, M., Bennett, R. E., Braun, H., Rock, D. A., & Powers, D. E. (1988). *Testing handicapped people.* Boston: Allyn & Bacon.

PART VI

PROSPECTS

The future of higher education assessment depends in large measure, as does the future of higher education itself, on developments in computer and audiovisual technology. The influx of technology into elementary and secondary education creates new modes of individualized learning that higher education will need to accommodate and extend to foster student development. The influx of technology into the workplace creates new demands for flexibility in learning and thinking that higher education will need to prepare students to cope with. The influx of technology into the larger society raises expectations about efficiency and value-added benefits that higher education will need to respond to in a new accountability.

In Chapter 18, Samuel Messick explores these themes by addressing three interrelated issues. He argues, first, that the new technology-based modes of learning will lead to a widening and deepening of individual differences in learning and thinking styles that will need to be accommodated by both assessment and pedagogy in higher education. Second, the technology-instigated rapidity of change in both education and the workplace requires that flexibility in thinking and problem solving become a high priority educational objective in its own right. Third, the cognitive and stylistic demands of the new media themselves will encourage the development of new information-processing skills in such areas as information search, visuospatial representation, and, especially, computer-enhanced problem solving, which will need to be validly assessed both for providing feedback during learning and for certifying competence.

Chapter 18 concludes with a discussion of the promise and threat of the virtual university. The promise is that electronic delivery of both assessment and instruction will dramatically increase access and efficiency while reducing costs for the major educational functions of the university—except those, such as the socialization of youth into the adult world, where human interaction appears to be imperative. Messick leaves the threat unspoken, lurking just beneath the surface of the promise. The threat is that technology may so alter the nature of the adult world, especially the world of work, that socialization into that world by means of technology may not only become feasible but necessary.

18

TECHNOLOGY AND THE FUTURE
OF HIGHER EDUCATION ASSESSMENT

Samuel Messick
Educational Testing Service

Computer technologies, including multimedia, are dramatically changing the way individuals learn as well as the way they work. Technological innovations are having a profound impact on the processes of instruction, selection, guidance, placement, and performance in both educational and employment settings. As a consequence, higher education needs to gear up to capitalize upon and extend the new technology-based modes of learning as well as to prepare individuals to cope with new and changing demands of the workplace. Meeting these challenges will require, among many other accommodations, a more extensive and varied role of assessment in higher education. The greatly expanded diversity of new demands on individuals and institutions will require new and more varied methods of assessing new and more varied aptitudes, competencies, and personal qualities, using new and more varied delivery systems to respond effectively and in timely fashion to new and more varied educational and societal needs.

Given the rapid pace and pervasiveness of technological change, some rationale is needed to guide proposed enhancements in higher education assessment, as well as in higher education itself, to minimize haphazard and trial-and-error responses. Of the numerous features of a technology-dominated future that are relevant to education and assessment, many of which bear common implications concerning the need for diversity in both the content and methods of learning and measurement, we will highlight three major ones:

First, the massive infusion of computer technology into education will lead to a heightened individuality in learning and performance as well as to a widening and deepening of consistent individual differences in learning and thinking styles.

Second, the explosion of computer technology in the workplace and in society at large will engender an enduring period of flux in which a premium will be placed on adaptive learning, on cognitive restructuring skills, and on flexibility in modes of thinking.

Finally, the cognitive and stylistic requirements of the new media per se convey an important message for the development and honing of congenial cognitive skills, cognitive styles, and performance consistencies, while the widespread deployment of these media creates expectations for how efficiently information should be processed and delivered.

These are by no means the only reasons, however, to revamp higher education and its supporting measurement system. Indeed, after exploring these three major forces, which in a sense impact higher education only indirectly by creating new educational needs to address, we will examine the impact of telecommunication networks, which will likely directly impact the nature of both higher education and its assessment requirements.

FUTURE DEMANDS ON ASSESSMENT

The three principles concerning the widening and deepening of individual differences, the need for flexibility in adapting to rapid change, and the message of the medium itself are not only interrelated but potentially in conflict. As a consequence, these issues should not be addressed separately but rather in various combinations. Many of the points that follow will sound familiar because they echo similar positions taken throughout this volume.

Heightened Individuality and the Need for Flexibility

The distinction between testing and instruction is becoming blurred, because the setting of tasks and the posing of problems, as well as the provision of feedback about the adequacy of performance, has come to be at least partly under the control of technology. There is thus a need for a variety of curriculum-embedded tests not just to certify the extent to which intended goals of instruction have been mastered or to signal progression or branching to next steps, but also to assess generalization and transfer skills and provide feedback about differential learning. In this sense, what is needed are not just tests as evaluators of learning but as vehicles for learning.

Because education is becoming more individualized, such curriculum-embedded tests (or various combinations of modular subtests) will have to cover a range of contents and formats to cope with the diversity of individualized learning. To accomplish this effectively, the tests will likely have to be computer-adaptive. Under these circumstances, the issues of fairness and choice become greatly exacerbated because the problem is not just one of assessment's responsiveness to diversity, but of education's responsiveness, as underscored by both Durán and Gordon in Part V. Furthermore, as anticipated by Gordon in Chapter 16, the problem is not just one of group or cultural *diversity* in education and assessment, but of *individuality*.

Education will become more individualized through technology because learners will be able to proceed through different instructional sequences at their own pace with differing amounts of recycling, even with changes in sequence and mode during repeated trials. They will be able to do this alone or in interaction with other learners, not only in school but in other settings where the technology is available, and not only during school hours but at other times of the day and night. Students may also be able to choose from among an array of instructional modules having the same general outcome goals but differing in the degree of structure provided, in mode of presentation, in inductive versus didactic approach, or in other stylistic features.

In the face of such options, unless they are placed under firm prescriptive control, individual learners will tend to choose modules and sequences and tempos that are compatible with their broad cognitive styles, their more specific learning styles, their patterns of developed abilities, and their interests. Learners will resonate to congenial instructional sequences that compensate for their weaknesses or capitalize on their strengths, with the consequence that existing ability patterns and styles of learning and thinking will tend to become intensified and more ingrained.

Such compensatory or capitalization strategies for matching instruction to learner characteristics may be fine with respect to the acquisition of skills and subject-matter knowledge, but anything that makes learning and thinking styles more ingrained and habitual is counter to the need for flexibility in thinking to be discussed in the next section. What is needed to foster flexibility in thinking is some systematic *mismatching* of instructional experiences to learner characteristics so as to confront existing cognitive styles with alternative modes of thought (Chickering, 1976; Messick, 1976). Given its importance in coping with change, flexibility of thinking should become a major educational goal in its own right and needs to be reliably measured as a key dimension of individual performance repertoires.

The question of matching or mismatching of instruction to learner characteristics in the name of individualization raises problems of either prescription or self-choice. Coping with either problem will require much more extensive assessment of functional characteristics of learners than is currently available, including measures of skill repertoires, knowledge structures, cognitive and learning styles, interests, and motivation, as emphasized by Everson and by Snow in Part III of this volume. Because students should probably have some say in the matter even when instructional prescriptions are well-grounded in empirical research (Glaser, 1977; Messick, 1996), this broadened array of learner measures will come to be used primarily in the service not of selection but of instructional guidance and placement, which will become much more important functions in individualized than in traditional education.

Along with this deepening or entrenchment of individual differences, there will also be a widening of individual differences because computer technology will not be uniformly available to all segments of the populace for some time. In addition to a widening gap between the haves and have-nots, however, there will also be a widening gap between the technology-minded and the technology-timid. That is, among those who have access to technology, some will embrace it enthusiastically while others will find it aversive because it somehow is not in harmony with their temperament, cognitive style, attitudes and values, or other personality dispositions. Thus, the educational measurement needs not only of the have-nots but of the want-nots will have to be served by a variety of alternative procedures, thereby further complicating the issues of comparability and fairness along lines akin to those discussed by Gordon and by Willingham in Part V.

Flexibility and Performance

The infusion of technology into the workplace and the larger society will lead to a continual structuring and restructuring of jobs as institutions attempt to accommodate their changing technology capabilities. As a consequence, individuals will need to cope with the cognitive requirements of change, which call for flexibility in learning and thinking, as well as with the emotional tensions and apprehensions that change is likely to precipitate. Because individuals will often have to cope with a changing interpersonal scene, adjusting to different casts of participants and different role relationships, a premium will also be placed on interpersonal sensitivity and social skills. These and other noncognitive characteristics will accordingly become goals or desired outcomes of higher education as anticipated by Chickering in Chapter 2 and by Ewell in Chapter 12. Measures of flexibility and of personal-adjustment and interpersonal skills will be needed if these variables are to be taken into account in guidance and placement or to serve as targets for skill development as higher education attempts to prepare students for realistic requirements of the workplace.

Because what a person needs to know and do may change numerous times during a career, there will be an increasing need to measure directly a person's readiness for learning in a particular area, as opposed to assessing the precursors or predictors of learning readiness. This might be done by gauging the difference between performance levels under standard test conditions and performance levels when hints, leading questions, or supplementary instruction are supplied. The larger the difference in these performance levels—what Vygotsky (1978) called "the zone of proximal development"—the greater the individual's potential for movement through further learning in the area (Feuerstein, 1980).

This is in the same spirit of stimulating further learning through student reflection and feedback as expounded by Cross, McKeachie, and Read in Part II. In this direct approach to assessing learning readiness, responsiveness to current instruction is used to predict responsiveness to subsequent instruction, which is a form of persistence forecasting (Wallach, 1976). This is in contrast to measuring functional learner characteristics such as abilities to predict responsiveness to instruction. This measurement approach is akin to the use of work samples, which are perennially the best predictors of job performance because they are measures not only of job skills but of the effective joint utilization of those skills in the job context—that is, they are realistic overall measures of complex task performance.

This emphasis on the measurement of complex performance, as opposed to measuring only requisite knowledge and skills, will become more widespread because of the apparent and quickly justifiable link to job and task performance for predictive purposes. At the same time, however, there will continue to be strong emphasis on measuring component skills and processes for diagnostic purposes (Anderson, Reder, & Simon, 1996; Messick, 1994b). Performance measurement is especially pertinent and straightforward in the assessment of generic competencies such as listening and speaking as well as reading and writing, but it is also being widely applied to the assessment of other complex skills. For example, performance on work samples or in simulated situations—whether simulated by means of paper-and-pencil, videotapes, live role playing, or computer presentation—provides an experimental means of assessing such complex skills as judgment and planning, decision making, entrepreneurial ability, and interpersonal sensitivity.

Thus, increased emphasis needs to be placed on performance measures of cognitive and interpersonal skills and of flexibility in their application under different circumstances. Because performance measurement of complex skills requires examinees to produce constructed responses, the development of technology for recording and reliably scoring constructed responses needs to have high priority for the immediate future, as stressed by Breland in Chapter 8. Apart from Vygotsky's (1978) proximal-development approach, which is endemic to education, the impetus for performance measurement stems from the standards-based reform movement in elementary and secondary education, as emphasized by Linn in Chapter 7, as well as from the pressures of change in the workplace. But in time, this emphasis on performance, not just knowledge, will come to permeate higher education as well, as predicted by Keeton in Chapter 4 and by Ewell in Chapter 12.

Impact of the Medium

Computer and multimedia technologies require a different mix and balance of information-processing skills than do static media such as books. For example, listening skills become more prominent in processing audiovisual presentations, as do skills of visuospatial representation and episodic visual memory—that is, memory for ordered sequences of episodes or scenes. Continual experience with these media may further develop and hone such formerly less practiced skills, as well as stimulate the emergence of nascent skills such as those involved in graphical and dimensional imagery. As another instance, the computer serves as a powerful extension of thinking in problem solving, so that problem solving with the computer is radically and perhaps qualitatively different from problem solving without it. Continual experience with computer-extended problem solving may stimulate the emergence of new or newly emphasized cognitive skills or lead to a reorganization of knowledge and skill structures more amenable to the computer medium, which is consistent with Everson's design framework in Chapter 9.

The measurement of specialized skills and structures especially conducive to the processing of information conveyed by technological media will likely have to entail in turn the presentation of test material via the same media and may have to be computer-based. Certainly the assessment of skill in computer-enhanced problem solving will have to be computer-based. As computer technologies become more widespread, the importance of measuring these new aptitudes or skills becomes more salient. But measurement of these medium-oriented aptitudes or skills will not replace the measurement of the more traditional aptitudes or skills of reading and writing—it is more a question of balance. This is so because although skill in configurational processing and visuospatial representation is critical in dealing with tangible and concrete information (where a picture may be worth a thousand words) as well as in mental modeling and problem representation (Baddeley, 1986; Lohman, 1996), skill in using the linguistic/propositional symbol system of reading and writing remains critical for dealing with nonvisible and abstract aspects of phenomena.

In any event, it should be emphasized that the impact of the medium is not universal but, rather, is contingent on the functional characteristics that individuals bring to the medium, especially their profile of abilities and their cognitive and learning styles. The content and form of the medium delimits what information one *should* address. The person's profile of abilities and cognitive skills determines what information one *can* address. The person's cognitive and learning styles determine what information one *does* address and *how*—as does a person's disabilities which, according to Bennett in Chapter 14, may also be potentially accommodated through technology. Thus, consistent individual differences in responsiveness to the media serve to circumscribe individual differences in learning, performance, and skill development via the media.

In addition to their cognitive impact, the media also markedly influence attitudes and expectations. For example, to the extent that instruction and testing in schools and colleges are computer-based, whether individualized or not, the students will expect all important testing to be computer-based because that would allow them to display in the same form the skills they acquired through formal education. Indeed, as technology becomes more pervasive in education, noncomputerized testing will be perceived to lack face validity as measures of school learning and academic aptitude.

Implications for Future Assessment

The heightened individuality of learning expected in the future, the increased need for flexibility in learning and thinking, and the impact of the medium as a vehicle for learning and performance all converge in highlighting a key set of implications for the future of higher education assessment. To begin with, the measurement armamentarium needs to be greatly expanded beyond the assessment of a few academic aptitudes and school achievements to provide a fuller reading of an individual's accomplishments and potential, as Snow maintains in Chapter 10.

This expansion should occur both within the domain of cognitive measures and beyond that domain to include the assessment of styles and of noncognitive or personal characteristics. Within cognition, assessment should be extended beyond the measurement of tried-and-true verbal and quantitative abilities to include measures of information-processing skills entailed in comprehension broadly conceived (not just reading comprehension), memory, reasoning, judgment, visualization, fluency, and flexibility. With respect to styles, assessment should include a number of cognitive styles such as field independence versus field sensitivity and converging versus diverging, as well as a number of learning styles such as holist versus serialist approach and deep versus shallow processing (Messick, 1994a, 1994c; Schmeck, 1988). In regard to so-called noncognitive or personal characteristics, the focus should be on measures of interests, attitudes, and motivation (Messick, 1996; Snow, Corno, & Jackson, 1996).

As a tactical suggestion, it would probably be best to begin the expansion of assessment by including at least some measures from all three domains (cognitive, stylistic, noncognitive) at the outset, filling in each domain with additional measures as soon as possible. This would insure that major distinct sources of examinee variance were included in higher education assessment in initial implementations.

The impetus for this expanded measurement stems from an increasing recognition of the utility of a broad range of examinee information in guidance and placement as well as of its usefulness in selection for evaluating a student's potential for growth in the context of his or her background opportunities, a value-added perspective advanced by Hargadon in Chapter 11 and by Astin in Chapter

13. In the context of guidance and placement, this broad range of measures is to be justified not so much by traditional predictive validity as by the usefulness of the information in individual and institutional decision making. However, while predictive validity is not the principle determinant for including a measure, construct validity will be because, as Willingham stresses in Chapter 17, comparable construct validity across individuals, groups, and settings is the sine qua non of test fairness.

Another measurement implication from this consideration of individuality, flexibility in response to change, and media impact is that increased emphasis should be placed on the measurement of performance. This implies a capability for presenting complex tasks as criterion samples or in simulated situations as well as a capability for scoring and interpreting constructed responses. This might entail the creation of computer simulations, for example, and the application of artificial intelligence techniques for natural language processing to the scoring of constructed responses.

The implications that the range of measurement should be expanded and the methods become more performance-based, taken together, suggest that a major commitment should be made to computer-based assessment. With computer technology, a wide range of short adaptive tests could be administered within a reasonable time frame without sacrificing reliability and precision of measurement. Computer simulation would also permit the presentation of complex tasks entailing dynamic interplay over time both between parts of the task and between the examinee and the computer, with the prospect of assessing both the sequence and timing of task activities. Such capabilities will permit both the assessment of overall task performance and the diagnosis of areas of deficiency as well as of expertise.

As emphasized throughout this volume, attention should be continuously focussed on the key measurement issues inherent in this future assessment. The key measurement issues are the same as they have always been—namely, the issues of comparability underlying considerations of equating, scaling, and norming; the issues of the validity and generalizability of score interpretations; of the demonstrated utility of the interpreted information; and, of the fairness of measurement when different methods and media are applied to the assessment of different individuals (Messick, 1995).

THE PROMISE AND THREAT OF THE VIRTUAL UNIVERSITY

As Everson noted in Chapter 9, the rapid expansion of telecommunication networks in the 1990s promises a powerful capability for administering tests, leading to likely improvements in access to testing programs, in the convenience of testing arrangements, and in the timeliness of score reporting. At the same time, the advent of electronic networking also affords a powerful means of delivering instruction, pedagogical materials, and educational experiences on line, with enormous potential for increasing efficiency and reducing costs in education.

Indeed, the two together—the electronic transmission of both instruction and assessment—promise to create a virtual university, with the prospect of dramatically changing the nature of higher education as we know it and of radically transforming the role of higher education assessment. Furthermore, the concept of a virtual university is no longer a will-o'-the-wisp or pipe dream. It is a reality discernible on the horizon, or at least a virtual reality.

A clear portent of the electronic future of higher education has already occurred in mid-1996. The governors of 10 western states have agreed to draw up a business plan for a virtual university that will allow students nationwide to take courses and eventually earn degrees on line. An on-line catalog is in the offing, which will be continuously updated to facilitate access to a variety of course offerings. Students can thus be exposed to the best of higher education experiences without being bound to options available at local colleges or universities. This range of choice at a homebase computer may substantially affect the pattern of college-going, especially for foreign students.

In such an electronic environment, the role of assessment in higher education can be expected to assume a much different cast. Admissions testing will no longer be a serious issue. Rather, testing will increasingly be in the service of instructional guidance and placement as well as of career guidance and decision making. These new or expanded testing requirements reinforce the need, reiterated throughout this volume, for assessment of a broader array of cognitive skills as well as of cognitive and learning styles, interests, values, and motivation to better serve a student-centered guidance function.

Moreover, in the virtual university, degrees are unlikely to be awarded on the basis of accumulated credits but, rather, in terms of demonstrated competence. Again, as stressed throughout this volume, the assessment of demonstrated competence will need to become more performance-based so that multiple aspects of competence can be evaluated, including affective and motivational as well as cognitive aspects. Thus, the point articulated by Ewell in Chapter 12—that to certify competence, knowledge and skill should be demonstrable in action and not just in theory—is likely to become greatly amplified in the virtual university as a means of legitimizing virtual degrees.

The remarks in this concluding chapter should not be taken to imply that the problems of higher education will be solved by expanded technology-based instruction and assessment per se. But rather that many of the problems will not be solved without expanded education and assessment. Notwithstanding, there are still critical functions of higher education, not the least of which is the socialization of students as citizens of the adult world, that will likely always require human and not just technological interaction and oversight.

REFERENCES

Anderson, J. R., Reder, L. M., & Simon, H. A. (1996). Situated learning and education. *Educational Researcher, 25*(4), 5-11.

Baddeley, A. (1986). *Working memory.* Oxford, England: Clarendon.

Chickering, A. W. (1976). The double bind of field dependence/independence in program alternatives for educational development. In S. Messick (Ed.), *Individuality in learning: Implications of cognitive styles and creativity for human development* (pp. 79-89). San Francisco: Jossey-Bass.

Feuerstein, R. (1980). *Instrumental enrichment: An intervention program for cognitive modifiability.* Baltimore, MD: University Park Press.

Glaser, R. (1977). *Adaptive education: Individual diversity and learning.* New York: Holt, Rinehart and Winston.

Lohman, D. F. (1996). Spatial ability and g. In I. Dennis & P. Tapsfield (Eds.), *Human abilities: Their nature and measurement* (pp. 97-116). Hillsdale, NJ: Lawrence Erlbaum Associates.

Messick, S. (1976). Personal styles and educational options. In S. Messick (Ed.), *Individuality in learning: Implications of cognitive styles and creativity for human development* (pp. 310-326). San Francisco: Jossey-Bass.

Messick, S. (1994a). Cognitive styles and learning. In T. Husen & T. N. Postlethwaite (Eds.), *International encyclopedia of education* (2nd ed., pp. 638-641). New York: Pergamon.

Messick, S. (1994b). The interplay of evidence and consequences in the validation of performance assessments. *Educational Researcher, 23*(2), 13-23.

Messick, S. (1994c). The matter of style: Manifestations of personality in cognition, learning, and teaching. *Educational Psychologist, 29,* 121-136.

Messick, S. (1995). Validity of psychological assessment: Validation of inferences from persons' responses and performances as scientific inquiry into score meaning. *American Psychologist, 50,* 741-749.

Messick, S. (1996). Bridging cognition and personality in education: The role of style in performance and development. *European Journal of Personality, 10,* 353-376.

Schmeck, R. R.. (Ed.). (1988). *Learning strategies and learning styles.* New York: Plenum.

Snow, R. E., Corno, L., & Jackson, D. N., III. (1996). Individual differences in affective and conative functions. In D. C. Berliner & R. Calfee (Eds.), *Handbook of education psychology* (pp. 243-310). New York: Macmillan.

Vygotsky, L. S. (1978). *Mind in society: The development of higher psychological processes.* Cambridge, MA: Harvard University Press.

Wallach, M A. (1976). Psychology of talent and graduate education. In S. Messick (Ed.), *Individuality in learning: Implications of cognitive styles and creativity for human development* (pp. 178-210). San Francisco: Jossey-Bass.

Author Index

A

Abedi, 195
Ackerman, 97
Algozzine, 188
Allen, 206, 210
Anastasi, 93
Anderson, 249
Andrews, 183, 184
Angelo, 58
Anrig, 217, 219
Armour-Thomas, 210
Astin, 15, 158, 159, 162, 167-169

B

Baddeley, 250
Baker, 96, 101, 103, 105
Bamford, 50
Belenky, 20, 21
Bejar, 95, 113, 121, 127, 138, 139
Belan, 122
Bennett, 93, 95, 113, 114, 115, 122, 123, 127, 183, 187, 233
Bereiter, 138, 139
Bersoff, 214
Birenbaum, 214
Bloom, 38
Bolus, 93
Boyer, 14
Braun, 183, 186, 193, 233
Breland, 99, 101, 249
Brennan, 120, 138
Brown, 214
Burton, 83, 99
Butler, 74

C

Camara, 214
Carroll, 134, 135, 136, 139
Carpenter, 139
Cashin, 37, 44
Centra, 37, 44
Chickering, 13, 146, 151
Chipman, 120, 138
Christian, 159
Cleary, 215, 216, 222, 235
Clinchy, 20
Coffman, 99, 101
Cohen, 37, 44, 38, 79
Cohen, 89
Cole, 215, 217, 220, 221-224, 226-228, 231, 235, 249
Collins, 92, 96, 97, 138, 139, 197
Coombs, 186, 187
Corno, 138, 251
Crittenden, 186
Crocker, 99, 101, 110, 115
Cronbach, 218, 223, 224, 233, 236
Cross, 35, 39, 160, 249
Crouse, 82

D

Diamond, 218, 219, 222
Darling-Hammond, 77
Darlington, 215, 217, 218, 236
Deutsch, 4, 235
Dewey, 78
DiQuinzio, 182
Donlon, 82, 83
Dowell, 38
Downey, 114, 127
Dribben, 184
Dunbar, 96, 99, 101-103, 105, 107
Durán, 101, 103, 193, 194, 196-198, 200
Durso, 187

E

Edgerton, 38
Embretson, 120, 124, 127
Ennis, 208
Epstein, 35
Everson, 113, 116, 120, 123, 127, 136, 249
Eyde, 230

F

Farmer, 183
Feldman, 196
Feuerstein, 248
Fine, 73
Fitzpatrick, 94, 109
Fishman, 224
Flaugher, 218, 223
Flower, 97, 98, 139
Fordham, 206

Frederiksen, 92, 96, 113, 124, 127, 138, 139, 138
Fuchs, 188
Fuess, 81, 82

G

Gamson, 51
Garner, 215, 218
Gaynor, 101
Geisinger, 188
Gentner, 97, 138, 139
Gioella, 186
Gipps, 218, 219, 223
Gitomer, 122, 127
Glaser, 78, 116, 121, 127, 138, 139, 247
Glazer, 214
Gleason-Weimer, 37, 60
Godshallk, 101
Goldberger, 20
Goldman, 197, 198
Golub-Smith, 187
Gordon, 162, 205, 206, 210
Gottfredson, 217, 218
Graue, 79
Gragg, 41, 44
Griswold, 101
Guilford, 136, 139
Gustaffson, 136, 139

H

Haertel, 100
Hambleton, 120
Hamilton, 208
Hammond, 77, 78
Hargadon, 71
Harmon, 77
Harris, 164
Hartigan, 215, 217, 218
Havill, 198
Hayes, 97, 98, 138, 139
Heller, 4
Henson, 159
Herrnstein, 207
Hilton, 215
Holtzman, 4, 9
Hoover, 96, 98, 99, 102, 109
Hopkins, 48
Houghton, 75, 85
Howe, 235, 236

Hunt, 118
Hunter, 214, 215
Hutchings, 43

J

Jackson, 138
Jacquemin, 186
Jensen, 218, 222
Jirele, 187
Jones, 123
Just, 139

K

Kamusikiri, 93
Kane, 233
Kaplan, 183, 186, 187
Katz, 121
Kay, 196
Keeton, 11, 19, 47, 48, 59, 236, 249
Kelly, 121, 127
Kerkhoven, 208
Kintsch, 138, 139
Klein, 93, 101, 109, 219
Klemp, 18, 19
Koretz, 96, 99, 102, 109
Kozol, 86
Krashen, 199
Kulik, 37, 44
Kupermintz, 208

L

Laing, 183
Lajoie, 116, 166
Lamden, 19
Lane, 116, 166
Langer, 58
Lauritzen, 122
Lesgold, 116, 121, 127, 138, 139
Levering, 182, 185
Lewis, 121, 221, 224
Light, 40, 41
Linn, 79, 83, 85, 86, 101, 103, 105, 169, 215, 218, 220, 221, 223, 224, 227, 249
Lloyd-Jones, 103, 109
Loeding, 186
Loevinger, 20, 21
Lohman, 93, 104, 114, 119, 250
Lomax, 79
Lord, 120

Lowell, 81
Lowman, 36
Lutz, 93

M

Machan, 184
Madaus, 79, 80
Marshall, 124
Martin, 122
Martinez, 121
McCamley, 224
McCamley-Jenkins, 221
McKeachie, 11, 37, 157, 168, 249
Mehrens, 96
Merrill, 137
Messick, 3, 4, 79, 84, 94, 96, 97, 103,
    113, 117, 118, 127, 194, 218, 220,
    222, 223, 225, 226, 233, 235, 236,
    247, 249, 251, 252
Miller, 99, 110
Mills, 187
Mislevy, 93, 113, 138
Mitchen, 116
Morley, 186
Morris, 108
Morrison, 94, 109
Moss, 92, 110, 199, 218, 221, 222, 223,
    228
Murphy, 104, 110, 218, 219, 223
Murray, 37, 59, 60, 207

N

Nathan, 84, 85, 89
Neal, 38, 44
Newcomb, 13
Newman, 16, 20
Nichols, 93, 103, 120, 138
Novick, 120, 214, 216
Nozick, 4
Nunnally, 121
Nussbaum, 208

O

O'Connor, 196
O'Day, 79
Ogbu, 206
Ones, 214
Okun, 4
Owen, 82

P

Pambookian, 59
Pascarella, 16
Pask, 137
Pearl, 122
Pennock-Roman, 193
Perfetti, 138
Perry, 20, 21
Petersen, 216
Postman, 171,
Powers, 183, 184, 233

R

Ragosta, 183, 185, 186, 233
Ramist, 221, 222, 224
Rawls, 4, 235
Read, 11, 157, 249
Reckase, 99, 120
Redden, 182, 185
Reder, 249
Resnick, 78, 80, 83, 92, 210, 226
Revlin, 198
Reynolds, 188
Robinson, 182
Rock, 95, 120, 127, 183, 187, 233
Rottenberg, 79
Rubin, 184
Ruth, 104, 110

S

Sackett, 217, 222
Sanders, 79
Scardamalia, 138, 139
Schaeffer, 187
Schmeck, 251
Schmidt, 214, 215, 224
Schwartz, 84-86
Scott, 137, 151
Scriven, 223
Sebrechts, 95
Shafto, 121, 127, 138, 139
Shanker, 85, 86, 89, 188
Sharf, 214, 215, 218
Sheckley, 19, 20
Sheehan, 120, 121
Shell, 139
Shephard, 79, 92, 184, 216, 218, 222,
    223,
Sherman, 182
Simon, 249

Singley, 186
Smith, 79, 97, 196, 197
Snow, 93, 104, 114, 119, 137-139,
    168, 208, 233, 251
Spiegelhalter, 122
Steffin, 186, 187
Steinberg, 122, 127
Sternberg, 117, 118, 138
Stewart, 75, 123
Stolurow, 137
Swaminathan, 120
Swineford, 101
Szymanski, 200

T

Talbert, 208
Tarule, 20
Tate, 48
Tatsuoka, 120, 121, 127, 138
Tenopyr, 215, 218
Terenzini, 16, 33
Thissen, 236
Thorndike, 215
Tittle, 218, 219, 222
Tobias, 116
Trusheim, 82

U

Undheim, 136, 139

V

VanLehn, 122
Verhelst, 120
Viator, 79, 88
Vygotsky, 249

W

Wallachn, 249
Wainer, 236
Ward, 121, 127
Weingartner, 171
Weinstein, 116, 117
Wendler, 185
Werts, 224, 227, 247
West, 79
Whitaker, 50
White, 93, 96
Wigdor, 215, 217, 218
Wiggins, 92, 111, 186

Wild, 218, 224
Wilk, 217, 222
Willingham, 7, 35, 67, 183, 184, 213,
    217, 224, 233
Wilson, 57
Wong-Fillmore, 199

Y

Yamamoto, 120, 127

Subject Index

A

AAHE, 35
ACHE, 52
ACT, 137, 167, 173
AERA, 184
AP, 142
APA, 184, 189
Academic Standards, 161
Admissions Testing, 3, 6, 69, 71, 72,
  91, 113, 114, 116, 124, 125, 133,
  137, 139, 140-142, 183, 185, 187,
  188
Adult Development, 26
  Learning, 51, 52, 55, 56
Auditory Perception, 134
American Association of Collegiate
  Schools of Business, 49
American College Testing, 19
Americans with Disabilities Act, 184,
  187
Apprenticeships, 53
Assessment, 9, 16, 32, 34-36, 47-55,
  57, 58, 60, 61, 63-68, 113, 114,
  116, 117, 121, 123-125, 127-132,
  147-150, 153-156, 157, 158, 161,
  193, 194, 203-211, 243, 245, 247
  Classroom, 10, 38-44, 58, 60
  Direct, 96
  Educational, 203, 204
  Issues, 32
  Performance, 54, 69, 70, 80,
    84, 98, 103, 106-108,
    115, 116
  Portfolio-Assisted, 48
  Quality, 149
Authentic, 92, 95-97, 118, 155

B

Bayesian Inference Networks, 122

C

CAEL, 35, 47-51
Carnegie Commission on the Non-
  Traditional Student, 52
CAT, 39, 40, 42, 43, 117

CBT, 181, 185, 186-189
CEEB, 74, 75, 81, 82
CIRC, 200
CIRP, 32, 167
CLEP, 52
COEP, 149
Cognitive 69, 70-72
  Abilities, 117
  Complexity, 107, 112
  Models, 139
  Psychology, 93, 117, 119,
    123,129,131
  Style, 22
  Theories, 123
College Admissions, 70, 71
  Testing, 73, 113
College Board, 52, 74-76, 78, 80-82,
  88-91, 193, 194, 201, 202, 215
  Achievement Tests, 173
  Computerized Placement
    Testing, 113, 124, 125
  Student Descriptive
    Questionnaire, 194
Comprehensive Reading, 64
Computer Based Testing, 113, 124,
  125, 178, 185
Computerized Performance Tests, 139
Conative, 134
Construct Domain, 98, 111
  Validity, 216, 222
Content Standards, 69, 70
Credential Learning, 9, 11
Critical Reading, 115
  Thinking, 117, 125
Cross-cutting, 4, 6

D

Depth, 133
Differential Validity, 213, 223
Diversity, 203-206, 209, 210, 245, 247,
  248, 257

E

ECS, 151
ECT, 97
Educational Measurement, 114-117,
  127, 130, 131

Ego Development, 22
Enhanced Score Reporting, 126
Equity, 1, 177
Essay Tests, 93, 96
ESL, 197, 198, 201
ETS, 35, 64, 68, 76, 124, 128, 129,
    131, 132, 174, 182-184-, 186, 187,
    190, 193, 214, 215, 243, 244, 246
Experiential Learning, 48-51, 53, 54,
    56

F

FIPSE, 63, 149
Faculty Performance, 38
Fairness, 1, 93, 98, 105, 111-113, 177,
    179, 181
Fluid-Analytical Reasoning, 134
Fluid Reasoning, 137, 139

G

GATB, 218
GED, 54
GIS, 156
Generalizability, 98, 101, 105
GMAT, 91, 101
GPA, 164, 167
GRE, 84, 92, 101, 124, 137, 139, 140,
    167, 173, 174, 183, 185, 187, 191
Group Fairness, 222

H

Higher Education, 1, 9-11, 26, 35, 36,
    63, 64, 66-69, 85, 245, 247, 249,
    250, 253, 255
        Assessment, 3, 4, 7, 8, 145,
        147
Human Development, 13, 16, 20, 21,
    26, 28
Human Diversity, 2, 179, 203, 204,
    209, 211

I

IBM, 115
ICEL, 53
IRT, 120, 122, 133
Individuality, 246, 248, 253, 254
Individualized Content, 66
Instructional Technology, 154
Institutional Objectives, 13, 15, 16, 34

Internships, 67
Interpersonal Skills, 18, 19

K

KIRIS, 103

L

LSAT, 92
Latent Trait Models, 120, 121

M

MCAT, 91, 101, 167, 173
Measurement, 114, 116, 118-121, 123,
    124, 126-132, 213, 214, 216, 217,
    219, 220-225, 240, 242, 243, 245,
    246, 247, 249, 250, 252-254, 257
        Model-based, 71, 119, 126
Mechanical Reasoning, 137
Memory, 134, 137
Meta-analysis, 36-38, 44
Metacognition, 117, 125
Minute Paper, 40-42, 57
Multiple-Choice, 78, 80, 84, 196, 197

N

NAEP, 195, 196, 200-202
NCHEMS, 147, 151
NCME, 184
NCTM, 77
NGA, 75, 76, 85
NRC, 218
NSEE, 53
NUCEA, 52
National Assessment of Educational
    Progress, 169
National Academy of Sciences, 182
National Education Goals, 156, 169
National Merit, 160
National Education Standards, 76
New Accountability, 149, 151

P

Perceptual Ability, 134, 137
Performance, 245-250, 253-255, 257
    Measurement, 250
    Standards, 69, 70, 74, 77-79,
        85-87, 161, 162, 166

Personal Qualities, 13, 16, 17, 20, 26, 36
Pluralism, 203, 204, 206
Problem Solving, 116-119, 121, 123, 125, 129
Proctored Examinations, 54
Project LEARN, 51
Psychological Measurement, 69
    Theory, 134
Psychometrics, 113, 115, 123, 128
    Modeling, 69, 123, 125, 132
    Principles, 50

R

Raven Matrices, 137, 139
Reading Comprehension, 195, 200, 201
Realism, 95, 98, 109, 111
Reform Movement, 69-71
Reliability, 64, 95, 101, 103, 105, 111, 116

S

SAT, 70, 82-84, 86, 88-90, 92, 97, 105, 113-116, 118, 119, 121, 122, 127, 137, 139, 141-143, 167, 173, 174, 183, 184, 187, 190, 191, 193-195, 223, 246
SCANS, 19
SDQ, 194
SPRE, 150
Self-Assessment 38, 44
Self-Awareness, 39
Spatial Ability, 134, 137
    Reasoning, 124
Standards-based Reform Movement, 73, 76-79, 81, 83-87, 98
Standardized Tests, 157, 158, 164, 166, 168, 169, 172, 174, 208
Statistical Cybernetics, 59
Statistical Pattern Recognition, 121-123
Student Development, 9, 10
Student Performance, 40, 43
Subjectivity, 96
Subjective Knowledge, 25-27

T

TSWE, 97
Test Fairness, 179, 180, 213-216, 219-223, 225-230, 234, 236, 238-240

Interpretation, 222, 235, 236, 238
Performance 215, 221, 238
Validity, 215, 228, 246
Tree-Based Regression, 122

V

Validity, 64, 193, 194, 196, 201, 202, 213, 215, 216, 218, 221-227, 229, 230, 232, 233, 236, 239, 241, 243-247
    Predictive, 105, 112
    Systemic, 70, 92
Values, 172
Visual Ability, 134, 137

W

Washback, 71
Worksite Learning, 55
Writing Assessment, 91, 93, 95, 98, 101, 105, 107, 108, 110-113